VOLUME 506   NOVEMBER 1989

THE ANNALS

of The American Academy *of* Political
and Social Science

RICHARD D. LAMBERT, *Editor*
ALAN W. HESTON, *Associate Editor*

HUMAN RIGHTS AROUND THE WORLD

Special Editor of this Volume

MARVIN E. WOLFGANG

President
American Academy of Political
and Social Science
Professor of Criminology and of Law
University of Pennsylvania
Philadelphia

Ⓢ **SAGE** PUBLICATIONS   *NEWBURY PARK   LONDON   NEW DELHI*

THE ANNALS

© 1989 *by* The American Academy *of* Political *and* Social Science

ERICA GINSBURG, *Assistant Editor*

Editorial Office: 3937 Chestnut Street, Philadelphia, PA 19104.

For information about membership* (individuals only) and subscriptions (institutions), address:

SAGE PUBLICATIONS, INC.
2111 West Hillcrest Drive
Newbury Park, CA 91320

From India and South Asia,		*From the UK, Europe, the Middle*
write to:		*East and Africa, write to:*
SAGE PUBLICATIONS INDIA Pvt. Ltd.		SAGE PUBLICATIONS LTD
P.O. Box 4215		28 Banner Street
New Delhi 110 048		London EC1Y 8QE
INDIA		ENGLAND

SAGE Production Editors: KITTY BEDNAR and LIANN LECH
*Please note that members of The Academy receive THE ANNALS with their membership.

Library of Congress Catalog Card Number 89-60677
International Standard Serial Number ISSN 0002-7162
International Standard Book Number ISBN 0-8039-3583-8 (Vol. 506, 1989 paper)
International Standard Book Number ISBN 0-8039-3582-X (Vol. 506, 1989 cloth)
Manufactured in the United States of America. First printing, September 1989.

Information about membership rates, institutional subscriptions, and back issue prices may be found on the facing page.

Advertising. Current rates and specifications may be obtained by writing to THE ANNALS Advertising and Promotion Manager at the Newbury Park office (address above).

Claims. Claims for undelivered copies must be made no later than three months following month of publication. The publisher will supply missing copies when losses have been sustained in transit and when the reserve stock will permit.

Change of Address. Six weeks' advance notice must be given when notifying of change of address to insure proper identification. Please specify name of journal. Send change of address to: THE ANNALS, c/o Sage Publications, Inc., 2111 West Hillcrest Drive, Newbury Park, CA 91320.

Origin and Purpose. The Academy was organized December 14, 1889, to promote the progress of political and social science, especially through publications and meetings. The Academy does not take sides in controverted questions, but seeks to gather and present reliable information to assist the public in forming an intelligent and accurate judgment.

Meetings. The Academy holds an annual meeting in the spring extending over two days.

Publications. THE ANNALS is the bimonthly publication of The Academy. Each issue contains articles on some prominent social or political problem, written at the invitation of the editors. Also, monographs are published from time to time, numbers of which are distributed to pertinent professional organizations. These volumes constitute important reference works on the topics with which they deal, and they are extensively cited by authorities throughout the United States and abroad. The papers presented at the meetings of The Academy are included in THE ANNALS.

Membership. Each member of The Academy receives THE ANNALS and may attend the meetings of The Academy. Membership is open only to individuals. Annual dues: $30.00 for the regular paperbound edition (clothbound, $45.00). Add $9.00 per year for membership outside the U.S.A. Members may also purchase single issues of THE ANNALS for $7.95 each (clothbound, $12.00).

Subscriptions. THE ANNALS (ISSN 0002-7162) is published six times annually — in January, March, May, July, September, and November. Institutions may subscribe to THE ANNALS at the annual rate: $66.00 (clothbound, $84.00). Add $9.00 per year for subscriptions outside the U.S.A. Institutional rates for single issues: $12.00 each (clothbound, $17.00).

Second class postage paid at Philadelphia, Pennsylvania, and at additional mailing offices.

Single issues of THE ANNALS may be obtained by individuals who are not members of The Academy for $8.95 each (clothbound, $17.00). Single issues of THE ANNALS have proven to be excellent supplementary texts for classroom use. Direct inquiries regarding adoptions to THE ANNALS c/o Sage Publications (address below).

All correspondence concerning membership in The Academy, dues renewals, inquiries about membership status, and/or purchase of single issues of THE ANNALS should be sent to THE ANNALS c/o Sage Publications, Inc., 2111 West Hillcrest Drive, Newbury Park, CA 91320. *Please note that orders under $25 must be prepaid.* Sage affiliates in London and India will assist institutional subscribers abroad with regard to orders, claims, and inquiries for both subscriptions and single issues.

THE ANNALS

of The American Academy *of* Political
and Social Science

RICHARD D. LAMBERT, *Editor*
ALAN W. HESTON, *Associate Editor*

————————— FORTHCOMING —————————

PRIVATIZING AND MARKETIZING SOCIALISM
Special Editor: Jan Prybyla

Volume 507   January 1990

ENGLISH PLUS: ISSUES IN BILINGUAL EDUCATION
Special Editors: Courtney B. Cazden
                                 Catherine Snow

Volume 508   March 1990

AMERICAN FEDERALISM: THE THIRD CENTURY
Special Editor: John Kincaid

Volume 509   May 1990

See page 3 for information on Academy membership and
purchase of single volumes of **The Annals.**

CONTENTS

PRESIDENT'S WELCOME AT THE
NINETY-FIRST ANNUAL MEETING .... *Marvin E. Wolfgang*   7

THE UNIVERSALITY OF THE CONCEPT
OF HUMAN RIGHTS .... *Louis Henkin*   10

HUMAN RIGHTS, THE NATIONAL INTEREST,
AND U.S. FOREIGN POLICY .... *Jerome J. Shestack*   17

HUMAN RIGHTS IN THE REAGAN ERA:
ACCEPTANCE IN PRINCIPLE .... *Aryeh Neier*   30

HUMAN RIGHTS AS AN
INTERNATIONAL ISSUE .... *Louise I. Shelley*   42

THE RIGHT TO LIFE AND
LATIN AMERICAN PENAL SYSTEMS .... *Eugenio Raúl Zaffaroni*   57

HUMAN RIGHTS AND THE U.N. COMMITTEE
ON CRIME PREVENTION AND CONTROL .... *Roger S. Clark*   68

GLASNOST — THE DAWN OF FREEDOM? .... *Richard Schifter*   85

PERESTROIKA, SOCIALISM, AND
THE CONSTITUTION .... *Valery Chalidze*   98

CIVIL RIGHTS IN THE SOVIET UNION .... *Arkady I. Vaxberg*   109

ASSESSING ISRAEL'S RECORD
ON HUMAN RIGHTS .... *Rita J. Simon*   115

THE ROLE OF SCIENCE AND SCIENTISTS
IN HUMAN RIGHTS .... *Carol Corillon*   129

HOMELESS CHILDREN: PHILADELPHIA AS A
CASE STUDY .... *Elaine R. Fox and Lisa Roth*   141

BOOK DEPARTMENT   152

INDEX   191

BOOK DEPARTMENT CONTENTS

INTERNATIONAL RELATIONS AND POLITICS

CARVER, LORD. *Twentieth Century Warriors: The Development of the Armed Forces of the Major Military Nations in the Twentieth Century.* Jean Bethke Elshtain 152

SHERR, ALAN B. *The Other Side of Arms Control: Soviet Objectives in the Gorbachev Era.* David Hecht 153

AFRICA, ASIA, AND LATIN AMERICA

BRANNON, JEFFREY and ERIC N. BAKLANOFF. *Agrarian Reform and Public Enterprise in Mexico: The Political Economy of Yucatán's Henequen Industry.* Kevin Gosner 154

MITTELBERG, DAVID. *Strangers in Paradise: The Israeli Kibbutz Experience.* Martin E. Danzig 155

SCHATZBERG, MICHAEL G. *The Dialectics of Oppression in Zaire.* Gary L. Fowler 156

WELFIELD, JOHN. *An Empire in Eclipse: Japan in the Postwar American Alliance System: A Study in the Interaction of Domestic Politics and Foreign Policy.* Hilary Conroy 156

EUROPE

BEISSINGER, MARK R. *Scientific Management, Socialist Discipline, and Soviet Power;*
SCOTT, HARRIET FAST and WILLIAM L. SCOTT. *Soviet Military Doctrines: Continuity, Formulation, and Dissemination.* Roger Hamburg 157

MEARSHEIMER, JOHN J. *Liddell Hart and the Weight of History.* Edward Hagerman 158

SHORROCK, WILLIAM I. *From Ally to Enemy: The Enigma of Fascist Italy in French Diplomacy, 1920-1940.* Spencer M. Di Scala 159

SIMKINS, PETER. *Kitchener's Army: The Raising of the New Armies, 1914-16.* Holger H. Herwig 160

SUNY, RONALD GRIGOR. *The Making of the Georgian Nation;*
McNEAL, ROBERT H. *Stalin: Man and Ruler.* Deborah Hardy 161

VIOLA, LYNNE. *The Best Sons of the Fatherland: Workers in the Vanguard of Soviet Collectivization;*
THORNILEY, DANIEL. *The Rise and Fall of the Soviet Rural Communist Party, 1927-1939.* Jonathan R. Adelman 162

WOOLF, STUART. *The Poor of Western Europe in the Eighteenth and Nineteenth Centuries.* Robert M. Schwartz 163

UNITED STATES

AMAKER, NORMAN C. *Civil Rights and the Reagan Administration.* Bernard D. Headley 164

COOPER, PHILLIP J. *Hard Judicial Choices: Federal District Court Judges and State and Local Officials;*

BARROW, DEBORAH J. and THOMAS G. WALKER. *A Court Divided:*
The Fifth Circuit Court of Appeals and the
Politics of Judicial Reform. Robert J. Sickels 165

CRESPI, IRVING. *Pre-Election Polling: Sources of Accuracy*
and Error. Robert E. Gilbert 167

HARGROVE, ERWIN C. *Jimmy Carter as President: Leadership and the*
Politics of the Public Good;
SPENCER, DONALD S. *The Carter Implosion: Jimmy Carter and the*
Amateur Style of Diplomacy. Raymond H. Gusteson 167

KOLKO, GABRIEL. *Confronting the Third World:*
United States Foreign Policy 1945-80. Ghulam M. Haniff 168

LANOUE, DAVID J. *From Camelot to the Teflon President:*
Economics and Presidential Popularity since 1960. Anne Permaloff 169

MUTCH, ROBERT E. *Campaigns, Congress, and Courts:*
The Making of Federal Campaign Finance Law. Carl Grafton 170

SOCIOLOGY

BOGDAN, ROBERT. *Freak Show: Presenting Human Oddities for*
Amusement and Profit. Norman K. Denzin 171

HAYES-BAUTISTA, DAVID E., WERNER O. SCHINK, and JORGE CHAPA. *The Burden*
of Support: Young Latinos in an Aging Society. Linda Liska Belgrave 172

IZOD, JOHN. *Hollywood and the Box Office, 1895-1986.* Edward T. Gargan 172

LAUREN, PAUL GORDON. *Power and Prejudice: The Politics and Diplomacy*
of Racial Discrimination. Howard D. Neighbor 173

OVED, YAACOV. *Two Hundred Years of American Communes.* Alan Lawson 174

VIGIL, JAMES DIEGO. *Barrio Gangs: Street Life and Identity*
in Southern California. Jorge Chapa 175

VINOKUR, MARTIN B. *More Than a Game: Sports and Politics.* James H. Frey 176

ECONOMICS

BAIROCH, PAUL. *Cities and Economic Development: From the Dawn of*
History to the Present. Thomas A. Reiner 177

DAVIDSON, GREG and PAUL DAVIDSON. *Economics for a*
Civilized Economy. Jon Harkness 178

DAWISHA, KAREN. *Eastern Europe, Gorbachev and Reform:*
The Great Challenge. Peter S. Elek 179

HOUNSHELL, DAVID A. and JOHN KENLY SMITH, Jr. *Science and*
Corporate Strategy: Du Pont R&D, 1902-1980. Barton C. Hacker 180

SIGLER, JAY A. and JOSEPH E. MURPHY. *Interactive Corporate Compliance:*
An Alternative to Regulatory Compulsion. Carolyn R. Dexter 181

SMITH, MICHAEL PETER. *City, State, and Market: The Political Economy*
of Urban Society. Joe R. Feagin 182

WEAVER, R. KENT. *Automatic Government: The Politics*
of Indexation. Phillip L. Gianos 183

WEISBROD, BURTON A. *The Nonprofit Economy.* G. S. Goldstein 184

PRESIDENT'S WELCOME AT THE
NINETY-FIRST ANNUAL MEETING

The American Academy of Political and Social Science was organized in Philadelphia on 14 December 1889; the current year is our centennial. The Academy was organized to promote the progress of political and social science, especially through publications and meetings. The Academy does not take sides on controversial questions, but seeks to gather and present reliable information to assist the public in forming an intelligent and accurate judgment. The Academy has had a charter from the Commonwealth of Pennsylvania since 1891 and in every sense has been a completely independent corporation. The officers and directors, myself included, often have come from the University of Pennsylvania, but there is no direct connection between the two organizations.

The membership of the Academy currently is about six to seven thousand from all over the world. Membership includes a subscription to *The Annals. The Annals* has been published since 1890, and we think of it as our outstanding bimonthly publication. It appears in January, March, May, July, September, and November. Each issue contains articles on some prominent social or political problem written at the invitation of the special editors. These volumes constitute important reference works on the topics with which they deal. *The Annals* is extensively cited throughout the United States and abroad. The papers that are presented today and tomorrow at this ninety-first annual meeting will be published in the November 1989 issue of *The Annals.*

I am pleased to welcome all of the faithful members and new members, students, and delegates from a variety of organizations to this meeting, where we will examine the theme of human rights around the world.

The topic of human rights is not new to the Academy. We have had issues of *The Annals* on topics related to human rights from the beginning of the journal's publication. In volume 1, printed in April 1891, Fred Taylor had an article, "The Law of Nature," which dealt with the topic of human rights. In January of 1900, Frederick Cleveland chose a very specific topic on human rights, connected with South Africa and its legal and political aspects. Also in 1900, in September, Inglis Clark had a very interesting article, "Natural Rights," which dealt with the topic. In 1903 several articles on labor, on child labor, and on convict labor were associated with the importance of human rights. In September of 1909, a special issue devoted to the Chinese and Japanese in America was concerned with these issues. The topics that I mention all had specific connection with human rights. In 1914 there was an issue on "reform in the administration of justice." In 1913 there was one on "prison labor," and in 1936 there was another, *The Constitution in the Twentieth Century,* and, specifically, in 1946 the title was *Essential Human Rights. Racial Desegregation and Integration* appeared in March 1956, *Internal Security and Civil Rights in America* in 1955. One of the latest issues I can refer to that had references to human rights is from 1979, which I edited, entitled *The Environment and Quality of Life.*

There is a difference between civil liberties and civil rights, as we know these concepts in the United States. There are individual rights, as civil rights; there are class-action cases for civil liberties. The distinction is not airtight, nor are the concepts mutually exclusive. But civil liberties apply, as I perceive them, in the abstract as principles of social justice for all persons in a democracy. Civil rights are more specific, concrete, individual case studies requiring litigation for specific cases of violations of due process: the Fourteenth Amendment; search and seizure, in the Fourth Amendment; the Fifth Amendment; cruel and unusual punishment, in the Eighth Amendment.

"Human rights," however, is a more global, collective macrosocial term. It is a term or concept that lies far beyond the legalities of an individual country and its statutes or constitutional protections of the individual. Human rights has become a universal concept, cross-culturally and across nation-states. I view human rights not as a condition that is imposed by Western societies on non-Western societies but as something closer to natural law, or the person's social condition, as a member of John Locke's status of prepolitical life as well as the person's social condition in Islamic, Hebraic, Confucianist, Christian, or current socialist law and philosophy.

The individual has a right, a human right, not to be harassed politically, economically, or socially. The individual has a human right to privacy of beliefs, religion, ethics so long as these do not injure others or promote violence between individuals and collectivities.

The cause of human rights requires nation-states to permit dissidence, criticism of the human condition. Human rights means freedom of expression in speech and in the press and in academia. Any state action that abrogates these freedoms is anathema to the cause of human rights.

"Free speech," claims the *New York Times* editorial as recently as Sunday, 16 April 1989, "is a universal good, not a Western idiosyncrasy. It grew out of the struggle for religious toleration and opens the way to peaceful co-existence of all faiths. The wise remedy whenever someone feels wronged by someone else's free speech is more free speech."[1] I am reminded also of Albert Camus's reference to patriotism, which, he said, is not blind acceptance or the following of one's country's actions; instead, the greatest expression of love of one's country lies in our willingness to criticize the policies and posture of one's country that do not match the notion of our ideal nation.

Human rights is a universal issue with universal appeal to all peoples, all cultures, to science and to the humanities.

I cannot hope, in these opening remarks, to enrich the language or logic of human rights resolutions, from the rhetoric of the United Nations to the metaphors of our poets. But I do wish to emphasize that the cause of human rights helps us to hold hands across many nations and disciplines of thought.

Over twenty years ago C. P. Snow wrote tellingly about the two cultures of science and the humanities or arts, claiming that they were two worlds of different patterns of thought and creativity. I have never fully accepted C. P. Snow's dichotomy. I think the story of the discovery of DNA is as exciting as the story of the writing of a Beethoven symphony. Our rallying around human rights has the same holistic unity as that which I see in science and the arts.

This annual meeting of the American Academy of Political and Social Science on this topic is why I mention science, the arts, and human rights. Relative to these three topics, I was impressed by a statement by Henry Fairlee in the 24 April issue of the *New Republic*. He said that, despite Copernicus and modern astronomy,

1. Copyright © 1989 by The New York Times Company. Reprinted by permission.

we will always say the sun climbs and the sun declines to the horizon, because that is what we see in sunrise and sunset, two daily spectacles of such profound beauty that no painter, not even Turner, has seriously thought to catch them. I find this immensely reassuring, because it means that we can have our science, one of the illimitable endeavors of the human mind, and still keep our poetry. We will always, with the poets, think of the sun as a chariot, while believing, with the scientist, that it is an unusually bulky fusion reactor.[2]

The issue of human rights blends diversities in the same way and binds us together. Personal examples include Einstein, Schweitzer, Sakharov, and many other scientists. Human rights brings us all together in a universal cause, in synthesis with peace and antithesis of war and repression. The human rights declaration, I repeat, is not an imposition of Western legal philosophical thought on Eastern or non-Western traditions. It is not a superpowers' imposition on the Third World. Relative to that point, I quote Senator William Fulbright's latest book, *The Price of Empire,* in which he says, "There is no greater vanity than the belief that one's own values have universal validity, no greater folly than the attempt to impose the preference of a single society on an unwilling world."

Human rights does refer to universal claims of individual rights and to the rights derived from social justice: the right to speak, to criticize, as well as the right to have proper education, housing, and medical care. Governments cannot, as Confucius claimed centuries ago, legislate love of parents for children or children for parents; but governments can legislate the right to speak freely, to hold religious and political beliefs, to educate society to care for its people, to offer health care, to provide jobs, education, and shelter.

At this ninety-first annual meeting of the Academy, which is celebrating its one-hundredth anniversary, we are proud to have human rights around the world as our theme.

We are especially proud about and pleased with our list of speakers at this annual meeting. Most of them are well-known advocates of human rights who have been speaking about this topic at many other meetings. Our papers at this meeting are not so much accounts of violations of human rights as they are of definitions, parameters, and concepts of human rights. We cannot cover all countries, but all countries may be mentioned by our speakers.

I am especially gratified to host this ninety-first meeting of the Academy on human rights on the eve of the meeting of Mr. Gorbachev and Mr. Deng in Beijing on 16 May. I hope they both will read our November issue of *The Annals!*

The Academy wishes to acknowledge with gratitude the donation of the William Penn Foundation toward this meeting and celebration of our centenary.

MARVIN E. WOLFGANG

2. *New Republic,* 24 Apr. 1989, p. 43.

ANNALS, *AAPSS,* **506,** November 1989

The Universality of the Concept
of Human Rights

By LOUIS HENKIN

ABSTRACT: Debate about the universality of human rights requires definition of "human rights" and even of "universality." The idea of human rights is related but not equivalent to justice, the good, democracy. Strictly, the conception is that every individual has legitimate claims upon his or her society for defined freedoms and benefits; an authoritative catalog of rights is set forth in the Universal Declaration of Human Rights. The rights of the Universal Declaration are politically and legally universal, having been accepted by virtually all states, incorporated into their own laws, and translated into international legal obligations. Assuring respect for rights in fact, however, will require the continued development of stable political societies and of the commitment to constitutionalism. Virtually all societies are also culturally receptive to those basic rights and human needs included in the Universal Declaration that reflect common contemporary moral intuitions. Other rights, however — notably, freedom of expression, religious and ethnic equality, and the equality of women — continue to meet deep resistance.

Louis Henkin is University Professor Emeritus and Special Service Professor at Columbia University, chairman of the Directorate of the university's Center for the Study of Human Rights, and a member of Columbia's War and Peace Institute. He is also a member of the Executive Committee of the Lawyers Committee for Human Rights. He is the author of several books and many articles in professional journals.

DISCUSSION of the universality of the concept of human rights begs for definition and interpretation of terms. I offer a word about the concept of human rights, another about universality.

HUMAN RIGHTS

Human rights are not the equivalent of justice, or "the good society," or, as some think, democracy, although the human rights idea is related to all of these. Briefly, the human rights idea declares that every individual has legitimate claims upon his or her own society for certain freedoms and benefits. Few, if any, human rights are absolute; they are prima facie rights and may sometimes bow to compelling public interest. Ronald Dworkin suggested that human rights ordinarily "trump" other public interests.

These claims upon society are not for some general and inchoate category of what is good; they have been authoritatively defined. They are specified in the Universal Declaration of Human Rights and in various other international instruments. The rights specified are commonly divided into two categories. Civil and political rights include rights to life and physical integrity; freedom from torture, slavery, and arbitrary detention; and rights to fair criminal process; as well as rights of personhood and privacy; freedom of conscience, religion, and expression; and the right to vote and participate in government. The other category comprises economic and social rights. These are essentially those associated with the welfare state: the right to work, to eat, to obtain health care, housing, education, and an adequate standard of living generally. A people's rights to self-determination and sovereignty over natural resources have been appended to the human rights catalog in two international covenants. Controversial candidates for inclusion as human rights are rights to peace, economic development, and a healthy environment.

The idea of human rights is a political idea with moral foundations. It is an expression of the political relationship that should prevail between individual and society. It implies that there are limitations on government, including limits on what can be done to the individual even for the welfare of the majority, the public interest, the common good. There are even limitations on law; one may think of human rights as a kind of higher law. The human rights idea implies individual entitlement and corresponding obligations on society. Our rights are not granted by society; we enjoy them not by the grace of society and not only because it may be good societal policy to respect them. Rather, we are entitled to them.

Implicit in the idea of human rights is a commitment to individual worth. The individual counts, and counts independently of the community. The idea suggests equality of human beings, not hierarchy among them. It implies that values of liberty and autonomy are sometimes more important than values of order. Justice Cardozo wrote of "ordered liberty."

Where the idea of human rights comes from is not agreed upon. In the contemporary world, human rights claims are justified rhetorically as required by human dignity, and by goals of freedom, justice, and peace.

UNIVERSALITY

The term "human rights" suggests the rights of all human beings anywhere and anytime. The principal contemporary articulation of human rights, the Universal Declaration of Human Rights, claims and prescribes universality.

The universality of human rights has been challenged from several perspectives. The idea has had an uphill struggle for political and philosophical acceptance. The strongest challenge has been to claims of cultural universality.

The political and philosophical idea of human rights has not always been universal, and it has not been universal for very long. It finds its authentic origins in the seventeenth century in the natural rights of John Locke. In America, we tend to proclaim Thomas Jefferson's restatement of Locke in the Declaration of Independence. But the idea was rejected by traditionalists such as Edmund Burke. It was rejected by progressives, even such eminent progressives as Jeremy Bentham. Bentham said: "Natural rights is simple nonsense: natural and imprescriptible rights, rhetorical nonsense — nonsense upon stilts." An American thinker once wrote that natural rights have been as much "the shield of conservatism as the sword of radicalism."[1]

In the nineteenth and early twentieth centuries, the idea of natural rights was challenged by positivists. It has been denied by utilitarianism, which implies that one can sacrifice individuals to achieve the greatest good of the greatest number or the maximum of total happiness. The idea of human rights has been attacked by socialists. Communitarians generally see human rights as egocentric, egotistic, and divisive. The human rights idea has also been challenged as undemocratic when claims to individual rights conflict with the will of the majority.

This political idea, so self-evident to Americans, took root in very few places. It

1. Jerome Frank, "Interpretations of Modern Legal Philosophers," in *Interpretations of Modern Legal Philosophies: Essays in Honor of Roscoe Pound,* ed. Paul L. Sayre (New York: Oxford University Press, 1947), p. 223.

found fertile soil in the United States in 1776 when Jefferson proclaimed it and the states included it in their constitutions; in 1789 Congress adopted what became the Bill of Rights. It is sobering to note, however, that while we amended the Constitution to include the Bill of Rights and continued to recite the Declaration of Independence, we maintained slavery for another eighty years, maintained racial discrimination for a hundred years more, and limited suffrage until recently. Minorities and women continue to claim invidious discrimination.

Our partner in the idea of rights in the eighteenth century, France, proclaimed its great Declaration of the Rights of Man and of the Citizen in 1789, then shelved it for about 150 years. Great Britain, our mother-in-law, continues to reject the idea of rights in constitutional principle, in favor of parliamentary supremacy. One hardly need mention countries in the twentieth century that rejected the idea of human rights in principle as well as in fact, in the name of fascism, national socialism, and Stalin's socialism.

Religions, too, have challenged the idea of rights. At various times, almost every religion — including Protestantism, whose stress on the individual contributed to the idea — has not received the idea of human rights warmly. Religions have not tended to favor ideas that could be seen as essentially anthropocentric. Autonomy and liberty have not been religious values and have been seen as anarchic.

Finally, some cultural anthropologists have charged that natural rights is a Western idea and that imposing it on others is cultural imperialism. In any event, they insisted, there is little hope for human rights if the world's cultures are not receptive to the idea.

EMERGING UNIVERSALITY

The human rights idea was not universal not too long ago. I believe it has now achieved universality in significant respects.

Political universality today can hardly be denied. World War II and the full realization of the enormities of Adolf Hitler ushered in what I have called "the age of rights." Human rights has been accepted as the idea of our times; no other political idea—not socialism; not capitalism; not even democracy, however defined, usually undefined—has received such universal acclaim. All states have accepted the idea of human rights in some form. Universal condemnation of apartheid, for example, also implies universal acceptance of the idea of rights.

The second half of this century has given the idea legal universality as well. The concept of human rights has been enshrined in the U.N. Charter, to which virtually all states are parties. The Universal Declaration of Human Rights has been accepted by virtually all states. The international covenants and conventions on human rights have been widely adhered to, and there is a customary law of human rights binding on all states.

The concept of human rights has been incorporated in virtually all state constitutions. Where it has not been fully incorporated, there is continuous demand for its inclusion and for constitutional guarantees of rights. Even the Soviet Union, even China have included human rights in their recent constitutions.

Needless to say, universal political and even legal acceptance does not guarantee universal respect for human rights. Many will see such acceptance as rhetoric or even hypocrisy. I have been sometimes tempted to offer two cheers for hypocrisy in human rights. Two cheers—though not three—recognize that "hypocrisy is the homage that vice pays to virtue"; it is important that the concept of human rights is the virtue to which vice has to pay homage in our time. Acceptance, even hypocritical acceptance, is a commitment in principle to which one can be held accountable. Hypocrisy requires concealment that can be uncovered. This homage is reflected even in the phenomenon of emergency rule that prevails in many countries today. When a country declares emergency rule, it declares its situation to be abnormal. In principle, emergency rule is only temporary. Regardless of how long it lasts, it continues to be abnormal.

There can be little doubt about the fact of the constitutionalization and the internationalization of human rights in our time, and of the popularity of the idea—in all senses of "popularity." With those political developments, even philosophical and religious opposition to the idea has been muted if not erased.

We may be approaching universality even among philosophers. Natural rights have had a rebirth. Philosophers who continue to eschew natural rights may nonetheless recognize a sense of common moral intuition that provides a basis for human rights. In any event, the human rights movement does not invoke natural rights with its historical baggage, and the battles with positivism are now moot since human rights are now established in positive national and international law. Philosophers, such as Professor Cranston in Great Britain, who continue to object to economic and social rights as rights do not challenge the concept of human rights and indeed reaffirm it, and other philosophers have shouted him down on economic and social rights, too.

The others I have mentioned — the utilitarians, the communitarians, the socialists — may continue to be opposed to the idea in abstract theory, but none of them is now prepared to submerge the individual completely. Utilitarians will not sanction slavery, or torture, even "for the greatest good." Communitarians increasingly recognize that a legitimate community can be maintained only with respect for individual human rights. Socialism recognizes that socialism is acceptable and viable only if it has a human face.

All the major religions have begun to emphasize their individualist, universalist, this-worldly — rather than other-worldly — elements. They have played down doctrines that are in tension with human rights, such as intolerance of other religions and subordination of women. Some fundamentalist actions taken in the name of Islam, however, continue to resist this trend. The rights of individuals now commonly are seen by all religions as a floor, a minimum requirement for the good society, especially in modern urban industrialized society. All societies and all religions today have accepted the notion of rights to have basic human needs satisfied. Modernization has brought the human rights idea even to the illiterate villager. In all parts of the world, it is increasingly recognized, the village will need law, institutions, education, organization, and human rights if it is to be part of modern society.

CULTURAL RECEPTIVITY

The core of the continuing challenge to the universality of human rights today is cultural. Essentially, the claim is that the concept of human rights is a Western idea, imposed on the rest of the world, and that many cultures are resistant and unreceptive to the idea.

That the idea has been imposed by the West is debatable. The idea of human rights has been accepted by leaders in every country, embraced not only by the early Western-educated elites but also by contemporary leaders. The Third World has had its Nyereres committed to human rights, not only its Idi Amins. Much of the resistance to human rights is resistance not to the idea of human rights but to some of its politics in the United Nations, to external scrutiny rejected as interference, to the imposition of sanctions for human rights violations — for example, by the United States — but not to the idea of human rights.

In any event, many contemporary ideas in the political world are Western — the concept of the state, socialism, the idea of the United Nations. Development is a Western concept, universally acclaimed. No one claims that these ideas are anything other than Western, yet no one claims that they are therefore culturally foreign and unacceptable.

Human rights may be a Western idea, but the West has not been more receptive to it than have other regions and cultures. The idea hardly flourished in the West before World War II, and it was in the West that Hitler perpetrated his monstrous deeds.

The political idea of human rights is rooted in interpersonal morality. The issue, I believe, is not the universality of the political idea but of the underlying morality. The question is whether the moral values of human rights are universal, whether the specifics in the catalog of rights in the Universal Declaration of Human Rights respond to that common morality. The important issue, moreover, is not even whether human rights reflects a common morality, but whether the morality it reflects, now universally politically prescribed, is culturally acceptable or will be rejected as foreign matter.

I am persuaded that there is, universally, a common contemporary moral intuition that responds to, and will not reject, most of the provisions in the Universal Declaration, those that constitute the core of human rights. I think there is universal cultural receptivity to the right to life and physical integrity; to freedom from torture, slavery, and arbitrary detention; to due process of law and the right not to suffer cruel punishment; to a right to property. These rights correspond to those alluded to in the phrase "consistent patterns of gross violations of internationally recognized human rights," a term of art in both U.N. doctrine and U.S. legislation. There is no reason to assume cultural resistance to universal political participation. There is surely no cultural resistance to societal responsibility for meeting basic needs for food, housing, health care, education, and the care of children and the aged.

On the other hand, some rights in the Universal Declaration are not universally favored and may meet cultural resistance. I cannot conclude that freedom of expression is universally accepted or even acceptable; I am not confident even about freedom of conscience and religion. Equality is not yet universally welcomed, and discrimination on grounds of race, ethnicity, or gender will be difficult to eradicate. The world has moved, but it has not yet moved far enough.

The world has been moved to accept new ideas, and in my view it is more receptive to the idea of human rights than to many others. The idea of human rights has been on the world scene for only some forty years. It has faced an uphill struggle in many countries, Western as well as Eastern, in the First and Second as in the Third World. Its political and legal acceptance has been universal, and philosophical and ideological resistance to it has subsided. The conception of human rights, and most of the rights in the authoritative catalog of human rights, I conclude, conform to a common moral intuition that is virtually universal today, and those rights are in fact congenial — or acceptable — to the principal cultures. Serious violations of these rights in many countries reflect, I think, not cultural resistance but political-social-economic underdevelopment and instability, and a still underdeveloped culture of constitutionalism, including an inability to keep the army in its barracks.

Some rights, on the other hand — freedom of expression, religious and ethnic equality, and the equality of women — appear not yet to be acceptable in fact in a number of societies. In that sense, those rights are not yet universal. I do not think that it is impossible to make them universal, but it will take dedicated effort by those who care.

* * *

QUESTIONS AND ANSWERS

Q (Ben Freedman, New Orleans, Louisiana): Where is the line between human rights and chaos?

A: In theory, the respect for individual autonomy can be carried so far as to lead to chaos, but we are far from that; all societies today have substantial respect for individual autonomy — certainly all societies in the West — and they have managed to avoid chaos. A line has to be drawn. The human rights instruments have recognized limitations on rights, but the limitations themselves are articulated in an international standard, and the international standard is monitored by international institutions — governmental, intergovernmental, and nongovernmental. The international standard seems workable.

———

Q (Anwar Barkat, Commission of the Churches on International Affairs, New York City): I think there has been a certain amount of simplification of the reaction of the Third World to human rights. It is not the concept itself that is under attack as much as the Western aspects of it. I do not think the Third World is willing to give that kind of honor to the Western world or to reject its own traditions and history. In the beginning, the interpretation and the language of human rights were so individualist that the Third World protested the exclusion of communitarianism from human rights discourse. As a result, the rights of communities, the right to national existence, and the right to ethnic existence are now addressed. The Universal Declaration of Human Rights and other human rights covenants are problematic also. When these instruments were negotiated, the Third World was not a party to the negotiations. It is not that we reject the contribution of the West, but we want to make contributions from our own tradition, culture, and history as well.

A: Actually, it has not been the Third World that has charged cultural imperialism but Americans speaking on the Third World's behalf. I think the Third World has been as dedicated to the human rights idea as the First World and certainly the Second, and perhaps more so in some respects. The Universal Declaration has been accepted by everybody, First, Second, and Third World. The Third World has not liked some of the means by which the West has enforced human rights, but that requires political rather than cultural discussion.

I do not think that communitarianism is inconsistent with the idea of human rights. But when the community begins to impinge unduly — the critical word — on the individual, communitarianism begins to swallow human rights.

Human Rights, the National Interest, and U.S. Foreign Policy

By JEROME J. SHESTACK

ABSTRACT: Foreign policy decisions are driven by conceptions of the national interest. It serves the national interest of the United States to pursue human rights goals because they advance our security interests; help establish a system of world order based on the aspirations of people and on the rule of law; are geopolitically advantageous by furthering peaceful evolutionary democratization of states; and command popular support, as they reflect fundamental values of the American people. Nonetheless, human rights had virtually no role in our foreign policy until the Carter administration. President Carter made human rights a key focus of U.S. foreign policy. When the Reagan administration began, it denigrated human rights policy, supporting many repressive authoritarian states. Gradually, the Reagan administration took a more positive stance toward human rights, largely accepting the Carter administration's human rights policies by the end of the Reagan years. Given the easing in East-West confrontation, the Bush administration now has a unique opportunity to strengthen and coordinate an international system of states that respect human rights. If the United States does this, our national interests will clearly be served.

Jerome Shestack was educated at the University of Pennsylvania and Harvard Law School. He is a former U.S. representative to the United Nations Commission on Human Rights and senior U.S. delegate to the Conference on Cooperation and Security in Europe. Since 1972 he has headed the International League for Human Rights. He founded the Lawyers Committee for Human Rights and chairs the Jacob Blaustein Institute for Human Rights. He is a senior partner and active trial lawyer at Schnader, Harrison, Segal & Lewis, Philadelphia, New York, and Washington, D.C.

CURRENTLY, human rights concerns seem alive and active in U.S. foreign policy. The president and secretary of state faithfully pledge allegiance to human rights in speeches and at press conferences. At congressional hearings, administration spokespersons parade their human rights initiatives and successes. A recent article by the assistant secretary of state for human rights proudly claims that human rights have been institutionalized in our foreign policy.[1]

Yet, as recently as 1974, human rights were not even a claimant in U.S. foreign policy decisions. In the State Department, human rights concerns were relegated to an obscure office, staffed by one official wielding no influence.[2] At the United Nations, our representatives were restricted from meaningful protests against human rights abuses.[3] Congress was largely apathetic on human rights issues and secretaries of state ignored them. In the indexes of

1. Richard Schifter, "Building Firm Foundations: The Institutionalization of United States Human Rights Policy in the Reagan Years," *Harvard Human Rights Yearbook*, 2:3-24 (1989). Schifter served as assistant secretary of state for human rights during the latter portion of the Reagan administration and proved to be a strong human rights advocate. His reappointment by Secretary of State Baker is to the credit of the Bush administration.

2. Jerome J. Shestack and Roberta A. Cohen, "International Human Rights: A Rule for the United States," *Virginia Journal of International Law,* 14:673, 678-80 (1984).

3. For example, Morris B. Abram, former U.S. representative to the U.N. Commission on Human Rights, commented in 1971, "Not once did we express our horror and disgust at the slaughter in Indonesia in any world forum. Nor have we raised a peep against the barbarities of our junta allies in Greece." *New York Times,* 26 Dec. 1971. Rita Hauser, also a former U.S. representative to the commission, reported similar restrictions. See U.S. Congress, House, *Hearings before the Subcommittee on International Organizations of the House Committee on Foreign Affairs,* 93d Cong., 1st sess., 1973, pp. 238-40.

leading texts on foreign policy published at the time, there are no entries on human rights. How is it then that, in the short span of some 15 years, the issue of human rights should bloom to its present flourishing prominence? Can a policy so embryonic be secure? Is it, in fact, secure?

What is particularly odd about the long period of neglect of human rights in foreign policy after World War II is that it represented a blunt disregard of history's lessons. The horrendous Nazi experience and the tragedy of the Holocaust epitomized the lack of international protection for the individual. Indeed, at its start, the new United Nations emphasized the need to protect individual rights through international law.[4] The Universal Declaration of Human Rights, adopted in 1948 by an almost unanimous U.N. vote, and subsequent international covenants established ample standards for human rights, encompassing both civil and political rights and economic and social rights.

Given such substantive support for human rights as well as our national tradition and sentiment in favor of individual rights, why did the postwar United States neglect human rights in its foreign policy?

Of course, there were various roadblocks to a human rights focus, such as fear of encroachments on sovereignty, and political concerns that a nation that protests human rights abuses by other nations inevitably risks a reciprocal limelight. These and other roadblocks were formidable — but not insurmountable. Had the United States determined to focus on human rights in its foreign policy, it could have done so.

4. The Preamble to the U.N. Charter affirms the dignity and worth and equal rights of each person. Article I states that the purpose of the Charter is to maintain peace and promote respect for human rights and fundamental freedoms. U.N. Charter, Art. I, paras. 1, 3.

To appreciate why the United States did not, it is necessary to address the basic questions: what ends should U.S. foreign policy serve, and what are the strategies to further those ends?

WHERE DOES THE NATIONAL INTEREST LIE?

Idealistic ends — peace, freedom, order, justice, harmony — are the staples of political rhetoric. But the engine that has driven foreign policy since World War II has been fueled by interests.[5] George Kennan expressed the prevailing view: foreign policy must be founded, not on "moral impulses," but on recognition of the national interest, "reasonably conceived."[6] Kissinger, too, endorsed this thesis: his realpolitik approach to foreign policy was his euphemism for pursuit of the national interest.

On the face of it, what can be wrong with furthering the national interest? The difficulty, of course, is in defining the national interest and, even more difficult, in choosing between competing interests. The contours of national interest are amorphous and imprecise. Kennan defines the national interest as military security, the integrity of a nation's political life, and the well-being of its people.[7] But that definition — which includes domestic issues — is fuzzy. What kind of military security is in the national interest? The security that

comes from Star Wars, or the security that comes from arms control treaties? What preserves the integrity of political life — judges selected on a merit plan or elected judges? What is the well-being of the people — pro-life or pro-choice, tax cuts or welfare programs?

Furthermore, who determines our national interest? The president, the Congress, and the public all believe they are legitimate articulators of the national interest. But what serves the national interest to one may well disserve it to another.[8] National interest propels both members of Congress who support aid to the contras and those who oppose it. At any one time national interest is no more than an amalgam of the policy motivations held by the ruling administration.[9] One is reminded of the two ministers who frequently quarreled. Finally, one said, "We men of the cloth shouldn't quarrel. After all, we are both doing God's work: you in your way, I in His."

Despite its definitional and normative deficiencies, national interest constitutes the rationale for foreign policy decisions.[10]

8. As James Chace put it, "In every case, there are elements of the 'national interest' on both sides of any difficult decision; too often those who invoke the phrase are trying to load the dice in favor of the outcome they think most important." James Chace, "Is a Foreign Policy Consensus Possible?" *Foreign Affairs,* 57:1, 15 (1978).

9. See Ernst B. Haas, "The Balance of Power as a Guide to Policy Making," in *Crisis and Continuity in World Politics,* ed. G. A. Lassy and W. C. McWilliams (New York: Random House, 1961), p. 326; Samuel Huntington, "Coping with the Lipmann Gap," *Foreign Affairs,* 66:453, 475 (1988). Professor Hoffmann has observed that "what is prudent or expedient [in the national interest] is itself greatly determined by what the statesmen consider right." Stanley Hoffmann, "Reaching for the Most Difficult: Human Rights as a Foreign Policy Goal," *Daedelus,* 112:19, 35 (1983).

10. Richard Bilder, "Human Rights and U.S. Foreign Policy: Short Term Prospects," *Virginia Journal*

5. See, for example, Henry J. Morganthau, *Politics among Nations* (New York: Knopf, 1948); George F. Kennan, *American Diplomacy: 1900-1980* (Chicago: University of Chicago Press, 1951); Henry Kissinger, *American Foreign Policy* (New York: Norton, 1969), p. 94.

6. George F. Kennan, "Morality and Foreign Policy," *Foreign Affairs,* 64:205, 217 (Winter 1985-86).

7. Ibid., p. 206. For critiques of Kennan's views on human rights, see Gordon A. Cristenson, "Kennan and Human Rights," *Human Rights Quarterly,* 8:345 (1986); Richard H. Ullman, "The Realities of George F. Kennan," *Foreign Policy,* 28:139 (1977).

Within the genus of national interest, various species of interest compete for preference — interests of trade, economics, alliances, human rights, and so forth. Hence, human rights will occupy a central role only if the molders of foreign policy are persuaded that a focus on human rights goals advances our national interest.

The Truman, Eisenhower, Kennedy, Johnson, and Nixon administrations were not persuaded. For a variety of reasons, some stemming from the Korean and Vietnam wars, some from overwhelming preoccupation with the superpower conflict, very little consideration was given to the question of whether human rights emphasis would further U.S. interests.

By the 1970s, the world had changed considerably since World War II. Rough military parity had been established between the two superpowers. The number of participants in the international order had multiplied, and their ability to affect each other had extended. We were moving from a bipolar to a multipolar society in which the global agenda was diverse and complicated. At least, by the early 1970s, compelling reasons had arisen to validate the proposition that a strong human rights policy would serve our national interest. Let us examine the reasons.

For one, human rights had become a major issue on the global agenda, appealing to the aspirations of people on every continent. The communications revolution had made people all over the world aware of human rights activity and its potential for bettering the human condition.

Championing human rights afforded the United States a unique opportunity to be relevant to this global agenda and to address those aspirations. Despite the fallout from Vietnam, the United States was generally regarded as having an immense potential to further individual freedom and development. This should have been — and should be — an appealing role for the United States.

Second, furtherance of human rights served our security interests. Peace and stability would be unattainable in a world in which people were impelled to rise up against their oppressors. Conversely, human rights furthered peace by advancing responsiveness to the will of the people and invoked restraints on aggressive action. Peace would be most likely to exist where states respected human rights. Kant's early insight proved valid; peace and human rights are interdependent.[11]

Third, human rights would further a just world order. Progress toward such a world order would require common ties, legalized international institutions, a web of common values, and an acceptance of domestic and international restraints based on law and reciprocity. Human rights advances these goals. Further, the legal order of the human rights law addresses economic and social rights, that is, elements of distributive justice without which a stable world order is unrealizable. International human rights thus offered the United States and other nations the opportunity to break away from the stalemate of bipolar policy and to generate broad coalitions of shared purpose.

Fourth, even under a geopolitical analysis, there were good reasons for a strong human rights focus in foreign policy.

of International Law, 14:597, 603, 607 (1978); Alan Tonelson, "The Real National Interest," *Foreign Policy,* 61:49 (Winter 1985-86). For a summary of opposing views, see Conway Henderson, *"Human Rights and Regimes: A Bibliographical Essay," Human Rights Quarterly,* 10:525, 527-28 (1988).

11. See Sissela Bok, *A Strategy for Peace* (New York: Pantheon Books, 1989), pp. 32-35.

Human rights values were those of liberal democracies. If one believed that furtherance of liberal democracies would provide this nation with more influence, security, and power, one should peacefully try to make those values prevail. As James Billington put it, "The cause of human rights provides a valuable vehicle for peaceful evolutionary democratization, throughout the communist world. . . . Out of the large literature on how wars start in the modern world, there emerges one heartening fact: democracies do not fight one another."[12] Our support of human rights would thus help build a coalition of liberal states, further peace, confound our adversaries, and reinforce our claim to world leadership based on elements other than military might.

Finally, it was in our national interest to have a foreign policy that commanded popular support because such a foreign policy would reflect fundamental values of the American people. A human rights focus could go a long way toward providing what Stanley Hoffman calls an "internal solidity" to our foreign policy. Moreover, there was a connection between the failure to support human rights abroad and the erosion of human rights at home. While the correlation was imprecise, we would enhance our own liberties by concern for the liberties of others.

These are compelling reasons why a human rights focus came to be in the national interest. Of course, as noted earlier, there are other interests in the marketplace of the national interest, and often they are competing ones. I shall come back to this shortly.

12. James Billington, "Realism and Vision in Foreign Policy," *Foreign Affairs*, 65:630, 652 (1987).

THE PRE-CARTER ERA

One might have expected that Kissinger, who conducted our foreign policy during the Nixon-Ford years, would have acted upon these factors. If human rights were not considered in the national interest prior to his reign, he had the influence and ability to redefine the national interest so that they would be taken into account. But he regarded human rights initiatives as moral exhortations, irrelevant to the national interest. His conception of the national interest, sparked by his personal brand of peripatetic diplomacy, essentially followed a balance-of-power approach with the United States maintaining its military power by superiority of arms and a network of alliances with nations adverse to the Soviet Union. As William Buckley succinctly put it, "Realpolitik crowded out human rights during the Kissinger years."[13] More devastating is William Bundy's requiem on the Nixon-Kissinger era: The "process by which . . . Nixon [read also: "Kissinger"] managed to get on strained terms with almost every democratic government in the world, while condoning and cultivating dictatorial regimes both in greater and lesser powers, set, I think, new records in making a vice out of necessity."[14]

It is striking that the impetus for inserting a human rights focus into American foreign policy came not from the executive branch but from a Congress disillusioned with executive unaccountability in Vietnam and anxious to assert its power in the aftermath of Watergate.[15] Deputy Secretary

13. William Buckley, "Human Rights and Foreign Policy," *Foreign Affairs*, 58:775, 784 (1980).

14. William Bundy, "Dictatorships and American Foreign Policy," *Foreign Affairs*, 54:51, 57 (1975).

15. For a review of the role of Congress in foreign policy during the Vietnam war period, see John F.

of State Robert Ingersoll had warned Kissinger in 1974 that "if the Department did not place itself ahead of the curve on this issue [human rights] Congress would take the matter out of the Department's hands."[16] Congress did. During the years 1974-76, Congress enacted a series of measures restricting military, economic, and financial assistance to gross violators of human rights and establishing in the State Department a new Bureau of Human Rights and Humanitarian Affairs, headed by an assistant secretary of state. These were important advances, not only because human rights standards became relevant in significant areas of foreign policy but also because Congress signaled its determination to compete with the president in foreign policy decision making. Edward Corwin said that, in this area, the Constitution is an "invitation to struggle." Congress accepted the invitation.

HUMAN RIGHTS UNDER CARTER

Jimmy Carter came from a strong civil rights background, but he was relatively unversed in international affairs. Nevertheless, early in his election campaign, he told the Foreign Policy Association that we "can take the lead" in promoting "global standards of human rights."[17] A sign that human rights was an issue that would find favorable response from the American people came during the Ford-Carter debate on foreign policy in 1976. In the course of that debate, Carter brought up the Soviet Union's failure to comply with the human rights provisions of the Helsinki Accords. Ford's startling response was that Eastern Europe was free of "Soviet domination."[18] Ford's odd bungle may well have won the election for Jimmy Carter. In any event, the debate projected human rights to the fore of the campaign. By the time of Carter's inaugural, he had made an "absolute" commitment to human rights, and by midterm he told the United Nations that "no force on earth can separate us from that commitment."[19]

But making an "absolute" commitment to human rights and carrying out an effective human rights policy are not synonymous. Carter's early pronouncements had a preachy tone, viewed by many as a display of American hubris. Three months into his term, a *Washington Post* headline read, "Administration Still Groping to Define Human Rights."[20] Soon thereafter, however, President Carter, Secretary of State Cyrus Vance, and Deputy Secretary Warren Christopher formulated a series of initiatives launching a vigorous and visible human rights program.

Looking back, we can see that Jimmy Carter's administration produced striking achievements on the human rights front. Carter's human rights emphasis significantly altered and bettered the international atmosphere.[21] For a period of time

Manley, "The Rise of Congress in Foreign Policy-Making," *The Annals* of the American Academy of Political and Social Science, 397:60 (Sept. 1971); cf. Lee H. Hamilton and Michael H. Van Dusen, "Making the Separation of Power Work," *Foreign Affairs*, 57:17 (1978).

16. Buckley, "Human Rights and Foreign Policy," p. 784.

17. Jimmy Carter, Address delivered to the Foreign Policy Association, New York City, 23 June 1976.

18. Elizabeth Drew, "A Reporter at Large: Human Rights," *New Yorker*, 18 July 1977.

19. Jimmy Carter, Speech on the Thirtieth Anniversary of the Universal Declaration of Human Rights, 6 Dec. 1978, printed in *Human Rights Reader*, ed. Walter Lacquer and Barry Rubin (New York: NAL, 1979), p. 325.

20. *Washington Post*, 16 Apr. 1977.

21. See Arthur Schlesinger, Jr., "Human Rights and the American Tradition," *Foreign Affairs*, 57:503 (1979); Hedley Bull, "A View from Abroad: Consistency under Pressure," ibid., p. 442.

Carter restored the American prestige that had been tarnished by our behavior in Vietnam and our association with dictators. He disengaged the United States from some egregious human rights violators, such as Argentina, Chile, and Brazil. He built human rights support at the United Nations and put repressive governments on the defensive for their human rights abuses.[22] He recognized that we were in a multipolar world and tried to restructure North-South relations. He encouraged human rights dissidents, helped release prisoners, and saved lives. These are not small achievements.

But there was also much to fault in Carter's human rights policies. He raised expectations that could not be fulfilled, and his policy was increasingly troubled by incoherence and inconsistencies. His administration overlooked human rights violations in China out of a fear of antagonizing Beijing. It became increasingly circumspect with Yugoslavia, the Soviet Union, and many of the African nations; it continued to support repressive regimes in the Philippines, Indonesia, Guatemala, Iran, and Korea because of supposed national security interests.

In large measure, the inconsistencies stemmed from the continuing influence of clientism and the absence of a cohesive working team within the State Department bureaucracy and from the administration's acceptance of ill-defined national security concerns as excuses for deflecting human

rights goals. Of course, complete consistency in international affairs is rarely possible and a foolish consistency can be a hobgoblin of foreign policy as well as of the small mind. Still, as Stanley Hoffman pointed out, "*ad hoc*-ism is particularly unbearable in a domain which seems to call for consistency."[23] In human rights, where values of human dignity and worth are at stake, there is good reason to call for a single standard, and there is a distinct vulnerability in selective application. Critics, even friends, focused on these and other vulnerabilities.[24]

Nonetheless, Carter's signal achievement was to redefine that national interest to include the human rights component. Writing midterm in the Carter administration, Professor Schlesinger said, "Human rights was now institutionalized as a claimant in American foreign policy decisions." Schlesinger, however, had the foresight to add, " . . . at least for the life of the Carter Administration."[25]

HUMAN RIGHTS UNDER REAGAN

Life after the Carter administration turned out to be precarious for human rights. The Reagan administration, determined to distinguish its policy from the so-called weaknesses of its predecessor, showed how quickly it could deinstitutionalize human rights as a claimant in American foreign policy decisions. At-

22. During the Carter administration, a number of dictators fell — Idi Amin in Uganda, Somoza in Nicaragua, and Bokassa in the Central African Empire. Disappearances declined in Argentina, and in Peru, Portugal, Ecuador, Bolivia, and Brazil, there were movements away from military regimes and toward constitutional governments. Annual emigration of Soviet Jews reached 51,000, the highest level ever. The Carter administration, of course, can hardly claim credit for all of these developments, but it did contribute to them.

23. Stanley Hoffmann, "A View from Home: The Perils of Incoherence," *Foreign Affairs,* 57:463, 479 (1979).

24. See, for example, Alan Tonelson, "Human Rights: The Bias We Need," *Foreign Policy,* 1982-83, pp. 57-98; Stanley Hoffmann, "The Hell of Good Intentions," *Foreign Policy,* 29:3 (1977-78); idem, "Requiem," *Foreign Policy,* 42:3 (1981).

25. Schlesinger, "Human Rights and the American Tradition," p. 521.

tacks on Carter's human rights policies became a cottage industry in the west wing of the White House. Reagan administration officials, with Jeane Kirkpatrick in the fore, quickly cuddled up to repressive regimes in Latin America, Asia, and South Africa and supported international monetary agency funding for a host of authoritarian governments. Ambassador Kirkpatrick visited Chile but declined to meet with human rights groups. She hobnobbed with South African military officials, while the vice-president traveled to Manila to toast Ferdinand Marcos for his "adherence" to democracy.[26] So much for the institutionalization of human rights in foreign policy.

What happened to the proposition that human rights goals were a vital component of the national interest? Very simply, the administration did not see it that way. The initial apocalyptic molders of the Reagan foreign policy were Jeane Kirkpatrick and a neoconservative coterie. In Schlesinger's apt term, the ship of state was captured by a "boarding party of idealogues."[27] They redefined the national interest to make it synonymous with national security. And national security was driven by the contest for world power against the Soviet Union; this called for alliances with anyone that was against the "evil empire." In this view of the national interest, human rights objectives were a kind of moralistic luxury that had to defer to a balance-of-power realpolitik.

This condition prevailed for the initial years of the Reagan administration. By 1982, the administration had somewhat eased its position. If one read the lips of administration officials, one heard splen-did pronouncements of evenhandedness. What was usually provided, however, was lip service. During the second Reagan term, the administration took a much more positive human rights stance. In part, this was in response to congressional pressure, as in the case of South Africa, or to external events, as in the case of Chile, or to popular pressure, as in the case of the Philippines and Haiti. In part, as Tamar Jacoby observed, the administration began to appreciate that human rights progress coincided with America's strategic interests.[28] Still, judged as a whole, the Reagan administration's human rights policies were marked and marred by double standards. Throughout most of its tenure, the administration focused on the use of human rights as a cold-war weapon against Marxist states, showed a disdain for internationalism,[29] and supported right-wing repressive governments—Argentina, Indonesia, Malaysia, Panama, Pakistan, the Philippines, Singapore, Somalia, South Korea, Turkey, South Africa, Uruguay, and Zaire—because these governments were regarded as allies against pro-Soviet states or as candidates for Communist takeovers.

Obviously, national security is a vital interest and, if at peril, its protection must override other interests, including, if need be, human rights. But "national security" is an imprecise term. When is the national security truly involved? When does it merit overriding human rights concerns? Jeane Kirkpatrick's view was that national security interests required alliances with any state that was adverse to the Soviet Union. To dress up and rationalize this balance-of-

26. Tamar Jacoby, "The Reagan Turnaround on Human Rights," *Foreign Affairs*, 64:1066, 1070 (1986).

27. Arthur Schlesinger, Jr., "Foreign Policy and the American Character," *Foreign Affairs*, 62:1, 5 (1983).

28. Jacoby, "Reagan Turnaround on Human Rights," p. 1084.

29. See, for example, Richard Gardner, "The Case For Practical Internationalism," *Foreign Affairs*, 66:827 (1987); Charles Maynes, "Lost Opportunities," ibid., 64:43 (1986).

power approach, Kirkpatrick advanced her infamous totalitarian-authoritarian model. Communist regimes were totalitarian and hostile, and their abuses were decried. Anti-Communist regimes were authoritarian and friendly; they were to be supported economically and militarily, and their human rights abuses were to be downplayed. This dichotomy was the neoconservative application of Machiavellian statecraft: a government's primary moral and political duty is to prevail in the struggle of us—the good—against them—the evil. In that struggle, the enemy of my enemy is my friend.

The Kirkpatrick thesis, which the administration embraced, has been so extensively analyzed and faulted by critics that it does not require extended discussion here.[30] From a human rights viewpoint, it ignored the essence of what was at stake: the existence of a human rights abuse depends on what is done, not the nature of the regime. Abuse is abuse and torture is torture, no matter who the perpetrators may be. It was certainly no solace to the mother whose son disappeared in Argentina or to the black man banned in South Africa to be told that the outrage was committed by an authoritarian regime rather than by a totalitarian one.

From an empirical perspective, the Kirkpatrick thesis was also faulty because it rested "on a confusion between the world of ideal types . . . and the world of political realities."[31] Authoritarian states, such as South Africa, Chile, Argentina, and Guate-

mala, were often harsher in their repression of human rights than were totalitarian states, such as Hungary, Poland, and Yugoslavia. Moreover, not all authoritarian states were friendly to the United States, nor were all totalitarian regimes unfriendly, as the Kirkpatrick model assumed. Artificial constructions can be dangerous when mistaken for descriptions of the real world.

Kirkpatrick tried to justify her disparate treatment by arguing that authoritarian states are susceptible to liberalization and should be helped. This is a flawed argument, however. On the contrary, the potential of authoritarian states for democratization should lead the United States to press such regimes for human rights progress and thus propel them toward democratic measures. Moreover, the United States often has the leverage to be effective with authoritarian governments because they need U.S. economic and military assistance. On the other hand, when the United States helps repressive governments, it prolongs repression, and when those governments fail, the United States risks the succeeding government's hostility. Kirkpatrick also wrongly assumed that totalitarian regimes were beyond redemption; recent history has dramatically demonstrated the shallowness of that perception.[32]

The principal defect in the Reagan outlook was not that it took national security

30. See, for example, Cyrus R. Vance, "The Human Rights Imperative," *Foreign Policy*, 63:3, 9-10 (1983); Tonelson, "Human Rights: The Bias We Need," pp. 57-62; Jerome J. Shestack, "The Rise and Decline of Human Rights in United States Foreign Policy," *Columbia Human Rights Law Review*, 15:19, 33-35 (1983).

31. Hoffmann, "Reaching for the Most Difficult," p. 19.

32. The Kirkpatrick model included a worst-case scenario. In her view, traditional authoritarian governments were in danger of being replaced by Marxists, reactionaries, or other revolutionaries. Hence to support authoritarian governments was to choose the lesser of two evils. But this is an artificial choice, not a moral imperative. One can reject both lesser and greater evils. Moreover, Kirkpatrick misunderstood the nature of autocracies and the desire of their citizens for democratic government. As it turned out, the worst-case scenario did not materialize in Argentina, Brazil, Bolivia, Chile, Peru, the Philippines, South Korea, or Uruguay.

seriously but that it misconceived national security and wrongly evaluated it to preclude other interests. Obsession with national security, of course, was not unique to Kirkpatrick or the Reagan administration. A great deal of bad policy has been justified in the name of national security. Concerns presumably about security were used to justify the Cambodian invasion, carpet bombing, chemical defoliation, free fire zones, and the destruction of villages, supposedly, in order to save them. Much bad domestic policy has also been rationalized on security grounds.[33]

Certainly, a nation's security must not be endangered, but national security must be realistically appraised. Illusory security interests should not be invoked to override human rights concerns. Consider the following cases. What national security interests would have been endangered had the Reagan administration not supported the junta in Argentina? When the confrontation arose between England and Argentina, the national security reason for supporting Argentina disappeared and the administration supported England.

What national security interests were served by the long support of Pinochet? Pinochet was defeated; U.S. national security does not appear to have been compromised. What security interest required the prolonged embrace of Marcos? The bases in Clark Field? Some military experts believed that, given other U.S. footholds in the Pacific, such bases were largely unnecessary. Even if the bases were necessary, would they have been jeopardized if Mar-

33. Justice William T. Brennan, Jr., has pointed out that "the perceived threats to national security that have motivated the sacrifice of civil liberties during times of crises are often overblown and factually unfounded." Brennan, "The Quest to Develop a Jurisprudence of Civil Liberties in Times of Security Crises" (Address delivered at the Law School of Hebrew University, Jerusalem, Israel, 22 Dec. 1987).

cos had not been supported? In the end, Marcos fell and the bases remained. What security interests would have suffered if the administration had pressed for elections in South Korea earlier and harder? Would Turkey have dismantled U.S. bases and given up some $750 million of foreign aid if the administration had vigorously opposed torture in Turkish jails? These attenuated and overblown national security excuses for deflecting human rights initiatives reflect the softness in the Reagan administration's commitment to a human rights policy.

A more forthright and probing approach to a claimed threat to national security would test each basis in fact and examine its relation to the human rights interests that are sought to be subordinated. If those measures were taken, I expect one would find very few situations in which national security interests constitute sufficient reason for shunting aside human rights concerns. In those few cases, an administration should be prepared to identify the fears and objectives that justify overriding human rights interests. The Reagan administration too quickly and too often found national security or strategic excuses for forgoing human rights pursuits. More often than not, the security and human rights interests are not mutually exclusive but compatible. In fact, in most cases, advancement of human rights serves the nation's strategic interests.

A FUTURE ROLE
FOR HUMAN RIGHTS

What we see from this review is the fragility of the role of human rights in foreign policy decision making. Before 1975, the role was nonexistent. Carter made human rights a strong component of foreign policy. But four years later, human rights were trumped often by perceptions of other interests. Gradually, human rights policy made a comeback, arriving by the very end of the Reagan administration close to where it had been, more or less, at the end of the Carter years.

What of the future? A new administration is in its freshman year. What role will it assign to human rights in foreign policy decision making? On the merits, the role should be significant. The reasons I gave earlier as to why a human rights focus is in the national interest should be equally relevant for the Bush administration. Indeed, implementing a positive human rights policy should be easier for the Bush administration. The means for furthering human rights are now well developed: disassociation from abuses; linkage in areas of security, military, and financing assistance; public and private diplomacy; pressure by multinational coalitions and regional bodies; marshaling of public opinion; cooperation with nongovernmental human rights organizations; sanctions in particularly egregious cases — the peaceful arsenal is large and can be used effectively.

The hurdles on the playing field are fewer. The United Nations is increasingly receptive to human rights initiation. In South America, except for some unfinished transitions, authoritarian regimes have been displaced with democratic governments. Human rights activity has increased in many African nations and in Southeast Asia, with China's future being in a highly precarious state. In portions of Eastern Europe, particularly in the Soviet Union and Poland, the condition of human rights has advanced considerably compared with its status five years ago. Current events have overtaken the Kirkpatrick-neoconservative view of the world. A solid case has been made for the congruence of human rights values and our long-term interests.

Does the progress that has taken place in realizing civil and political human rights mean that a need for a human rights focus in foreign policy no longer exists? Hardly. Human rights abuses still abound in the world. The storming of a few Bastilles has not razed the many that still exist. Many of the recent democracies that have replaced authoritarian governments are fragile and vulnerable to an authoritarian comeback. The United States needs to encourage and help shore up these governments. The United States must also face up to those states where democracy is still only a facade for military control. Human rights advances in the Marxist world obviously need to be addressed with sensitivity and care.[34]

We must also, at long last, cope with the neglected aspects of human rights that will, in the years ahead, undoubtedly cause ferment. These are the lack of economic and social rights that distress and unsettle most of the Third World. These rights involve concepts of distributive justice that we have been reluctant to accept. They involve the need to reassess the quantity and quality of our assistance programs. Ultimately, they involve the need to transfer substantial resources as the price for a stable and more equitable world order. The urgency of these rights must be faced. A world in which large masses of its inhabitants are deprived of basic needs, let alone a decent standard of living, cannot be a stable or a just world.[35]

34. For an excellent analysis of the case of the cold war and human rights programs, see Michael Mandelbaum, "Ending the Cold War," *Foreign Affairs*, 68:16 (1989).

35. See David P. Forsyth, "Socioeconomic Human Rights: The United Nations, United States and Beyond," *Human Rights Quarterly*, 4:433 (1982); Philip Alston, "Making Space for New Human Rights: The Case of the Right to Development," *Harvard*

Of course, enormous problems exist in realizing economic and social rights for poor nations. It is not a task for the short-winded or the short funded. Addressing this need cannot be done by the United States alone; it calls for a coalition of shared purpose among all of the developed states. The United States, however, has the opportunity to be a leading and constructive force in forging that coalition.

CONCLUSION

Each administration has to define the national interest in its own terms. The Bush administration, relieved of the burdens of superpower confrontation, has an opportunity, as Secretary of State Baker observed, to structure a foreign policy for "new times."[36]

The "new times" require responses to new challenges: environment, international economics, the drug trade, terrorism, arms reduction.[37] But the challenge of human rights continues. Including a strong human rights component in U.S. foreign policy would express political vision, contribute to individual development and dignity, build coalitions in a multipolar world, and further world order. Sakharov's insight is compelling: "The ideology of human rights," he said, "is probably the only one which can be combined with such diverse ideologies as communism, social democracy, religion, technology and those ideologies which may be described as national and indigenous."[38] The opportunity to strengthen and coordinate an international system of states that respect human rights appears greater now than at any time in history. This is an exciting time.

Archibald MacLeish prophesied that human rights may turn out to be the true revolutionary movement of the twentieth century. Can there be any doubt that our national interest will be served if the United States helps make that prophecy come true?

* * *

QUESTIONS AND ANSWERS

Q (Gerald Porter, Committee of Concerned Scientists, New York City): I find your analysis a little bit wanting in one regard. The picture you paint of American policy is one of a bunch of people sitting in Washington making decisions and re-

moved from other sorts of reality. But American popular pressure seems to be an influence on U.S. policy, too. The emergence of the Jewish emigration movement in the USSR and the resulting formation in the United States of a special interest group to support that, plus the anticommunists, who found a way of attacking the Soviet state, put a lot of pressure on the U.S.

Human Rights Yearbook, 1:3 (1988); Jerome J. Shestack, "An Untimely Focus: The Vulnerability of the Reagan Administration's Human Rights Policy," Harvard Human Rights Yearbook, 2:25-53 (1989).

36. James Baker, "Power for Good: American Foreign Policy in the New Era," Current Policy, 14 Apr. 1989, no. 1162.

37. See, for example, Charles W. Maynes, "Coping with the '90s," Foreign Policy, 74:42 (1989); Henry Kissinger and Cyrus Vance, "Bipartisan Objectives for Foreign Policy," Foreign Affairs, 66:899

(1988). Both articles instruct the new administration in policy goals and stratagems but do not see fit to emphasize human rights — a sobering reminder, perhaps, that human rights is still far from the recognition it requires in U.S. foreign policy.

38. Quoted in Burns H. Weston, "Human Rights," Human Rights Quarterly, 6:257, 281 (1984).

government. I think that we have seen among the people in the United States at various times greater and lesser emphasis on human rights. Popular pressure does not play a decisive role in the formulation of U.S. policy, but it seems to play a large one.

A: Certainly, popular pressure is important with respect to human rights. Nongovernmental organizations are very important, but it takes time for them to have an effect. The American people were against the Vietnam war for many years before the government took action to end it. President Johnson left office due to popular dissatisfaction with the war, yet the war continued for the first four years of the Nixon administration. With human rights, the Reagan administration did nothing more than issue a few statements on the matter for the first year. The influence of the American people and pressure groups is important, but, at least in the short run, it does not control U.S. human rights policy. But the fundamental values of the American people do support human rights, and in the long run they will support a foreign policy that has human rights as part of its focus.

Q (William Fernekes, National Council for the Social Studies, Washington, D.C.): The United States has an increasingly multicultural student population, particularly in areas that are near the southern U.S. border. There are, for example, many multicultural groups throughout the United States in urban school systems. Can you give us some priorities in the human rights area for refugees and how the United States might structure its response?

A: There is no doubt that there is an interrelationship between refugees and human rights. Many people become refugees because they are deprived of human rights. If human rights were observed, we would have fewer refugees around the world. The other reason, to a large extent, that there are refugees — leaving aside the cataclysmic effect of war — is the deprivation of economic and social rights. People leave a place because they cannot live there, they cannot satisfy their basic needs. The basic reason why people leave Mexico is that they cannot make a living in Mexico; their basic needs are not fulfilled, and they see America as the land of opportunity. To address that huge problem, one must deal with economic and social rights. It means an enormous transfer of resources. The issue is distributive justice — human rights not only in terms of liberty but also in terms of equality. Achieving distributive justice is very difficult because it means taking resources away from somebody. But we will not have a stable order unless the developing nations address the problem of distributive justice. In the future, distributive justice will be a very high priority, just as the environment and Third World poverty will be. So long as we have a world of haves and much more numerous have-nots, we shall have a lot of refugees.

ANNALS, *AAPSS,* **506,** November 1989

Human Rights in the Reagan Era: Acceptance in Principle

By ARYEH NEIER

ABSTRACT: Over eight years, the Reagan administration's policy on human rights shifted dramatically. At the outset, some in the administration repudiated promoting human rights internationally as a foreign policy goal of the United States; others argued that the United States should condemn abuses by hostile totalitarian governments but not by friendly authoritarian governments. By the time the Reagan administration left office, it accepted that promoting human rights was a major goal and that the United States should be evenhanded in condemning abuses. Despite the seeming headway, much remains to be done. The Reagan administration equated elections and democracy with human rights and failed to condemn abuses by ostensible democracies such as the Philippines and Guatemala; it promoted human rights in high-profile countries such as Chile while ignoring abuses in obscure countries such as Somalia; and it failed to condemn abuses by Communist governments, such as Yugoslavia and China, that had broken with the Soviet Union. In the Bush years, the task of the human rights movement is to secure implementation of principles that are now accepted.

Aryeh Neier has been executive director of Human Rights Watch since 1981. Previously, he served with the American Civil Liberties Union for 15 years, including 8 as national executive director. A graduate of Cornell, he holds honorary degrees from Hofstra, Hamilton, and the State University of New York at Binghamton and serves as an adjunct professor of law at New York University. His books include Defending My Enemy *(1979) and* Only Judgment *(1982).*

"A principal goal of the foreign policy of the United States," according to a law first enacted in 1974, "is to promote the increased observance of internationally recognized human rights."[1] A decade and a half later, that proposition probably commands more support than at any time previously. An essential factor in the development of the current consensus is that, by the time the Reagan administration had ended at the beginning of 1989, it had persuaded itself, and the nation, of the rightness of this goal.

Eight years earlier, when the Reagan administration assumed office, its secretary of state, Alexander Haig, informed the Congress that a concern for combating terrorism would replace a concern for human rights. Today, it is unthinkable that Secretary of State James Baker would propose replacing a concern for human rights with a concern for any other cause. Indeed, when the subject of human rights arose at his confirmation hearing on 18 January 1989, the comments of Secretary Baker echoed the words of the 1974 law.

Senator Christopher Dodd of Connecticut referred to one of the early themes of the Reagan administration in posing a question to Baker on human rights. "We all recall," Dodd said, "earlier statements distinguishing between totalitarian and authoritarian governments in applying a different standard of human rights in those situations. . . . [Do] you believe a different standard ought to be applied? If so, why? And if not, why not?"[2] Baker responded:

I think . . . human rights . . . is one of the very basic foundations of our foreign policy, and for that matter, our national security policy. . . . I don't think that we should distinguish in our human-rights standards in application between situations where human rights are violated on the left or situations where human rights are violated on the right. I think our standards ought to be straight and we ought to play it down the middle.[3]

Baker's response to Senator Dodd was predictable. By 1989, it would have been shocking if he had said anything substantially different. It is that predictability that seems remarkable just eight years after Alexander Haig and Jeane Kirkpatrick testified at their confirmation hearings and eight years after President Reagan nominated Ernest Lefever to be assistant secretary of state for human rights. Lefever, it will be recalled, had earned his nomination by statements like this one in congressional testimony on 12 July 1979:

In my view the United States should remove from the statute books all clauses that establish a human rights standard. . . . It should not be necessary for any friendly state to "pass" a human rights "test" before we extend normal trade relations, sell arms, or provide economic or security assistance. This approach, I believe, should be adopted toward adversary states like the Soviet Union.[4]

On another occasion, moreover, Lefever had also opposed a human rights "test" for the Soviet Union. As he wrote in the winter of 1978:

Our policies of nuclear deterrence should be determined by our understanding of the Soviet nuclear threat and our trade policies toward Moscow should be determined by our economic and security interests. Neither should be influenced, much less determined, by the extent of human rights violations in the Soviet Union. Likewise, in dealing with Third World countries, their foreign policy behavior should be

1. Sec. 502B(a)(1) of the Foreign Assistance Act of 1961, as amended.
2. *Washington Post,* 19 Jan. 1989.
3. Ibid.
4. U.S. Congress, House, Committee on Foreign Affairs, Subcommittee on International Organizations, "Human Rights and U.S. Foreign Policy," testimony, 12 July 1979.

the determining factor, not their domestic practices.[5]

The first milestone on the path that led from the views espoused by Haig, Kirkpatrick, and Lefever — not that their views were identical — at the time that Ronald Reagan assumed the presidency to the views stated by James Baker at the time that George Bush took office was the rejection of the Lefever nomination in a 13-4 vote by the Senate Foreign Relations Committee in May 1981. For most of that year, any further movement along that path was forced upon the administration by its critics in the Congress, in the press, and in private organizations concerned with human rights. In subsequent years, the Reagan administration continued to proceed in the direction that led to Secretary Baker's testimony, sometimes at the prodding of these critics but also sometimes through its own initiatives.

THE CASE OF CHILE

Despite the great changes that took place between 1981 and 1989, some of those who were critical of the Reagan administration's stand on human rights at the outset were still dissatisfied when it left office eight years later. Before exploring the reasons for that dissatisfaction, however, it is worth citing an example of the movement that did take place. Perhaps the most striking is the trajectory followed by the administration in developing and implementing its policy toward Chile.

In 1981, the new team in Washington manifested support for the regime of General Augusto Pinochet. The Reagan administration reversed the practice of the Carter administration that had opposed multilat-

eral development bank loans to Chile on human rights grounds. It sent a prominent spokesperson, Jeane Kirkpatrick, to Santiago to state that the hostility of the Carter years was at an end. In the following year, 1982, it dispatched James Theberge to Santiago to serve as U.S. ambassador, a post he had previously held in Nicaragua during the Somoza years. During those years in Managua, Theberge was noted for his assurances to visiting members of the U.S. Congress that the Somoza government did not practice abuse of human rights, and the signal sent by his appointment in Chile was that he would perform a similar service in Santiago. Despite congressionally imposed restrictions that would have made it difficult to provide the Pinochet regime with direct military assistance, it appeared for a period in 1982 and 1983 that the Reagan administration would send such aid.

By the time it left office, the Reagan administration had reversed itself completely and had demonstrated its opposition to the Pinochet regime. On 17 December 1987, President Reagan and Secretary of State George Shultz issued a joint statement asserting that the United States "share[s] the aspiration of the Chilean people to have full democracy" and that this meant elections in "a climate of freedom and fair competition,"[6] including freedom of assembly and access to television for the opposition. Later the same month, the administration stripped Chile of trade benefits under the General System of Preferences for its violations of labor rights. The U.S. embassy in Santiago was making strenuous efforts to secure prosecution and punishment of the murderers of Orlando Letelier even though more than a decade

5. "The Trivialization of Human Rights," *Policy Review,* Winter 1978.

6. "U.S. Statement on Support for Democracy in Chile" (U.S. Department of State, press advisory, 12 Dec. 1987).

had passed since he was killed. Also, the United States abstained on votes on some loans to Chile by the multilateral development banks. The National Endowment for Democracy and the U.S. Agency for International Development funneled money to the Chilean opposition during 1988 to finance voter registration and, thereby, to help ensure that the no vote prevailed in the plebiscite held 5 October 1988 to determine whether Pinochet should hold onto his office as president for another eight years. On the eve of the plebiscite, to make clear the strong commitment of the United States that the vote should go forward, Deputy Secretary of State John Whitehead summoned the Chilean ambassador to his office in response to rumors that Pinochet planned to cancel the vote. U.S. Ambassador Harry Barnes, who succeeded Theberge in 1985, wound up his service in Santiago after the votes were counted in the plebiscite with everyone regarding him as the friend of democracy and human rights and as the enemy of Pinochet.

The Chilean case is regularly cited by those who claim that the Reagan administration's policies, at least during its later years, included the evenhanded defense of human rights. To some — such as myself — who continued to be dissatisfied with the way that the Reagan administration's policies on human rights evolved, the Chilean case is also emblematic. For these critics, the Pinochet regime in Chile had all of the characteristics that made it an easy and logical target for those intent on giving the appearance of evenhandedness without the actuality. That is, it was an avowedly military regime that came to power by a coup and ruled dictatorially, with no veneer of democratic government; it continued to be ruled by the same figure — that is, Pinochet — whose hands were covered with blood at the time of the coup; it figured

prominently in international attention to human rights abuses, both because of the purported and actual involvement of the United States in the overthrow of the predecessor Allende government and because its human rights community was extraordinarily sophisticated and had many articulate spokespersons inside and outside the country who were well known internationally; it was not located in one of the regions of the world that had been a strategic battleground between the superpowers; and the almost certain alternative to the military regime would be a politically centrist democratic government that would be friendly to the United States.

From the standpoint of such critics of the Reagan administration's policies on human rights, picking on Pinochet had high rewards and low costs. The principal reward was to be able to point to firm opposition to abuses of human rights on the Right as well as on the Left and thereby to establish credibility for a policy that purported to be devoted to the promotion of human rights. Moreover, it helped to legitimize criticism on human rights grounds of left-wing regimes, particularly those elsewhere in Latin America, such as Cuba and Nicaragua. As for the cost, it was minimal, amounting to little more than the disaffection of such die-hard supporters of Pinochet in the United States as Senator Jesse Helms of North Carolina.

Even to the critics of the way that the Reagan administration's policies on human rights evolved, of course, the stand against Pinochet was far from valueless. The efforts of the United States helped to open political space within Chile and contributed significantly to the likelihood that a democratic transition would take place in 1990. Also, on a broader scale, those efforts represented a rejection of the views espoused by Haig and Lefever in 1981 in that they represented the acceptance, at least in principle, of the importance of promoting human rights as a foreign policy goal of the United States. Finally, the evolution of U.S. policy toward Chile represented a rejection of the Kirkpatrick dichotomy and an acceptance of the view that our policy should be applied evenhandedly; in Secretary Baker's words, "our standards ought to be straight and we ought to play it down the middle." Much as this represented progress, however, it left a sizable gap between the policies of the United States as they were applied in practice even at the conclusion of the Reagan era and the policies espoused by the leading private groups in the United States concerned with human rights.

GLOBAL SURVEY

One way to understand the nature of that gap is to consider the application of U.S. policies to governments that are not client states of the Soviet Union and that practice significant abuses of human rights but otherwise do not share the essential characteristics of the Pinochet regime in Chile. How was the shift in U.S. policy on human rights from 1981 to 1989 manifested in the case of governments that are ostensibly democracies even if their armed forces wield actual power; or that came to power by elections rather than by a coup; or that are not headed by a despot who carries the symbolic freight of a Pinochet but by a gray figure or by a representative of a party or military bureaucracy who may be readily replaced by some other representative; or that do not have a high profile in international affairs or in attention to human rights abuses; or that are located in regions that have become strategic battlegrounds; or that may be susceptible to left-wing takeovers, either in elections or by other means,

if the governments that currently practice abuses should be weakened and fall?

In such circumstances, some critics of the Reagan administration's human rights policies contend, when the rewards were fewer and the costs were higher than those that followed from opposing Pinochet, the Reagan administration's practices even during its final years were generally not to serve as an advocate of human rights. Worse, it frequently defended the practices of such governments and, thereby, acted as an apologist for abuses.

The point can be illustrated by examining briefly the record of the Reagan administration during its final years with respect to several governments in different regions of the world. None of these governments is a client state of the Soviet Union but all have practiced, in varying degrees, significant abuses of human rights. In other respects, they differ in crucial ways from the Pinochet regime in Chile and from each other. In an effort to demonstrate that these examples are representative, I have focused on U.S. policy with respect to one country in Africa, one in Asia, one in Europe, and one in Latin America.

An African country that may illustrate what the evolution of the Reagan administration's policies on human rights has meant in practice is Somalia. Its relative obscurity, at least as far as most Americans are concerned, probably means that few would place it on a list of the world's human rights disaster areas. If the extent of abuses and the suffering they have caused were criteria, however, Somalia belongs on such a list. Yet the Reagan administration did little or nothing to promote human rights in Somalia, probably because what happens in that country or elsewhere in the Horn of Africa attracts little domestic debate in the United States and also probably because Somalia does lie in a region of considerable strategic importance. It has hundreds of miles of coastline, both on the Indian Ocean and on the Gulf of Aden; for nearly a decade, the United States has operated military facilities at the port of Berbera; and Somalia shares long borders with a Soviet client state, Ethiopia, and an important U.S. ally in the region, Kenya. Another consideration in the case of Somalia is that, after Ethiopian forces defeated Somalia in the Ogaden War in 1978, the Somali government — which was previously backed by the Soviet Union — switched sides and now enjoys the backing of the United States. This makes the application of a human rights policy in Somalia particularly sensitive, from a strategic standpoint, as the United States may not wish to convey the view to Third World governments that this is one of the costs of joining our side.

In the two decades since the government of Mohamed Siad Barre seized power in a military coup, political repression in Somalia has been pervasive. It is a capital offense to belong to an opposition group or to an organization that has not been approved by the government. The media are all operated by the government and no breath of criticism of its policies is permitted. The judges are subservient to the executive branch of the government. The National Security Service conducts warrantless searches and detains suspects for limitless periods. The death penalty is used to punish a wide range of political crimes.

During 1988, intense fighting erupted in the northern part of the country between an insurgent group, the Somali National Movement, and government forces. The counterinsurgency measures by the government — ground and aerial attacks on areas populated by presumed civilian supporters of the Somali National Move-

ment — were so fierce that, in a period of a few weeks, 300,000 to 400,000 civilians fled across the border into impoverished Ethiopia. Another 600,000 or so were internally displaced. The Somali government barred journalists and human rights groups from access to the conflict areas, and relief agencies departed because their personnel were endangered or because they were not permitted to carry out their humanitarian programs in a manner that accorded with their determination to remain neutral in the conflict.

Neither before the period of intense fighting nor subsequently did the United States speak out against human rights abuses by the Siad Barre government. Indeed, after some of the most extreme abuses against civilians were committed during the conflict in 1988, the Reagan administration sent new shipments of military assistance to the Somali government. For all intents and purposes, the Reagan administration's policies with respect to human rights in Somalia were no different at the end of its tenure from when that administration entered office in 1981. The transformation in rhetoric and principle from the days of Haig, Lefever, and Kirkpatrick had no practical consequence.

There are, of course, many more differences than similarities between Somalia and the Philippines, the Asian country that I have chosen to illustrate the deficiencies that are perceived by some critics of the Reagan administration's policies on human rights. The Philippines ranks much higher in strategic importance. Far from being obscure, before the student revolt in China in the spring of 1989, the Philippines may have been the only Asian country whose chief of state could be named by most Americans. It, too, is engaged in a guerrilla war, though of the low-intensity-conflict variety. Perhaps the greatest difference from Somalia for those concerned with human rights is that whereas the latter is a totalitarian dictatorship, the Philippines is a democracy. Extensive abuses of human rights currently take place in the Philippines despite the central government rather than at the direction of the central government.

In the last few years, the Philippine armed forces and vigilante groups linked to them have engaged in a large number of assassinations and disappearances and in the use of torture against civilians suspected of links to the Communist New People's Army or of sympathizing with it. Among the victims have been a number of journalists whose reporting has earned the enmity of the army and the vigilantes, and several human rights lawyers, apparently murdered because of hostility toward their clients. Many of the most grisly abuses are attributable to the vigilante groups that emerged subsequent to Corazon Aquino's assumption of the presidency following the ouster of Ferdinand Marcos in 1986. At the outset, instead of condemning the vigilantes, the United States appeared to endorse them. Secretary of State George Shultz said during a visit to Manila in June 1987, "As far as the citizens' groups are concerned, as I understand it, they are being organized within the framework of government authority. They are not sort of free-floating vigilante groups, and President Aquino has supported that approach and we support what she is standing for."[7]

It was an astonishing comment six and a half years into the Reagan administration, at a time when these groups had compiled a record of unrestrained brutality and lawlessness. Yet it reflected not only support for those resorting to any means to defeat a Communist insurgency but, perhaps

more important, an unwillingness to oppose a president who had become a symbol of the triumph of democracy over dictatorship. Even a year later, following extensive public criticism of his comments in Manila, and many additional killings by the vigilantes, Secretary Shultz was not ready to oppose them unambiguously. Testifying before the Senate Foreign Operations Subcommittee in June 1988, he described the vigilante groups as "a development that . . . has pluses, but it also has minuses. Vigilante groups are always a problem . . . because they tend to take the law into their own hands, so to speak, and that can be a dangerous trend." He added that it was important to be "wary" of such groups, not exactly a ringing condemnation of the Philippine counterpart to the death squads of Central America.[8]

In Europe, the Reagan administration's responses to abuses of human rights in Yugoslavia are particularly illustrative. At the end of the administration's tenure, there were more known political prisoners in Yugoslavia — some 1300 — than in the seven Warsaw Pact countries combined. This does not mean that Yugoslavia is the most repressive country in the region. The fact that the names of few political prisoners are known in Romania, for example, reflects the fact that repression is so severe that few Romanians dare even express dissenting views and risking prison. Also, information gathering on human rights is extremely difficult in the case of Romania, and there may be political prisoners other than those whose names are known to human rights groups.

---

7. "Shultz Endorses Philippine Paramilitary Groups," *New York Times*, 17 June 1987.

8. U.S. Congress, Senate, Committee on Appropriations, Subcommittee on Foreign Operations, "Foreign Assistance and Related Program Appropriations, Fiscal Year 1989," pt. 3, "Hearings before the Senate Committee on Appropriations," testimony, 100th Cong., 2d sess., 16 June 1988.

Despite these caveats, the high level of political imprisonment in Yugoslavia does signify that human rights abuses warrant denunciation. Most of the political prisoners in Yugoslavia were imprisoned simply for what they said. Yet, though the Reagan administration was outspoken in denouncing abuses of human rights in other Communist countries, it maintained almost complete silence about abuses in Communist Yugoslavia because Yugoslavia is not aligned geopolitically with the Soviet Union. In this respect, the Reagan administration's position was similar to its stand with respect to the People's Republic of China: that is, a Communist government that broke with the Soviet Union was rewarded by silence about its violations of human rights. By following a similar approach when the Chinese student revolt broke out in the spring of 1989, the Bush administration found itself with little to say at one of the great moments in the history of the struggle for human rights.

Finally, the Latin American example I have chosen is Guatemala. Though the human rights situation improved to some degree during 1986, the first year in office of Vinicio Cerezo, its elected civilian president, subsequently it deteriorated rapidly so that, at this writing, the number of political assassinations and disappearances is running at a higher rate than during the last two years of military rule that preceded Cerezo. Aside from suffering such violent abuses, Guatemalans are victimized by coerced, unpaid, onerous service in "civilian patrols" in which they engage in surveillance over each other and their neighbors under the direction of the army. Despite the elimination of any serious guerrilla threat several years ago, hundreds of thousands of Indian males in the highland regions are still required to participate in patrol duty.

The Reagan administration did not spare the Guatemalan government criticism on human rights grounds out of special affection for President Cerezo. Though documents released during the trial of Oliver North suggest that Cerezo had concluded a secret agreement in September 1986 with the Reagan administration to support the contras in Nicaragua, his part subsequently in undermining the contras by promoting the Central American Peace Plan cannot have endeared him to Reagan administration officials. Even so, he was a democratically elected president and criticizing his government would actually have meant denouncing the Guatemalan military, which has been the author of horrendous abuses but which also supported the transition from a military regime to democracy. Accordingly, the Reagan administration was either silent about the continuing human rights abuses in Guatemala or defended its government against criticism.

Are the examples discussed here in fact representative? Many other governments around the world could have been chosen to illustrate the same point: that the commitments to promote human rights, and to do so evenhandedly, that were accepted in principle by the Reagan administration were applied in practice only to the Soviet Union and its client states in Eastern Europe and the Third World; to a few old-style right-wing military dictatorships such as those in Chile and Paraguay; and to a few governments that have become enemies of the United States for reasons not directly related to their abuses of human rights, such as those in Iran and Panama. There were exceptions from time to time when abuses in one or another country became particularly notorious: it is possible to cite occasions when the Reagan administration criticized violations of human rights by such governments as those of El Salvador, Israel, Liberia, Turkey, and Uganda. But it did not maintain ongoing pressure on these governments to end human rights abuses as it did with respect to governments such as those in the Soviet Union and Chile. Yet because it ended by doing so in Chile as well as in the Soviet Union, the Reagan administration's claim that it promoted human rights evenhandedly acquired considerable public credibility.

THE REAGAN LEGACY

Despite the Reagan administration's shortcomings in practice, as far as some critics in the human rights movement are concerned, its legacy is another matter entirely. In accepting, at least rhetorically, that efforts to promote human rights are central to U.S. foreign policy and that such efforts should proceed evenhandedly, the Reagan administration effectively ended debate over those issues. These propositions are now taken for granted. Eight or nine years ago, they could be dismissed as idiosyncrasies of the Carter administration. Indeed, when President Reagan nominated Ernest Lefever for the post of assistant secretary of state for human rights, it appeared that the United States was reverting to an earlier era when the human rights issue was not part of the foreign policy agenda. In contrast, at the end of the Reagan administration, concern with human rights appeared to have secured a permanent place in the formulation of our policy toward other nations.

For those seeking a Bush administration human rights policy that carries into practice the commitments that the Reagan administration adopted in principle, there are three main challenges. The first is to persuade the Bush administration that democ-

racies should not be immune to human rights criticism. The second is to persuade it that strategic interests should not deter speaking out on human rights, either because there is no conflict between the two foreign policy concerns or because, except in circumstances of extreme danger to national security, the national commitment to promote human rights internationally should take precedence. The third is to get the Bush administration into the habit of attempting to curb gross abuses even when these attract little public attention.

The Reagan administration's reluctance to criticize democratic governments for their abuses of human rights — or abuses by military or paramilitary forces over which they exercise scant control — was ideologically rooted. President Reagan and leading members of his administration seemed to consider it a given that democratic government itself would solve most ills. These views were set forth forcefully in an address by President Reagan to the British Parliament on 8 June 1982 that was an important early milestone in his administration's commitment in principle to promote human rights and also in redefining human rights. Previously, a concern with human rights meant, first and foremost, a concern with ending such gross abuses as extrajudicial executions, disappearances, torture, and long-term imprisonment without charges or in reprisal for peaceful expression or association. Indeed, it is such abuses that are enumerated specifically in U.S. laws that require that promoting human rights shall be a "principal goal of the foreign policy of the United States." Those laws are silent on the question of democracy, or on such elements of democratic government as elections, freedom of expression, and freedom of association. To the Reagan administration on the other hand, a concern with human rights meant, above all else, a concern with establishing democracy.

President Reagan's 1982 address to the British Parliament was delivered at a time when the most hotly debated human rights issue in the United States was military aid to El Salvador. It was a time when thousands of civilians were being killed by death squads and almost every day's newspapers seemed to carry accounts of additional horrors. To President Reagan, however, not only did democracy offer a way to end such abuses, but the fact that a democratic process was under way itself negated what was being reported about those abuses. As he told the Parliament:

For months and months the world news media covered the fighting in El Salvador. Day after day, we were treated to stories and film slanted toward the brave freedom fighters battling oppressive Government forces in behalf of the silent, suffering people of that tortured country.

Then one day those silent suffering people were offered a chance to vote to choose the kind of Government they wanted. Suddenly the freedom fighters in the hills were exposed for what they really are: Cuban-backed guerrillas who want power for themselves and their backers, not democracy for the people.[9]

In effect, President Reagan was saying, by lining up to vote, Salvadorans had not only repudiated the guerrillas but had erased from the pages of their history the military massacres, death-squad killings, disappearances, and torture. He never said this in so many words, of course, but that was the impression that he and other spokespersons of his administration seemed eager to create.

9. "Text of President Reagan's Address to Parliament on Promoting Democracy," *New York Times,* 9 June 1982.

Unfortunately, though governments such as those in Guatemala and the Philippines may be fairly described as democracies, violent abuses of human rights on a large scale have persisted. These countries have a free press and a significant number of free institutions, and officials of their governments hold office as a result of free and fair elections, but they have not established the rule of law and do not control political violence by their own armed forces. If the purposes stated in U.S. laws on promoting human rights are to be fulfilled, the Bush administration will have to be persuaded, as the Reagan administration was not persuaded, to go beyond celebrating the advent of democracy in such countries and to seek actively an end to violent abuses.

The possibility of persuading the Bush administration that strategic concerns are not damaged by speaking out on human rights may be enhanced because the Reagan administration helped us to enter into a new era of détente with the Soviet Union. In particular, because the Soviet Union has been withdrawing support from some Third World governments and guerrilla forces and abandoning some imperial ambitions, policymakers in the Bush administration may be less fearful that criticizing human rights abuses by U.S. allies will destabilize them and serve the purposes of hostile neighbors or Soviet-backed opposition forces. In this scenario, the cause of promoting human rights could prevail not because it is perceived as independent of strategic concerns but because certain strategic concerns are considered less urgent.

Of course, almost any administration would wish to maintain security assistance to some governments that practice gross abuses of human rights. Turkey, which is an important ally in the North Atlantic Treaty Organization because of its geographical location but which also has systematically used torture against political detainees, is an example. U.S. laws requiring the promotion of human rights take into account situations of this sort and provide a way to maintain aid. There should be no reason, however, for the United States to fail to exert pressure on such a government to curb abuses. Though threatening to withhold security assistance may be an inappropriate means of pressure if an administration has no intention of fulfilling such a threat, it still should speak out publicly about gross abuses of human rights. Much of the time, this is the most effective means of exerting pressure to end abuses, and it is difficult to imagine many circumstances in which this would conflict with strategic concerns.

Indeed, it could be argued that if the United States spoke out consistently and evenhandedly to criticize human rights abuses wherever they occur, the possibility of a conflict with strategic concerns would be diminished or eliminated. No government could feel that it was being singled out for criticism. It would simply be accepted that one of the functions the United States has assumed in world affairs is always to speak out in defense of human rights and in opposition to gross abuses.

Finally, there is the task of persuading the Bush administration to speak out with respect to abuses that attract little public attention — such as the extreme abuses in Somalia — because of where they take place. This may be the most important change from the practices of the Reagan administration that is sought by some human rights advocates. The reason is that, quite aside from what is done by the U.S. government, it is possible for human rights groups themselves to generate pressure to curb abuses in those parts of the world that attract the spotlight of public attention. On the other hand, the government of the United States has a unique capacity to focus attention on more obscure regions. If it will not speak out about gross abuses in such regions, the expressions by others may be little heeded.

Though it may seem a difficult task to persuade the Bush administration to speak out on human rights abuses in democracies, in situations where there are apparent conflicts with important strategic concerns, and in situations that would otherwise escape public attention, in 1981 the task of persuading the Reagan administration to travel the distance that it did travel by the time it left office in 1989 appeared even more formidable. What is required in eliciting a strong policy on human rights from the Bush administration involves the implementation in practice of principles that are now accepted. In contrast, what was required in dealing with the Reagan administration in 1981 was persuading it to alter its principles. The fact that such a revision actually took place provides the opportunity that is now available.

* * *

QUESTIONS AND ANSWERS

Q: Although the Khomeini regime has proved to be one of the most brutal regimes ever known, was there any particular reason that you have not elaborated on the gross violations of human rights that have taken place in Iran and on its relations and behavior? Please comment on the behavior of the Reagan administration with respect to the Khomeini regime.

A: Certainly, the Khomeini regime has a disastrous human rights record. I myself try to avoid ever saying that one government or another government has a worse record on human rights. It seems to me that when one engages in comparisons, there is always a tendency to excuse the government that is somehow described as not engaging in such severe abuses. The Khomeini regime is a horrendous regime from the standpoint of human rights, but there are also other horrendous regimes elsewhere in the world. I did not cite, for example, the government of the Sudan; and yet one could say that if genocide is being committed anyplace in the world today, it is probably being committed in the Sudan so far as the Dinka population in the south is concerned. I was not trying to give a catalog of the worst human rights abuses in the world. If I had, there would be quite a few more governments that I would name. I would have named the North Korean government, for example, which is probably the most systematically totalitarian government in the world, as one of the great abusers of human rights. But I think it is, in general, best not to get into that kind of catalog — or hierarchy, if you will — of horrors. As far as the Reagan administration's approach to the Khomeini government is concerned, I would not say that it has been primarily shaped by concerns about human rights. I would say it has been shaped primarily by a variety of strategic concerns of the United States. Strategic concerns probably animated the attempts to deal with so-called moderate elements in the Khomeini government during the affair that we know as Irangate or Contragate. I would mention one other set of concerns. The Bush administration has been, I think, less than outspoken in dealing with the Salman Rushdie affair recently and the Khomeini government's attempt to purchase the execution of Salman Rushdie. I have wondered why the administration has so deliberately downplayed that affair, why the president has never spoken out forcefully on that particular episode. I have heard explanations, such as the desire not to inspire terrorist acts against U.S. facilities in various other countries. But I do not know if, in fact, that is the reason the administration has soft-peddled the Rushdie affair so much or whether it reflects a desire at some point for a strategic rapprochement with the Iranian government. It does seem, however, to be the strategic concerns that have been the dominant impetus behind U.S. policy toward Iran.

COMMENT: I am a born Muslim. At the turn of century there will be some 1 billion Muslims throughout the world. I think that intolerance in the name of piety is not exclusive to any religion. The Khomeini regime has for the past ten years been massacring the Iranian people, has been threatening the free nations of the world, and so on; yet there has not been much fuss about that regime. But all of a sudden, once Rushdie insulted the prophet of Islam and Khomeini responded, there was an outcry. I am not against Mr. Rushdie's book. I think he has the right to write. But we also have to consider the fact that we as human beings do have the right to worship.

Human Rights as an International Issue

By LOUISE I. SHELLEY

ABSTRACT: Human rights currently constitute an issue of great concern. Several conditions, resulting from cumulative postwar developments and the current political situation, account for the present change in attitude toward human rights. They are (1) institutional developments of the past forty years; (2) the growth of citizen human rights organizations; (3) decline in superpower involvement in international and regional military conflicts; (4) the current focus of national leaders on human rights; and (5) significant political changes in the most abusive nations. This article focuses on the change in the conceptualization of human rights in Latin America and the Soviet Union and the current priority given in these areas to the issue of human rights. It also focuses on the utility of the human rights issue for these countries. The dynamics in the human rights arena have changed in the 1980s, but there is no guarantee that the present conditions will continue.

Louise Shelley is chair of the Department of Justice, Law and Society as well as professor in the School of International Service of the American University. She has written Crime and Modernization *and* Lawyers in Soviet Work Life *as well as numerous articles. She has been the recipient of Guggenheim, National Endowment for the Humanities, Fulbright, Kennan Institute, and International Research and Exchanges Board fellowships.*

NOTE: My thanks to Professor Tom Farer for his thoughtful suggestions.

HUMAN rights constitute an intellectual and legal problem as well as a political issue of extraordinary concern. The issue of human rights is now part of an intellectual dialogue that assumes headlines in many leading newspapers throughout the world. There appears to be growing consensus in the Western world and in certain socialist societies that human rights are definable, should exist, and may be an achievable objective.

The international rock concerts sponsored by Amnesty International have brought the concept of human rights to a broader and more general audience than the readers of leading newspapers. At this time of greater agreement on human rights, there is a concomitant risk that the movement's message has been appropriated by its enemies.[1] So many countries, long violators of human rights, have become their advocates. Has the issue of human rights been so generalized as to be trivialized?

There are harsh reminders that the growing consensus is certainly not a universal trend. The terroristic death threats against Salman Rushdie and the banning and burning of his book, *The Satanic Verses,* indicate that many human rights, as currently conceived, are a Western concept not sought or institutionalized by many non-Western countries. Although these countries are signatories to the United Nations' convention on human rights, their political and social cultures do not conform to many of the provisions expressed in this document. The issue of human rights, as it has emerged out of the ideas of the Enlightenment, still remains alien to many of the world's nations.

The growing consensus in many Western and Western-oriented societies does not necessarily herald the institutionalization of human rights in these societies. The fragility of the new democracies, the debt crisis in Latin America, and the failure as yet to institutionalize law reform in the Soviet Union mean that the new approach to human rights is reversible. The present situation may be an interlude, albeit a desirable one, in the international arena.

The change in the international dialogue on human rights is significant. Human rights now command the attention of national leaders of major political powers, as well as enjoying broad support among political conservatives and liberals of different social classes. Several different political factors account for this evolution. Some of these factors represent the evolution and consolidation of human rights policy in the postwar period while others are conditions unique to the mid and late 1980s.

This article will focus on the conditions that have most recently contributed to the present prominence of human rights. The changing conceptualization and attention paid to human rights in Latin America and the Soviet Union will be emphasized.

THE EMERGENCE OF THE HUMAN RIGHTS ISSUE

The international human rights movement emerged out of the ashes of World War II. The Allies declared during World War II that the purpose of victory was to "defend life, liberty, independence and religious freedom, and to preserve human rights and justice."[2] Following the war, the United Nations was founded and the Commission on Human Rights was established to prepare an international bill of rights.

---

1. Tom J. Farer, "The United States and Human Rights in Latin America: On the Eve of the Next Phase," *International Journal,* 43(3):473 (1988).

2. Warren Lee Holleman, *The Human Rights Movement* (New York: Praeger, 1987), p. 1.

The Universal Declaration of Human Rights adopted by the United Nations is now forty years old. Born out of the Holocaust and the atrocities of World War II, the declaration outlaws murder, torture, and political imprisonment. These steps reflect "the lessons of the Second World War which demonstrated that internal regimes were not just a domestic matter but could themselves become a menace to world peace."[3]

The Universal Declaration of Human Rights, adopted in the final years of Stalinist rule, when mass repression was still institutionalized, seemed to many to be a hypocritical gesture. In many of the signatory countries this characterization remains true, but the human rights issue has recently acquired greater prestige and respect in the international arena. It is no longer exclusively the sphere of a limited number of do-gooders but is a concern of many politicians with a mass constituency. The observance of human rights has become a key gauge by the international community of a country's performance.

Human rights did not acquire visibility until recently. But concern for human rights has grown gradually in the postwar period, accelerating in the last ten years. The reasons for the current prominence of this issue are primarily political, although economic conditions have contributed to the changing status of human rights. Those dependent on American foreign assistance are evaluated annually to determine their aid eligibility, and the foreign debt, particularly of the Latin American countries, has in some ways made them more vulnerable to external pressure. Political changes at the top of the political hierarchy as well as mobilization at the grass-roots level have also contributed to this change.

3. I. F. Stone, "The Rights of Gorbachev," *New York Review of Books*, 16 Feb. 1989.

Let us examine more closely some of the major changes, first by focusing on long-term changes in the postwar period and subsequently by analyzing the dynamics of the late 1980s. These major changes include institutional developments for the past forty years, the growth of human rights organizations, a decline in superpower involvement in international and regional military conflicts, priority paid to human rights by many national leaders, and significant political changes that have occurred in some of the most abusive countries.

The United Nations' declaration is still viewed as the cornerstone of human rights developments, but it is only the first step of many that have been taken. Human rights have been pushed onto the international level through covenants and legally binding agreements as well as the establishment of international and regional human rights organizations. Many of these have produced much more tangible developments in the human rights arena than the more famous U.N. declaration.

The development of human rights legislation and institutions has been well documented.[4] For the purpose of this article, I will merely enumerate the major covenants and official human rights bodies. These include the International Covenant on Civil and Political Rights and the International Covenant on Economic, Social and Cultural Rights, both adopted by the General Assembly of the United Nations in 1966. In the postwar period there has also been an elaboration of human rights institutions. The first steps were taken in Europe. The Commission and Court of Human Rights in conjunction with the

4. See, for example, A. H. Robertson, *Human Rights in the World*, 2d ed. (New York: St. Martin's Press, 1982); Louise B. Sohn and Thomas Buergenthal, *International Protection of Human Rights* (Indianapolis: Bobbs-Merrill, 1973).

Council of Europe was authorized in 1950.[5] Subsequently, these institutions developed in the Americas. The Inter-American Commission on Human Rights of the Organization of American States was established, and its enforcement body, the Inter-American Court of Human Rights, now operates in San José, Costa Rica. The Organization of African Unity has adopted a human rights charter and has indicated its commitment to enforcement through a court to be based in the Gambia. These legal documents and organizations have given prominence to human rights in many parts of the world.

One of the strongest pushes for human rights in the Western world has been provided by the agreement establishing the Commission on Security and Cooperation in Europe. Popularly known as the Helsinki accords, it was not originally conceived of principally as a human rights document. Adopted in Helsinki in 1975, it has had a very significant impact on the U.S.-European-Soviet dialogue on human rights. Initiated by the USSR in the 1950s to gain legitimacy for its dominance in Eastern Europe, the Helsinki accords were finally signed by 35 nations but only after a compromise had been reached. In exchange for the first two baskets on military and economic cooperation, the Soviet Union and Eastern Europe agreed to a variety of human rights provisions, the so-called Basket III. With many countries feeling that they had made very significant compromises and with the USSR and the East European countries in very clear violation of many of the provisions agreed to, the Eastern bloc left itself open to criticism by state bodies and numerous citizen groups that sprang up in Western Europe and the United States to monitor the observance of the accords.

5. Robertson, *Human Rights in the World,* p. 82.

Although the Helsinki accords may be one of the most visible success stories on the official level, progress has been made in other parts of the world in recent decades. The reports of the Inter-American Commission on Human Rights focusing on numerous abuses in Latin American dictatorships have had a major impact in many countries. More recently, a landmark victory was secured in a case concerning disappearances in Honduras before the Inter-American Court of Human Rights.[6]

Second, in the last two decades since the formation of Amnesty International, the approximately 1000 human rights organizations have acquired a large, socially and geographically diverse following. Amnesty International, with the largest constituency and the most broad-based agenda, and the other, more narrowly focused groups have raised the consciousness of large numbers of individuals worldwide and have become important pressure groups. This has been done by forming locally based citizens' groups and also through mass publicity efforts such as the recent live rock concerts sponsored by Amnesty International throughout the world. Human rights groups, enjoying much popular support in the mass media of democratic and democratizing countries, are able to exercise their influence in this forum as well.

The research and fact-finding missions conducted by independent human rights organizations bring credibility to human rights concerns that is not possible when the issues are researched by governmental bodies. Rarely tied to a particular party or movement, the independent organizations are able to serve as a credible voice with

6. "Inter-American Court Finds Honduras Responsible for Disappearance," *Human Rights Watch,* no. 3, p. 1 (July-Aug. 1988).

different political administrations. Human rights for these groups is a primary concern that does not have to be balanced with the general political strategy of an individual nation.

Third, international superpower conflicts are at a nadir. There have been no major world wars for four decades. Furthermore, there is lessened superpower involvement in regional wars. The Iran-Iraq war has been terminated, and the USSR has withdrawn from Afghanistan. The tensions generated by the lengthy and costly cold war are subsiding as the Soviet Union has seemingly abandoned its commitment to the exportation of revolution. The unanimity of the Soviet bloc is ending. Some have gone so far as to suggest that peace is breaking out throughout the world, although this is certainly an overstatement, considering the amount of nonideological conflict still present. Nonetheless, these changes provide an atmosphere conducive to human rights.

Fourth, the international dialogue on human rights has been accelerated by the prominence given to this issue by many national leaders. Speaking from the American perspective, human rights have assumed a prominent place on the agenda of recent American presidents. The United States, albeit possibly a declining superpower, has a significant influence on the international political dialogue. The recent prominence given to human rights in the Soviet Union and, to a lesser extent, in Latin America and Asia by successive American presidents has made them an issue that is impossible to ignore.

President Carter, the first American president to place such emphasis on human rights, was first viewed as a Don Quixote figure or a sign of American weakness. But his policy achieved more momentum as its themes, initially abandoned, were subse-

quently appropriated by President Reagan[7] and pursued during the remaining years of his presidency, although with a very different political orientation. The national attention to human rights was not just a presidential effort, as Congress and its individual members joined to promote this policy objective sometimes in conjunction with the White House and sometimes at cross-purposes. A standing congressional subcommittee of the House Foreign Affairs Committee was dedicated to human rights.

The United States is certainly not alone in the Western industrialized world in the prominence it has attached to human rights issues, but it places more emphasis on them than many other large developed countries. Within Europe, Scandinavia and the Netherlands have also made human rights a key feature of their foreign policy.

The human rights thrust that was once clearly identified with the United States in the superpower dialogue is no longer solely in the American domain. Gorbachev, since his ascent to the Soviet leadership, has made human rights both a national and an international priority.[8] The USSR seeks to abandon a defensive stance on this issue as it arranges to host a major human rights conference in the USSR in 1991.[9]

Fifth, major political changes have occurred in the Soviet Union and Latin American countries, previously among the most abusive of nations, which have made human rights into an acceptable, even desirable, issue in the international arena. The tenor of discourse between the Soviet Union, the United States, and Western Eu-

7. Tom J. Farer, "United States and Human Rights in Latin America," pp. 475-76.
8. "Vienna Breakthrough: Human Rights in the USSR," *Moscow News*, no. 13, p. 10 (1989).
9. Natan Sharansky, "Rights Parley—or Sham," *New York Times*, 22 Jan. 1989.

rope has changed. Moreover, it has become a domestic Soviet issue by which the proponents of *perestroika* are trying to break permanently with the Stalinist legacy.

"An upsurge of human rights violations in the 1960s and 1970s produced a concomitant proliferation of efforts—local, national and international—to combat them."[10] These efforts were a major factor in forcing military governments in Latin America to transfer power to democratic governments. With the transition to democratization, the human rights issue is a significant way of discrediting past military governments and of delegitimizing the opponents of pluralistic regimes. The willingness of many Latin American countries to engage in international and domestic dialogue on human rights indicates the change in attitudes toward this issue.

The major political changes have made human rights a central issue on the international political agenda. Progress in this area has by no means been universal, however. In some societies there has even been a deterioration of the human rights situation. But that deterioration has become an important measure of the development of those societies, a reflection of the changing appraisal of the significance of human rights.

The changed perception of the importance of human rights and of the possibilities for institutionalizing guarantees of personal and political freedom do not necessarily reflect a permanent change in the international climate. The debt crisis in Latin America and the economic difficulties in the Soviet Union may jeopardize the current political situation. Consequently,

there is no guarantee of the permanence of the present congenial climate for human rights.

THE CONCEPTUALIZATION OF HUMAN RIGHTS

Many analysts have long suggested that there is no single conception of human rights, asserting that there are very different perceptions of human rights in Western, Communist, Muslim, Latin American, and African countries. Although so many countries are signatories to the United Nations' documents on human rights, these legal agreements have not necessarily universalized the conception of human rights.

The violent reaction to the Rushdie book, the negative Chinese reaction to President Bush's invitation of a dissident to an official reception,[11] and harsh Cuban reaction to Gorbachev's new human rights thrust reveal that great differences still remain in the conception of human rights. Much of the Muslim world believes that individual freedom should not threaten the interests of the community. According to the Sharia, "It is the state's duty to enhance human dignity and alleviate conditions."[12] In this view, human rights are not granted through individual initiative. Marxism, the ideological basis of Communist societies, also emphasizes the importance of collective values and the subordination of individual needs to the interests of the state. Furthermore, many Latin American countries accepted the national security doctrine, which subordinated individual rights

10. Margaret E. Crahan, "Human Rights and U.S. Foreign Policy: Realism versus Stereotypes," in *The United States and Latin America in the 1980s*, ed. Kevin J. Middlebrook and Carlos Ricos (Pittsburgh, PA: University of Pittsburgh, 1986), p. 417.

11. Nicholas D. Kristof, "'New Authoritarianism' Seen in Chinese Actions," *New York Times*, 28 Feb. 1989; Dan Southerland, "Chinese Police Stop Dissident," *Washington Post*, 27 Feb. 1989.

12. Abdul Aziz Said, "Human Rights and Islam," in *Understanding Human Rights: Cultural and Ideological Perspectives*, ed. Adamantia Pollis and Peter Schwab (New York: Praeger, 1979), p. 87.

to state interests. The collective interests of these different groups provide a fundamental contradiction to the Western conception of human rights embodied in the Universal Declaration of Human Rights, a document that reflects the ideas of individual rights originating in the Enlightenment.

The present change in the international atmosphere concerning human rights can be ascribed to a very dramatic change in the conception of human rights in the Soviet Union and many Latin American countries. These major world regions are moving toward acceptance of the predominant Western views of the supremacy of individual rights to free speech and political expression. There is no longer unanimity in the Communist world. China and Cuba have not abandoned the view that a social safety net of assured employment, housing, and medical care is the preeminent human right, but fundamental change on this issue is evident in the USSR, Poland, and Hungary.

The Soviet Union, under Gorbachev, has been de-ideologized and no longer places its emphasis on Marxist doctrine. It has currently tempered its traditional view that communal rights are more important than individual ones. As a Soviet law scholar contends, "One of the principal tasks that is being accomplished during the democratization of our society is the ensuring of unconditional respect for human rights and liberties and their protection against all violations."[13] The most visible recognition of this transformation is the Soviet decision to accept the International Court of Justice's binding arbitration over five important human rights agreements concerning genocide, trafficking in prosti-

tution, guaranteeing the political rights of women, banning racism, and the outlawing of torture.[14]

The growing focus on human rights in Latin America has permitted individuals of different social classes and political views to form a consensus on the given major issues at hand.

Having rejected the revolutionary path, and being conscious of the extremely serious economic difficulties that future governments must face, democratic leaders of the left and center (as well as some emergent "democratized" sectors from the preceding authoritarian regime) know that they have no alternative other than negotiation and compromise if the authoritarian stage of the cycle is not to be reproduced.[15]

No longer are communal values emphasized to the detriment of those protecting the individual from the abusive authority of the state. This movement in Latin America is by no means unilateral, nor does it suggest the abandonment of the collective values that have been so strong for centuries. Rather, as in the Soviet Union, this new approach to human rights can be seen as an effort to institutionalize democratic values that are closely linked with Western concepts of human rights.

The historical legacies of the Soviet Union and Latin America help explain their approach to human rights. As has been pointed out by a distinguished historian, not only Russia but also Spain was outside the Enlightenment.[16] The Soviet Union is the heir of the Russian legal tradition, a culture in which individual rights

13. Yu. Kudriatvsev, "We Learn Democracy: Restructuring and Human Rights," *Current Digest of the Soviet Press*, 39(42):6 (1987).

14. Paul Lewis, "Soviets to Accept World Court Role in Human Rights," *New York Times*, 9 Mar. 1989.

15. Guillermo O'Donnell, "The United States, Latin America, Democracy: Variations on a Very Old Theme," in *United States and Latin America in the 1980s*, ed. Middlebrook and Rico, p. 363.

16. James Billington, *The Icon and the Axe* (New York: Knopf, 1967).

were consistently subordinated to the state.[17] Russia was never directly exposed to the ideas of the Enlightenment, although some of its values were transmitted via the czars. Latin America has been shaped by the Spanish tradition. "Many Latin American scholars trace their notions of human rights back to Spanish philosophers . . . who antedated the Western Enlightenment and who thought more in communal than individualist modes."[18]

In the USSR, human rights are now tied to the formation of the *pravovoe gosudarstvo* ("rule-of-law state"). Human rights are linked with legality. Individual rights are to be respected as both the party and state institutions are to be subordinate to the law.[19] The doctrine of previous Soviet leaders that social solidarity must be supported even if it jeopardizes the rights of individuals is a concept considered inconsistent with the *pravovoe gosudarstvo*. The concept that citizen responsibilities are more important than individual rights, a formulation currently incorporated in many articles of the existing Soviet constitution, is being reconsidered. As the state has abandoned its promise of full and guaranteed employment, so, too, has it loosened its hold on the expected conformity of the citizenry to state objectives. Numerous voluntary associations have been permitted to form as individuals are being permitted to express their interests outside the state-controlled channels. The censorship of the mass media has been reduced, permitting extensive criticism of the society and its institutions. All of this permits a civil society to develop outside party control. Despite these changes, the USSR has yet to relinquish the concept that the socialist structure must be upheld even if it infringes on the rights of the citizenry to express their opinions.

Very recent amendments to the criminal code still make it a punishable offense to denigrate Soviet officials or to threaten the constitutional order. The newly conceived socialist *pravovoe gosudarstvo* is thus more intrusive into the lives of the citizenry and grants less autonomy to the individual than in Western societies. The Soviet Union has announced its willingness to respect the decisions of the World Court of Justice concerning human rights conventions, but it has yet to make the intellectual leap that would permit it to accommodate itself to the provisions of all the international accords. State control is still too great to allow human rights to the extent granted in less regulated societies.

The national security doctrine that was so present in Latin America during the period of dictatorships in the 1970s has been discredited with the advent of democratic rule in most countries. This doctrine, which reached its fullest expression in the Southern Cone, provided the most long-term threat to human rights. According to the national security doctrine, the state is "held to be an organism with natural rights and its own needs, which take precedence over individual rights."[20] Thus the state is entitled to take extraordinary measures against its citizenry in order to protect the integrity of the state from subversives. With such an ideological justification for repression, numerous individuals were tortured and disappeared in Argentina, Uruguay, Brazil, and Chile. During the period

17. Richard Wortman, *The Development of a Russian Legal Consciousness* (Chicago: University of Chicago Press, 1976).

18. Holleman, *Human Rights Movement*, p. 22.

19. V. N. Kudriavtsev and Y. A. Lukasheva, "Socialist Legal State," *FBIS Daily Reports*, 20 Sept. 1988, p. 5 annex.

20. Crahan, "Human Rights and U.S. Foreign Policy," p. 419.

of military dictatorship, extensive repression also took place in many other countries, sometimes with this intellectual justification and oftentimes without.

The discreditation of the national security doctrine has not led to its replacement with a substitute ideology. But the rule of law, which under the national security doctrine was subordinated to the decisions of the ruling elite,[21] has again acquired value. As in the Soviet case just discussed, the observance of legal norms and the adherence to international human rights covenants represent a desired direction for many Latin American countries trying to democratize.[22] Yet the problem remains of how to establish a state of law in societies without democratic traditions and with strong bureaucratic, populist, or charismatic authoritarian legacies. To do this, Latin American society must also look to voluntary organizations, relying on the growth of voluntary religious, social, and academic associations as well as the development of a free press. These organizations are necessary in societies in which many citizens "do not adhere with conviction to the principles and precepts of a constitutional and pluralistic system."[23] Yet the movement toward the rule of law is slow as the legacy of a hierarchical structure and the great disparities in wealth and social status limit the transformation of these societies to a Western model of individual rights.

21. Ibid., p. 418.
22. Comite internacional de la cruz roja and Instituto interamericano de derechos humanos, *Seguridad del estado, derecho humanitario y derechos humanos* (San José, Costa Rico: Educa, 1984).
23. Rafael Braun, "The Human Rights Question in U.S.-Latin American Relations," in *United States and Latin America in the 1980s,* ed. Middlebrook and Rico, p. 392.

The increasing acceptance of common values of human rights in North and South America, Western Europe, and the USSR has had a very profound effect on the level of international dialogue. With growing consensus on the ways that the state should treat its citizenry, the level of confrontation in international discourse has been reduced. But is this evolution in attitude toward human rights an end in and of itself, or does it perform other functions?

THE UTILITY OF
HUMAN RIGHTS

Human rights are often conceived of differently by the national leaders and the citizen activists who espouse human rights objectives. For some leaders, the advocacy of human rights does not necessarily reflect a growing humanism but may instead be an example of enlightened self-interest. Consequently, the present situation does not assure a permanent commitment to human rights by current leaders. Furthermore, the pressure that is applied to particularly abusive countries by the major powers may diminish as the latter find it no longer in their self-interest to press countries to improve their human rights situation.

The institutionalization of democratic structures has always been a cornerstone of American foreign policy. Human rights are seen as an inextricable part of the democratic tradition that is based on the principles of the Constitution and the Bill of Rights. Because they constitute an issue that is deeply rooted in American values, human rights are supported by both conservatives and liberals. The United States has tried to foster these values in its relationship with other countries, but it has not done this evenhandedly. Standards applied to countries that are allies of the United

States have been very different from those applied to countries outside its sphere of influence.[24]

Pressure from the United States, often combined with that of its Western European allies, has made countries respond to criticisms of human rights abuses. Throughout the 1970s in Eastern Europe and the USSR, presidential and congressional pressure resulted in improvements of individual rights cases but in no major structural or legal changes that would alter the inherent political systems. The same might be said for South America. Pressure applied to the military regimes would help particular individuals but did not alter the practice of disappearances. The internal dynamics of these societies had to change to produce the currently observed conditions.

The human rights equation at the superpower level has changed recently as the USSR has realized the utility of altering its stance on human rights. Yuri Kashlev, the head of the Soviet delegation to the recent Vienna talks at which new human rights agreements were signed, commented that the new aim "'to make humanitarian cooperation one of the Soviet Union's priority foreign policy lines, made it possible for our delegation to act in Vienna and put forward a number of serious initiatives rather than hugging the defensive.'"[25] At this conference the Soviet Union agreed to provisions more encompassing than those of the Helsinki accords, granting greater religious freedom, rights to ethnic minorities, reunification of families, and the right

to emigration.[26] The USSR has chosen to change its stance on human rights not only for foreign policy advantages but also because such a change has significant domestic utility.

One noted American political critic has suggested that Gorbachev is turning "back the clock on human rights" and attempting to "seal them from outside intrusion."[27] Parts of this evaluation are misleading. Recent changes in the Soviet Criminal Code pertaining to political crime are not advances and may indeed be a step backward.[28] But the USSR is now a more open society. Although parts of the country under military rule enjoy limited international scrutiny and there is restricted access to areas with nationalist disturbances, Gorbachev has recently enhanced access of human rights monitors to the Soviet Union.[29]

The USSR has changed its stance on human rights not only because it seeks to abandon its traditionally defensive position but also because it sees concrete domestic payoffs. The rule of law and respect for individual rights have been justified in

24. This point was made very forcefully by Jeane J. Kirkpatrick in a piece that contributed to her rise to prominence in the Reagan administration. See Kirkpatrick, "Dictatorship and Double Standards," *Commentary*, Nov. 1979, pp. 34-35.

25. "Vienna Breakthrough," p. 10.

26. "East-West Talks Better Promises," *Economist*, 21 Jan. 1989, pp. 46-47; U.S. Commission on Security and Cooperation in Europe, *Concluding Document of the Vienna Follow-Up Meeting* (Washington, DC: Government Printing Office, 1989).

27. Stone, "Rights of Gorbachev."

28. "Ukaz Presidiuma Verkhovnogo Soveta SSSR," *Izvestiia*, 10 Apr. 1989, p. 2. The provision on insulting and defaming state organs and public organizations is so broad as to threaten *glasnost*.

29. I was recently part of the juridical commission of Helsinki Watch that visited the USSR with an official invitation. Our hosts arranged talks with high-level Soviet legal officials on human rights questions. This visit was unusual but not totally unprecedented, as an American journalist had been permitted to visit a camp for political prisoners and American psychiatrists had been given access to psychiatric patients.

terms of their economic utility. For the Soviet Union to invigorate its economy and to promote economic initiative, it must convince citizens that they are no longer subject to arbitrary legal authority. Human rights in the USSR are not some lofty agenda but constitute more practical goals such as the establishment of an independent judiciary, a presumption of innocence, and a legal system in which the individual is not helpless at the hands of the state. To achieve this objective there must be a firm break with Stalinism and Stalinist legal norms. Without such a firm schism and the institutionalization of human rights, individual citizens may always fear that the law will be used against them as a weapon to force conformity and stifle innovation. In the Soviet Union the new emphasis on human rights is a utilitarian objective. It is a tool of democratization and economic efficiency, a wedge that separates the past from the present.

Latin America is not a unified political structure as is the Soviet Union, but a dramatic political change has occurred throughout South America in the 1980s as most of the countries have moved from military to elected civilian governments. For these countries, respect for human rights is fundamental to the institutionalization of democracy. Although Latin American countries have not abandoned their traditional Hispanic-based concept of human rights,[30] they are placing more emphasis on such fundamental Anglo-American legal concepts as freedom of the press and speech, free elections, and civil-

ian supremacy over the military. Yet movement toward these objectives is hindered by the legacy of past military governments, many of which had committed such human rights abuses that the societies cannot smoothly make the transition from a dictatorship to a democracy.

Only in Argentina have the former military leaders been held responsible for the abuses committed under their leadership. Following an extensive investigation of human rights abuses,[31] nine former commanders who had ruled Argentina were tried between April and September 1985 for such terrible human rights abuses as kidnapping, torture, rape, and execution. This widely publicized trial discredited the military and facilitated the transition to democratic rule. But this bold step has not been followed in other South American countries. The Uruguayan military and police were granted an amnesty preventing their punishment for the torture and murder committed during their years of rule. This amnesty has been challenged and upheld in a plebiscite, in part because President Sanguinetti argued that its repeal would not be accepted by the military, thus risking the return to democracy.[32] Brazil has also not brought its abusive military personnel to trial.

The failure to try former military personnel does not mean that the problem of human rights is ignored. Brazil, in conjunction with the fortieth anniversary of the Universal Declaration of Human Rights, devoted much attention to past violations of political rights. Even current problems of excessive police force and the large number of police killings of civilians are

30. For a discussion of this, see Howard J. Wiarda, "Democracy and Human Rights in Latin America: Toward a New Conceptualization," in *Human Rights and U.S. Human Rights Policy: Theoretical Approaches and Some Perspectives on Latin America,* ed. Howard J. Wiarda (Washington, DC: American Enterprise Institute, 1982), pp. 30-52.

31. Argentine National Commission of the Disappeared, *Nunca más* (New York: Farrar, Straus & Giroux, 1986).

32. Shirley Christian "Uruguayans Vote, at Ballot Box and in the Streets," *New York Times,* 17 Apr. 1989.

highlighted on television. The public consciousness on these issues is raised, a necessary prerequisite for democratic rule, but the clear discrepancy between present practice and the ideals espoused undermines citizen faith in the existing political structure and its ability to secure human rights.

In many Latin American countries, despite the transition to democratic rule, there is limited civilian control over the military. Death squads operated either by government security forces or by wealthy landowners kill civilians sometimes in very significant numbers.[33] The focus of repression has changed from the time of military rule. While many of those who disappeared were intellectuals, present-day victims are of working-class or peasant origin. The freer electoral structure does not necessarily benefit these individuals.

Citizen recognition of the need for and desirability of human rights is important for both the transition to democratization and the maintenance of democratic rule. It is a point that is recognized by the current Soviet leadership and many leaders of Latin American countries that seek to break with their traditions of military rule. Yet advocacy of human rights that have not yet been institutionalized may prove to be a double-edged sword as the discrepancy between professed intentions and reality may increase hostility toward the existing government. Protest and uprisings, as has been noted, are more frequent in periods of rising expectations. The recent wave of nationalist protests in the USSR is evidence of individuals trying to exercise their constitutional rights. Growing citizen dissatis-

33. See U.S. Department of State, *Country Reports on Human Rights Practices for 1988,* submitted to U.S. Congress, Senate, Committee on Foreign Relations and U.S. Congress, House, Committee on Foreign Affairs, Feb. 1989.

faction is heard in many Latin American countries where the general population in the difficult economic situation sees few tangible improvements in their lives. Attention to human rights may have more political benefits for a political leadership in the international rather than in the domestic arena.

HUMAN RIGHTS: RHETORIC OR REALITY?

Human rights now command a level of unprecedented political and popular attention. Major diplomatic efforts have recently been made to formulate further human rights agreements and to press cases in international tribunals. Significant media attention in different continents is now devoted to the problems and achievements in the human rights arena. Citizen human rights groups command the ear of the public to a previously unrealized extent. But has the issue of human rights been so universalized in the Western-oriented world that it is now trivialized?

Human rights are now in fashion. Advocating human rights is no longer associated with the weak or idealists. But with this growing acceptance of human rights and their advocacy by leaders of very different political stripes, the issue may have lost some of its potency. One reason is that leaders of complex societies, shaped by their existing foreign and domestic policies, are forced to make compromises. Second, issues cannot remain permanently in the forefront. Human rights, deemed to be of such centrality today, may be sidelined tomorrow as the Western world chooses to emphasize the primacy of some other political concern.

Gorbachev speaks of human rights and legality at the same time that Armenia and Azerbaijhan are under military rule and peaceful demonstrators are killed in Soviet Georgia. Prime Minister Thatcher presses for human rights abroad while military involvement exists in Northern Ireland and English intellectuals proclaim that the media are losing their independence and academic freedom is threatened.[34] American presidents criticize human rights abuses in Nicaragua but tread lightly in criticizing allies in South Korea or Israel. With such inconsistency in the advocacy of human rights, has much been gained by the greater acceptance of the issue?

Looking at the issue more positively, it is clear that great strides in human rights have been made in what were previously among the most abusive of nations. The phenomena of torture and disappearances have largely vanished from Latin America. New political rights have been gained in the Eastern bloc as Communist hegemony has given way in Hungary and Poland. In the USSR, the recent elections, the newspapers, and the cultural and religious life give evidence that there are greater individual and political freedoms, particularly in the Baltics and the Russian Republic. Probably little of this would have been accomplished without the increasing awareness of and pressure to institutionalize human rights.

Despite these improvements in human rights, violations of individual rights remain all too common not only in those countries that advocate democratization but also in many that have eschewed this form of government. In 1988 the Iraqi government used chemical warfare to quash a Kurdish insurgency, interethnic conflict in the Sudan resulted in 100,000 to 250,000 deaths from starvation, and major human rights violations were observed in Burma

and Burundi.[35] In these cases, international protests had limited impact, but the number of countries that can remain untouched and unaffected by the criticism is certainly limited. In this respect, the growing recognition of human rights makes it more difficult to mistreat one's citizens and live within the international community. Large-scale citizen mobilization combined with governmental pressure has made it harder for many states to abuse citizen rights. Human rights have not been institutionalized but they are no longer rhetoric.

CONCLUSION

An important dynamic has changed in the human rights arena in the late 1980s. The decline of military conflicts and the ascent of leaders seeking to democratize has given a new impetus to the human rights movement. But will this process be temporary, or does it herald a new world order?

This analysis has suggested that despite the marked improvement, there is no certainty that this situation will prevail with other political leaders or in the face of a domestic backlash in the currently democratizing society.

Human rights cannot be imposed on a society. Institutions that foster and nurture human rights must develop in a society. This is a gradual process. In societies without such a tradition it is unnatural to expect that such a transformation can occur in the face of a different historical legacy and in the face of other pressing economic and political problems. A straight progression in human rights cannot be anticipated; rather, one can expect a process of advancement and subsequent retraction of

34. James Atlas, "Thatcher Puts a Lid On," *New York Times Magazine,* 5 Mar. 1989, pp. 36-38, 97.

35. Department of State, *Country Reports on Human Rights Practices for 1988,* pp. 2-3.

rights. One can only hope that there will be two steps forward for every one taken backward.

Although the present emphasis on human rights cannot be expected to endure, it can be hoped that this increasing consciousness will preclude a return to the mass genocide of the Hitler period, to the Stalinist repression, or to the disappearances of the 1970s. Even if successor governments pay less attention to human rights, the present period will provide a legacy for the future.

* * *

QUESTIONS AND ANSWERS

Q (Anwar M. Barkat, Commission of the Churches on International Affairs, New York City): I have doubts about whether one can pin the growth of human rights — both in terms of ideology and otherwise — on the Enlightenment. The Enlightenment tradition alone does not account for the human rights agenda. Second, how could you ignore the impetus to the human rights movement of the issue of colonialism? Imperialism and colonialism form an important aspect of this discussion. My question is whether you consider work on human rights to be complete now. I would rather think of it as evolving.

A: What I was suggesting was that the emphasis on human rights that has been so significant in the documents that have been produced in the last forty years is one that is traced to the concept of individual rights. I do not see this as being the only way of approaching human rights, but it has become the dominant international focus and it contradicts some of the cultural and social bases of other societies that place an emphasis on collective rights. I think that the point that you make about the change in colonial societies is very, very important; the Latin American experience is relevant to that point. Finally, I share with you the hope that the human rights agenda is evolving. The problem is that the human rights issues peaking at the moment may inhibit some of the progress that still needs to be made.

———

Q: We heard Louis Henkin's paper regarding the universality of the notion of human rights and the issue of whether this has been a concept imposed by the West on non-Western societies. How do you view that particular issue? Is there real universality, or is the issue of human rights an Anglo-American concept?

A: The concept is not Anglo-American. Some of the ideas of the Enlightenment are very French, not just Anglo-American. I think that in some respects one can talk of a certain imperialism of this Western agenda. Imperialism was certainly felt in areas of the world with which I am familiar. For example, in Latin America, there was a feeling that the issue of human rights was tied particularly to American democratic structures and was an imposition of our way of conceiving of human rights. There is not enough appreciation of the collective consciousness with respect to human rights. This has been repeatedly said in the Soviet Union, that is, that we have provided an economic safety net, which is more important for the individual than the expression of political rights is. What is so startling in the Soviet Union is that they have retracted this position and that there is so much emphasis now on individual rights.

Q (Joseph Ostroy, Long Beach, New York): Will you please enumerate the human rights in the Arab countries?

A: I am not a specialist on Arab countries.

Q (Ostroy): You made a comment about one of the countries in the Middle East, Israel. The reason I asked that question is that yesterday's *Philadelphia Inquirer* reported that 34 Palestinian Arabs were assassinated by Arafat's hoodlums and 46 were severely wounded. What can we suppose their relationship is with Israel? So why do you pick on one Middle Eastern country, thereby assuming that human rights exist in Arab countries? I say human rights do not exist in Arab countries.

A: I do not think I said anything like that. The only mention I made of Israel was that there is an inconsistency in American policy. U.S. policy criticizes certain countries more than others, and it has been quite hesitant to criticize human rights abuses in Israel. I also talked about the different conception of human rights in Muslim societies in accordance with the Sharia. That is all that I said on the subject.

COMMENT: I am from Jamaica. I wish your paper had included Jamaica and the Caribbean. This is an area that suffers tremendously from the lack of human rights. You could bring the New World greater perspective.

ANNALS, *AAPSS,* **506,** November 1989

The Right to Life and
Latin American Penal Systems

By EUGENIO RAÚL ZAFFARONI

ABSTRACT: Deaths at the hands of the state in Latin America, through the penal system, are a serious menace to democracy in the region, and they are the worst attacks on human rights. According to the public portrayal of these deaths, it seems necessary to project a continuous war, sometimes as a political war and sometimes as a war against common delinquency. Human rights organizations are usually worried about the first phenomenon and its deaths, but they do not perceive the enormous importance of the deaths produced by the war against criminality, which is publicized by the police agencies to justify the use of their illegal power. Social contamination with common delinquency — and with marginalization in general — is the tool used to inhibit the public denunciation of these deaths — the number of which is frequently higher than the number of deaths caused in cases of open political violence — and to delegitimate any action along that line, especially through the journalists and social operators of the law-and-order campaigns that create the public war atmosphere.

Eugenio Raúl Zaffaroni is professor of criminal law and criminology at the University of Buenos Aires and deputy secretary general of the International Association of Criminal Law. He is also a judge on the Criminal Court of Appeals in Buenos Aires and a member of the Senate Committee for the Study of a New Argentinian Penal Code. He is the author of many publications, including Tratado de derecho penal *and* Manual de derecho penal.

THE present work is an advance report of the final results of an investigation of the subject, which is part of a project set up by the Interamerican Institute of Human Rights. This investigation comprises the first three years of the project, which will be in progress for another two years. The general topic is that of human rights and the penal systems in Latin America; this subject was examined in a general study that was concluded in 1986. In the course of the earlier study, some alarming information emerged about the large number of deaths caused by the direct action of the penal systems in the region and about the indifference of penal systems in the face of other phenomena that were causing an even larger number of deaths.

The importance of this fact moved us to undertake the first factual study of the subject. The data that disturbed us most concerned the public image of those deaths: except for the cases of missing people, generally related to open political violence, the deaths are announced publicly, that is, they are reported in different ways by the mass media and, in many cases, in complete detail. It is outstanding that police agencies provide exact information and statistics to the mass media. This means that they show an involvement in the publicity as a sign of efficiency in the repressive acts.

The first hypothesis was that the phenomenon was measurable through investigating the press. The facts later showed this to be wrong, as we will see. However, our first investigation was of the press. With the available information we cannot measure the phenomenon exactly, but we can describe in detail its public portrayal and we can establish as well a firm hypothesis concerning its function and mechanics. No less important are the conclusions we can extract about the real function and the operation of the penal systems.

The study was first faced with the selection of serious newspapers and following in them the image of this phenomenon over five years. This task was done by local teams in the following cities: Mexico City, San José (extended to the whole country), Bogotá, Quito, Lima, Caracas, Maracaibo, Córdoba (Argentina), Buenos Aires, Montevideo (extended to the whole country), Rio de Janeiro, São Paulo, Salvador (Bahía), and Recife. The results were presented in a seminar in Salvador (Bahía) in December 1988 and were discussed with specialists from the United States and Europe, which enabled us to use comparative data and to enrich the hypothesis. The results of the study in the four Brazilian cities were finished too recently to analyze them for this article, so we include only preliminary discussion of this work presented in the seminar in 1988. At present, we are entirely dedicated to preparing the final work. It is a quite difficult task because of the quantity of information. In this article we will consider some hypotheses that have emerged so far and seem to be confirmed by the available information that has been analyzed.

We must comment that these provisional conclusions can be improved and enriched with the addition of more information.

THE PATTERN THAT EMERGES FROM A FIRST APPROACH

The construction of a hypothesis requires, in some way, a theoretical frame. We believe that this study confirms the fact that in no way is a theoretical frame satisfactory for the Latin American criminological questions. Until now, at least, the most common versions of functionalism, Marxism, and the sociology of conflicts have not allowed us to explain the phenomena adequately and satisfactorily. In a more extensive way, an approach is achieved through the structuralist version of the Foucaultian "microphysics of power," but it requires an approach that can be nearer to the criminology of dependency as the key to the understanding of the phenomena in the so-called developing countries.

There are two theoretical and undeniable consequences. First, the originality of this phenomenon obliges us to use a syncretic theoretical frame, because the known frameworks do not offer any satisfactory explanation. Even more, the extreme dangerousness of this phenomenon requires, from a human rights point of view, the adoption of a pragmatic criterion: the main aim must be the necessity of controlling the death phenomenon in the region. The second consequence is that all the hypotheses based on theory that pretend to explain the problem on a macro level can completely distort the perception of this phenomenon. This consequence seems to be obvious in any contemporary criminological study, but it needs to be specified because it follows from the first one: the nonexistence of a suitable theoretical frame and the lack of satisfaction caused by the constrained application of the usual ones. As a result, a sequence of intuitive hypotheses is generated, full of emotion, when we, as investigators, are also "cognitive subjects" that have introjected the messages of the penal system and its social control. Whether for conformity or as a reaction, we frequently have politicized intuitions that suppose the presence of a dark hand that controls everything. That is, there is an intentionalism

typical of the conspiracy thesis that, according to preference, explains the problem by the action of national or international complexes.

The phenomenon under study includes different kinds of deaths or threats to the human right to life: (1) deaths in real or simulated encounters with agencies of the penal systems, including executions without due process; (2) deaths caused by jail violence; (3) deaths caused by persons authorized or allowed to carry guns; (4) murders committed by the personnel of the penal systems when off duty; and (5) murders committed by extermination groups. The other subject that was also studied is that of transit deaths, which will be explained in less detail.

The analysis of the recorded information showed us a primary classification of the countries, according to the peculiarities of the phenomenon. On the one hand, there are the countries convulsed by open political violence — that is, an encounter that takes place in the presence of large and violent groups, organized with considerable offensive capacity, with a clear and confessed political design, and that is carried on against both military objectives and executive agencies of the penal system. On the other hand, there seem to be two broad categories of countries that are not beset by such violence: countries with evident social contradictions and an increasing level of conflict; and countries with social conflicts controlled in some way.

Even though it is not possible to analyze the information here, I must explain that this classification does not follow any previous hypothesis but emerges from information that was gathered. Examination revealed how this phenomenon works in urban concentrations, according to where the country falls in the classification. The public portrayal of the deaths differs, or at least shows a clear tendency to differ, according to the classification.

COUNTRIES WITH
OPEN POLITICAL VIOLENCE

It is evident that in two cities in this study, Bogotá and Lima, the deaths caused by the penal system are largely depicted as deaths of subversive elements after armed encounters. The trend is much more evident in Bogotá: there seems to be a large number of deaths corresponding to subversive or countersubversive activities, as well as a considerable number of deaths as a result of ordinary murder. The press does not seem to deliberately intend to hide deaths due to ordinary murder, but news stories on them are relegated to the interior pages and printed with reduced titles. They constitute generic news; they are stereotypical, lacking the details that ordinarily distinguish one death from another.

We must observe that in comparison to Lima, Bogotá has the greater degree of violence, that is, the greater number of deaths. We must agree that, even though our study is not quantitative — the nature of the information forbids this — the fact emerges from it that the number of deaths from Peruvian violence is lower than the number in countries without open political violence, as in the Brazilian cities or Buenos Aires.

In Lima, the other deaths resulting from the penal system are publicized in more detail but not in a sensationalist way. This fact leads us to think that the number of deaths caused by the penal system outside of the open political violence should not exceed the number that is published in the newspapers or at least that the newspapers' figure can be taken as a more or less accurate indicator. In any of these countries we can say there is not a deliberate intent to hide. There is less information on these deaths in Bogotá because the deaths are not considered newsworthy.

Briefly, then, where open political violence exists, the deaths by the action of penal systems are not considered hidden. Rather, they seem to be considered less important and are therefore given less prominence.

COUNTRIES WITHOUT
OPEN POLITICAL VIOLENCE

The cities that attract our attention because of their contrast with the rest are the urban concentrations of the countries that seem to control their own social contradictions without publicizing the deaths. In the context of our study, these are the main characteristics of Costa Rica and Uruguay. Uruguay never had the social contradictions caused by or inherited from the existence of intensive culture, and Costa Rica resolved them by means of a so-called natural democratization that took place.

Both countries — with some exceptions in the past decade in Uruguay — have known a long tradition of constitutional government. The subversive violence and state terrorism in Uruguay in the 1970s was not up to the Argentine level, according to some trustworthy evaluations, such as those coming from human rights organizations in Uruguay. In the case of Costa Rica, one of the main favorable conditions that allowed resolution of the social contradictions is the position that it occupies in the power balance of the Central American region. For Uruguay, it is necessary to remember the notorious emigration of young people. Both Costa Rica and Uruguay have much lower urban concentrations than the rest of the countries, and generally their total population represents one-third of the population of one of the great Latin American urban concentrations, such as São Paulo, Buenos Aires, Rio de Janeiro, or Mexico City.

The deaths caused by the penal system and publicly made known in these countries are many fewer than in the rest of the countries that are not plagued by open political violence. There are no reasons to suppose that the phenomenon is being hidden. In addition, the evidence leads us to think that the figures are not alarming. The logical deduction is that it was not necessary for social control to seek remedy in publicity and that the corporate interests of the executive agencies do not give rise to any death.

We can say that something similar occurs in the mediterranean region of Ecuador, where the publicity about deaths is limited. We have some information on Quito, and we hope to have more information on Guayaquil, which would be very interesting, given the different characteristics of both cities as urban concentrations in different regions of the same country. With the information coming from Quito, we can affirm that Ecuador seems to be in the middle of both subgroups of not openly politically violent countries.

PORTRAYAL OF
PENAL-SYSTEM DEATHS
IN COUNTRIES WITHOUT
OPEN POLITICAL VIOLENCE

The rest of the cities analyzed present the most interesting and alarming portrayals of penal-system deaths not only because of their seriousness but for what they mean for human rights and for the future of democracy in the region.

Without considering Mexico City for the moment, we can affirm that in these cities, the public announcement of deaths

caused by the penal system has turned into a daily and normal element of information. The number of suspects dead in real or supposed encounters with police forces is indeed high. We must add that in some countries, a considerable number of deaths are attributed to conflicts between marginal groups, but the penal system does not interfere with any preventive action. One cannot dismiss the possibility of alliances between the agencies of the penal system and some marginal groups. We can finally observe in some cities — Rio de Janeiro, Recife — the existence of extermination groups that act with total impunity. All these deaths are publicized in detail. Most of the time they are cruel and unnecessary, especially if we consider that our data come not from the sensationalist press but from the serious media.

It is impossible for us to provide here the figures for each city and country analyzed. Nevertheless, we will mention some figures to illustrate what we have been observing through the analysis of the available information. The figures that we provide fully prove two things. First, the deaths related to the penal system are not the necessary response to violent criminality, because their number is known to vary according to phenomena that have nothing to do with violent criminality. Second, the daily announcement of the deaths does not extend to the international press because it is considered a normal element of information, even though the magnitude of the deaths can be higher than in the openly politically violent countries.

BUENOS AIRES AND
FACTORS EXTERNAL TO
CRIMINAL VIOLENCE

Part of the city of Buenos Aires belongs to the province of Buenos Aires, and part of the city is federalized. In the provincial part, the city provincial police operate, and in the other part, the federal police do. In 1982 there were a total of 61 deaths by the penal system, 44 of them attributed to provincial police and 17 to federal police. In January 1983 a new wave of deaths occurred in the province of Buenos Aires. These deaths occurred because two months earlier an underground group had emerged among the provincial police backing salary increases and better working conditions. The military dictatorship constructed a convincing image of public security and so the press was controlled; it was not possible to install a law-and-order campaign.

After 1984 the press was not under censorship. At first, with the constitutional government, a liberal reaction was produced in the population, causing police authority to be rejected, public opinion to go against the genocidal army, and so on.

The response was immediate, and a law-and-order campaign was undertaken. The result was a considerable increase in the number of deaths, compared to the time when the democratic government took power. During 1985 the number increased even more. In July the number was considerably higher in the province of Buenos Aires, coinciding with the reform of the procedure code, which forbade the police to give instruction in procedures. The instruction was a task that they had been performing unconstitutionally and that was the source of great corruption. For March we can also observe an increase that coincided with the declaration of the unconstitutionality of the arrest and detention of any citizen for 24 hours — another fount of corruption. A decrease in the number of deaths can be observed for the second half of 1985. The decline coincides with a brutal event — the slaughter of a whole family by the provincial police — with the elec-

tions, and with the broadcast of alarming facts by ultrarightist sectors — according to official reports. For 1986 a recrudescence in the law-and-order campaign is noticed until the middle of the year, when the interior minister was questioned by the Congress, doubting the investigative capacity of the authorities and causing the dismissal of both police chiefs, in addition to the discovery of the participation of police officers in the most savage criminal events emphasized by the press. An abrupt decrease is observed in deaths by the police and it is maintained for some time by the federal police, but it is promptly discontinued in the province. There are obviously different policies emerging from the two police agencies.

Taking the year 1982 as a base, it is fairly clear that with the beginning of the election campaign of 1983 a framework of insecurity was established in the police agencies that increased the number of deaths by 44.26 percent in 1983, still during the dictatorship. This figure rose to 113.11 percent in 1984, during a broad constitutional government, and reached 311.48 percent in 1985, sheltered by a law-and-order campaign that provoked the citizens' insecurity with the approval of the government and certain journalists who held notorious roles during the dictatorship.

In 1986, with the peculiarities that I have already mentioned, the number of deaths decreased, but it was still 145.10 percent higher than in 1982. In data gathered later, we can notice that the time when the figures were lower, even lower than in 1982, was November 1987, the month of the province governor's election and the renewal of deputies at Congress.

If we carefully examine the information we have, it becomes evident that at certain times when the number of deaths increased notoriously, the number of wounded and arrested in real or supposed encounters diminished, until we have months in which there are no wounded or arrested but only deaths resulting from those encounters. This reveals that on some occasions the aim is to kill. As there is no explanation in the criminal violence for changes in the figures, the percentage of wounded cannot be altered easily. Of every hundred persons participating in real or supposed armed encounters with police agencies in 1985, 81 were killed and 19 arrested; in 1986, 92 were killed and 8 arrested.

It is useful to add that the deaths by the penal system are concentrated. We can establish geographical areas of deaths that correspond to well-defined jurisdictions and police headquarters and that vary with the changes of chiefs.

During the period analyzed, police news passed from the interior pages of the newspapers to the front pages, the amount of space devoted to police news was doubled, and the advertising space on those pages was tripled. This information has been requested from a journal that prints 1.5 million copies per issue and that has a national circulation. It can be considered the most powerful journal in Argentina and the one with the best status, after the breakdown or the public setback of the two old, traditional journals. The total population of the city — federal and provincial sectors combined — is nearly 8 million. We have determined the total number of deaths caused by the penal system to be approximately 700 between 1984 and 1987.

COMPARISON WITH PERUVIAN FIGURES

Because the situation of Peru is much more publicized internationally, due to its open political violence, it is useful to compare Peruvian figures to the figures we have given for Buenos Aires. It is possible to object that the center of the open political violence in Peru is not located in Lima, the city we used in our study. But it is useful to know that the mean number of missing persons in all Peru from 1984 to 1988 was 105 a year: 177 in 1984, 94 in 1985, and between 111 and 117 in the years 1986-88. Besides, we have collected information from the whole country to meet this objection.

The following deaths were attributed to the violence of the penal system: in 1982, 18; in 1983, 20; in 1984, 21; in 1985, 26; in 1986, 62. The public officers who were victims of this violence numbered: 40, 84, 92, 75, and 149 in those same years. The figures for deaths in jail are high: 14, 45, 36, 37, and 256, respectively. The number of citizens killed by terrorist violence is also high: 38, 407, 678, 157, and 198, respectively. This means that facing this violence — which is quite considerable if we judge it by the number of dead citizens — were a number of now dead and missing persons. Those who faced violence in jail or death at the hands of police agencies or were missing persons totaled 307 in 1983, 174 in 1984, 156 in 1985, and 425 in 1986. This last figure includes the deaths caused in Lima's jails in the horrible ways that are publicly known. If we compare these figures with those of Buenos Aires, we will find that sometimes they were higher than or equal to those of Buenos Aires. In 1985 there were 156 dead or missing persons in Peru, but in Buenos Aires the state deaths totaled 251 without any open political violence. For 1986, if we do not count the deaths that occurred in Lima's jails, the figure for Buenos Aires is still superior.

This must alarm us about the nature of the phenomenon: the deaths in a penal system of an openly politically violent country can be fewer than the ones produced in a country where this kind of violence does not exist. That is, the penal system can be more violent than when reacting against open political violence but, because this circumstance is not being hidden — because the news is published in newspapers of major circulation — announcement of it is not capable of causing internal or international alarm. The deaths are accepted as normal phenomena that do not even mobilize the human rights organizations.

THE CASE OF MEXICO CITY

Mexico City presents a special case in the publicizing of deaths in the penal system. There are solid reasons to suppose that even though news is not hidden, there is at least a carelessness about it, especially about citizens' deaths at the hands of police. There is no available information about the real facts, but the news registered by newspapers is practically incredible, especially if we have in mind the magnitude of urban concentration and the incidence of conflict in Mexico City. Facing this panorama, we cannot believe that the numbers of cases broadcast — 7 in 1982, 22 in 1983, 17 in 1984, and 16 in 1985 — reflect real figures. There is an obvious interest in not announcing the deaths. The numbers of police officers' deaths are announced, however, and they are high: 42 in 1982, 62 in 1983, 55 in 1984, and 60 in 1985. It can be observed that the number of deaths caused by off-duty police officers was 79 in four years and, of these, 33 were also police officers.

In Mexico City, it is quite clear, there is no interest in showing the deaths caused by the penal system. On the contrary, there is a special stress on publicizing the police officers' deaths, although, at the same time, there does not seem to be a serious effort to protect the officers' lives. The latter fact

obviously emerges from the number of victims who are police officers.

WHAT ARE THE CONSTANTS?

What can we infer from a panorama that seems to be so varied? Over the well-known differences there really seems to be a prevailing note that emerges when a conflictive overflow takes place instead of social contradictions.

When open political violence exists, the executive agencies of the penal system feel secure, because they are needed and there is no way to take away the power they possess. When this situation is not present, the efficacy of the agencies is not evident through the exhibition of their so-called war deaths, and these agencies try to recover their secure position by means of projecting another war; because open political violence does not exist any more, there should be a war against ordinary delinquency.

The power of police agencies is transferred in the corporate interests of the agencies, and to preserve them, the power must not be diminished. Police agencies are necessary to political agencies, or at least the latter need the former not to declare a sort of strike of indifference that could allow a chaotic atmosphere to endanger the political system. To face this extortion, political agencies maintain the power of police agencies. Nevertheless, there are sectors of political agencies and judicial sectors that cut or try to cut this power. In addition, the democratic process itself can cut this power, despite resistance by political groups.

The reduction of the police agencies' power in a constitutional system is a structural result of the democratic system and not an effect of the politicians' desire in particular; politicians frequently would prefer to avoid conflicts. This reduction affects the corporate interests and particularly reduces corruption, which is more or less institutionalized; that is, it decreases licit or illicit incomes. The agencies can maintain their power only by generating another war situation, and that explains the way in which deaths arise in the penal system and their publicity: the determination to show that the penal-system deaths can be explained only by showing publicly the existence of a war and exhibiting the dead enemies.

Such an excuse is not necessary in openly politically violent situations; it is needed only when these situations do not exist or when they end.

Mexico City does not escape this rule. It shows only a different kind of death: police officers'. We must not forget that in Latin America the criminalized, the victimized, and the police belong generally to the same social stratum. The war image is projected in the same way, by showing the enemies' dead bodies or by showing their own dead soldiers. In either case, an image of public war is being projected.

The exhibition of deaths causes public interest. Attempts have been made to explain this interest, and the explanations have taken many forms, from a morbid interest to a natural interest. Whatever type the interest is, the certain fact is that publicizing the deaths attracts and increases the attention. Without censure, the publicity agencies whet the appetite of attention and thereby produce a multiplier effect for the phenomenon. The law-and-order campaign is established easily, reinforced by some journalists who make a more or less conscious contribution by proposing repressive solutions to every single social conflict. We must not forget that the most privileged sectors of Latin American societies are seriously alarmed by any attempt at popular organization in a horizontal form.

POLITICAL PERSPECTIVES

Through these constants we can perceive the political perspectives of the phenomenon. We have already said that we cannot search for a conspiring theory. Maybe only some privileged sectors, with a more or less real degree of consciousness, join their voices through some public opinion operators. But they only join a course already in process; in no way are they the conductors or the promoters of it.

What is certain is that this panorama allows us to conclude that the manifest function of penal systems in Latin America, as being in charge of the guardianship of fundamental rights and principally the right to life, is false. Our penal systems cause an extraordinary number of deaths in comparison with those of Europe, the United States, Canada, and Japan. Those deaths are broadcast in order to maintain an atmosphere of continuous war, which sometimes seems to be a political war and, on other occasions, a war against common delinquency.

This situation is even more evident if we analyze the deaths that occur in transit. The figures are very high, involving nearly 6000 in Argentina and nearly 50,000 in Brazil. The penal system does not take any effective precautions, and the whole normative order does not care about the problem. We have to take into consideration that there is not even provision for a civil reparation, which would be a serious countermotivation. In Peru, for instance, the amount of an indemnity for death is nearly $300. The penal system's indifferent omission on this subject is plain. From now on, the penal-system discourse is false and the judicial discourse is completely empty of content.

All this has deeply serious consequences for the political perspective of the region and especially for its democratic future. It is impossible to ignore the fact that nowadays the productive systems of our countries are suffering a severe contraction, that every day there are more young people rejected by the system, as well as more adult people who are expelled from it. Juvenile marginalization and aggression are a result of the phenomenon of penal-system deaths, as is the adult self-aggression that is transferred into a high number of suicides. The Argentine suicide rate, for instance, is similar to the number of deaths by transit and exceeds the Swedish rate, even if the information on this topic is mostly unknown. Heteroaggression and self-aggression are two effects with the same origin, namely, the anomie produced by the severe contraction of the productive system in a so-called developing society. In this emergency, police agencies that, because of their corporate interests, want to build a war scenario do not contribute to the pacification of a nonpeaceful situation.

We must add that showing the deaths as a daily and normal element in public information—that is, exhibiting the state victims as an everyday source of security—contributes to distorting the public image of the state as supplier of security. It banalizes the deaths and generates the conviction that murder by the state is necessary to control the enemy at war.

The vocabulary used in publicizing these deaths is warlike and generates the paradox that the people perceive death by the state as something easygoing. Such aberration is introjected so much that thinking in any other way becomes disagreeable, a result of a logic branded as idealistic, if not dissolving, subversive, anarchic, or Marxist. Behind all this, the police agencies regain and occupy more positions of power without control, which menace democracy, because they foreclose

the possibility of community organization, something perceived as dangerous by the privileged sectors. The danger then arises of stopping any social development and of producing, in the long term, bursts of irrational public violence.

In the people's sentiment, troubled in a vindicatory sense, there is an enormous disdain for the judicial warranties that are always considered as obstacles to the revenge claimed by social operators, sowing hatred and instigating death. The deformation of the public conscience is also alarming.

In addition to this, the judicial discourse is evidently false in the face of the real social impact of the penal system. We are not far from public disdain for rights and their limits. Under these conditions, our penal systems, because of the number of murders caused and tolerated, turn into genocide machinery in our countries. In Argentina, with a population of fewer than 30 million, the penal system causes in Buenos Aires alone four times the number of deaths caused in five years by acquired immune deficiency syndrome in the whole country, and it remains motionless in the face of the primary cause of death among the young: transit.

We believe that there are possibilities for controlling the phenomenon and that some of them are now emerging spontaneously. Despite the violence of the penal system, community action is apparent. Such is the case in Peru: nearly two-thirds of the population solve their conflicts outside the state institutions.

We feel that the process of neutralizing this genocidal phenomenon must be supported and stimulated. At the level of regional human rights organizations, it should be noted that not only should deaths by the penal system in an openly politically violent climate be amended, but so should deaths that occur where there is no such violence. The deaths are even more dangerous where this kind of violence does not appear. In this article we have not included Brazilian data, but the Brazilian figures are remarkably higher than the ones listed herein. Nor have we considered the rural violence of Brazil, which is a phenomenon left aside in our study.

It is very interesting to note that many human rights organizations only notice the politically violent deaths; when this violence is not present, they do not act. Fear of being discredited as a result of the violation of the prohibition of coalition — that is, the fear of being contaminated by the victim, who is labeled as an ordinary delinquent — paralyzes those human rights groups from taking any action. What they do not perceive is that this paralysis is extremely dangerous to the political future of the region because the executive agencies feel sheltered and omnipotent, and their power cannot be admitted in any democratic system and particularly in a region that requires effective solutions to problems and where conflict is increasing, because of the crisis in the productive system.

We hope this study can help at least to call attention to the extreme gravity of the phenomenon.

* * *

QUESTIONS AND ANSWERS

Q (Paul Chevigny, New York University, New York City): I have a question about the causal relationship between the authoritarian dictatorships in countries like Argentina. In your talk you say that the creation of a fear of crime replaces the control of a state of war under a dictatorship. Do you think that there was similar police violence before the dictatorship began in 1970? I would ask the same question about Brazil — do you think there was similar police violence in the 1960s? I understand that no one knows for sure. Also, do you think that police violence against ordinary people is one of the causes of the development of the dictatorship?

A: We studied police violence in Argentina for only five years but my personal impression is the following: police violence in Argentina was high for several years, but in the dynamic of our society the power of the police agencies increased and it was power without control. This power without control means corruption, and corruptions means increased incomes to the police agencies. Of course, during the dictatorships the possibility of extra income is increased, and when a dictatorship ends, police agencies want to expand all of this power, and then we are in a continued process of giving more power to the police agencies without control. There are some accidents that are natural or structural to democracy although the political agencies do not want to have trouble with the police agencies. Sometimes groups, political or civic, try to contain or to control the police power, and here we must be very clear about this problem. Sometimes, we, especially we lawyers, think that if we change laws, we change reality. Sometimes when we change, the effects in Latin America are greater reactions, killing more persons to defend the power of the police against the new liberal legislation. So sometimes liberal legislation, introduced with a worthwhile motive, increases the number of executions without due process practiced by the police.

Human Rights and the U.N. Committee
on Crime Prevention and Control

By ROGER S. CLARK

ABSTRACT: Numerous subsidiary organs of the General Assembly and of the Economic and Social Council have played a part in the human rights program of the United Nations. For the first thirty years or so of its life the organization concentrated primarily on the development of normative texts; more recent efforts have emphasized implementation. The United Nations Committee on Crime Prevention and Control has been expanding its role both in the creation of human rights standards in the broad criminal justice area and in endeavoring to implement those standards on the ground. On first exposure, the Committee's main area of activity is a category of civil and political rights, namely, the protection of rights in the administration of justice. Further examination of its work in such areas as the prevention of juvenile delinquency or domestic violence suggests that its role encompasses various aspects of economic, social, and cultural rights as well. The author examines the work of the Committee with the particular aim of increasing its visibility.

Roger S. Clark is a Distinguished Professor of Law at Rutgers University School of Law, Camden, New Jersey. In 1986 he was elected by the U.N. Economic and Social Council to a four-year term as an expert member of the U.N. Committee on Crime Prevention and Control. He is vice-president of the International League for Human Rights and an adviser to several other organizations devoted to furthering human rights and decolonization. He has written widely on international law, human rights, and criminal law.

F OLLOWERS of the U.N. human rights program are familiar enough with a number of organs of the program that are serviced primarily through the Centre for Human Rights in Geneva. These include, notably, the Commission on Human Rights, the Subcommission on Prevention of Discrimination and Protection of Minorities, the Economic and Social Council (ECOSOC), the Third Committee of the General Assembly, and the various treaty bodies, such as the Committee on Human Rights, which function in a supervisory role under a number of specific treaty regimes distinct from the U.N. Charter itself. In 1987, I began a four-year term on a subsidiary of ECOSOC, the Committee on Crime Prevention and Control, which, operating out of Vienna, has been expanding its role as a standard-creating catalyst in the broad criminal justice area. Increasingly as well, it is devoting its attention beyond standard setting to follow-up, or implementation, a tentative step down the road that other human rights bodies describe as "enforcement."

My intention in this article is very simple — to increase the visibility of the Crime Committee and its human rights functions.

At first blush, the Committee's human rights creation area is primarily that of a subheading of civil and political rights, namely, the protection of rights in the administration of justice. Further reflection suggests that its role is wider than this and encompasses economic, social, and cultural rights as well. Its secretariat arm in Vienna, the Crime Prevention and Criminal Justice Branch, is anchored in the United Nations' Centre for Social Development and Humanitarian Affairs, and much of the Committee's work output — in areas such as the prevention of juvenile delinquency and strategies for dealing with domestic violence — is decidedly in the social sphere.[1]

HISTORY OF THE COMMITTEE AND ITS FUNCTIONS

The interest of the United Nations in the criminal justice area stems from the basic statement in Article 1, paragraph 3, of the Charter of this purpose of the organization: "To achieve international cooperation in solving international problems of an economic, social, cultural, or humanitarian character, and in promoting and encouraging respect for human rights and for fundamental freedoms for all without distinction as to race, sex, language, or religion."[2] As early as 1946, ECOSOC established a Temporary Social Commission, which, inter alia, was to "report to the Council on the advisability of bringing under the Council . . . such . . . activities as the work on the treatment of offenders now carried on by the International Penal and Penitentiary Commission."[3] The United Nations in fact set up a secretariat unit — originally known as the Social Defence Section — to

1. By being located in Vienna, the Crime Prevention and Criminal Justice Branch runs the risk of being marginalized in the U.N. system. It has succeeded, however, in developing fairly good liaison with the Centre for Human Rights in Geneva.

2. See also U.N. Charter, arts. 55, 56.

3. United Nations, Economic and Social Council (ECOSOC), Res. 7(I); United Nations, *Economic and Social Council Official Records,* 1st sess., 1946, 1:166-67. The history is discussed in Thorsten Sellin, "Lionel Fox and the International Penal and Penitentiary Commission," in *Studies in Penology Dedicated to the Memory of Sir Lionel Fox, C.B., M.C.,* ed. Manuel Lopez-Ray and Charles Germain (The Hague: Martinus Nijhoff, 1964), p. 194; Benedict Alper and Jerry F. Boren, *Crime: International Agenda* (Lexington, MA: Lexington Books, 1972), pp. 77-112; John Robson, "Criminology in Evolution — The Impact of International Congresses," *Otago Law Review,* 3(1):5 (1973).

work in the area in 1948. In 1950 it accomplished the transfer to itself of the functions of the International Penal and Penitentiary Commission.[4]

The most notable of these functions had, since 1885, been the holding of quinquennial congresses in the correctional field except when world wars intervened. These congresses would become the most visible part of the United Nations' activities in the criminal justice field. The first of them under U.N. auspices was held in Geneva in 1955 and the eighth is scheduled for the end of August 1990, in Havana.

The General Assembly's 1950 resolution on the matter called for the secretary-general to assemble a small international Ad Hoc Advisory Committee of Experts to advise the secretary-general and the Social Commission in "devising and formulating programmes for study on an international basis and policies for international action in the field of the prevention of crime and the treatment of offenders." This ad hoc committee of seven members evolved in 1965 into a ten-person Advisory Committee of Experts on the Prevention of Crime and the Treatment of Offenders.[5] In May 1971 ECOSOC made the committee a subsidiary organ of the council, continuing its status as a body of experts, renamed it the Committee on Crime Prevention and Control, and increased its membership to 15 persons elected by ECOSOC on the nomination of governments.[6] In 1979 a further increase to its present 27 members was

accompanied by an explicit geographical distribution of seats: seven to African states, six to Asian states, three to East European states, five to Latin American states, and six to West European and other states.[7]

At the same time, ECOSOC summarized the "main functions" of the Crime Committee as follows:

a) Preparation of the United Nations congresses on the prevention of crime and the treatment of offenders with a view to considering and facilitating the introduction of more effective methods and ways of preventing crime and improving the treatment of offenders;

b) Preparation and submission to the competent United Nations bodies and to those congresses for their approval, of programmes of international cooperation in the field of crime prevention on the basis of principles of sovereign equality of States and non-interference in internal affairs, and other proposals related to the prevention of offences;

c) Provision of assistance to the Economic and Social Council in the co-ordination of the activities of the United Nations bodies in matters concerning crime control and the treatment of offenders, and preparation and submission of findings and recommendations to the Secretary-General and the appropriate United Nations bodies;

d) Promotion of exchanges of experience gained by States in the field of crime prevention and the treatment of offenders;

e) Discussion of major issues of professional interest, as a basis for international co-operation

---

4. United Nations, General Assembly, Res. 415(V), 1950.

5. United Nations, ECOSOC, "Organizational Arrangements for the United Nations Social Defence Programme," Res. 1086 (XXXIX)B, 1965.

6. United Nations, ECOSOC, Res. 1584(L), 1971. See also United Nations, General Assembly, Res. 32/60, 1977, solidifying the principle of geographical representation and providing that members

would be elected to a four-year term with half the membership elected every two years. Nominations for election were to be made by states.

7. United Nations, ECOSOC, Res. 1979/30, 1979. The author, elected by ECOSOC on the nomination of New Zealand, holds one of the West European and Other Group seats. On New Zealand and the congresses, see John L. Robson, *Sacred Cows and Rogue Elephants* (Wellington, New Zealand: Government Printing Office, 1987), chaps. 14, 29.

in this field, particularly those related to the prevention and reduction of crime.[8]

Plainly, a substantial part of this mandate of the Committee is to foster the exchange of information, to give policy advice, and to facilitate networking between criminal justice professionals, with the congresses as a focal point. Yet much more than exchange has been going on. The Committee and its predecessors have been deeply involved in generating standards against which state performance may be judged. I speak of the Committee in terms of catalyzing or generating the standards, bearing in mind that only some of the drafting has been done by Committee members themselves, either at meetings of the full group or at various regional and interregional preparatory meetings for the congresses. Much of the nitty-gritty work is, of course, done by the very able but understaffed secretariat, by paid consultants, and by an army of underpaid nongovernmental representatives, many of whom have given freely of their time and expertise to lobby or to participate directly in the work. But as preparatory body for the congresses, the Committee has a central role in shaping the whole agenda.

STANDARD-SETTING INSTRUMENTS

With this in mind, let us look at some of the major documents generated by this part of the U.N. system.

The Standard Minimum Rules for the Treatment of Prisoners

The best known of the U.N. instruments in the area is the Standard Minimum Rules

8. United Nations, ECOSOC, Res. 1979/19, 9 May 1979.

for the Treatment of Prisoners.[9] Major credit for the formulation of this document does not, in fact, belong to the United Nations, although the Ad Hoc Committee of Experts and the 1955 congress both had a hand in final drafting. The Standard Rules were first developed by the International Penitentiary Commission — as it was then known — in 1926 and revised in 1933. The League of Nations took note of the rules in that year. The Ad Hoc Committee recommended further updating in 1949 and the International Penal and Penitentiary Commission put forward a new draft in one of its last official acts before its dissolution in 1951. The 1955 congress adopted a revision of this work and ECOSOC duly approved in 1957.

The rules deal with a whole range of institutional issues, such as maintaining a register of prisoners, separation of categories, accommodation, personal hygiene, clothing and bedding, food, exercise and sport, medical services, discipline and punishment, instruments of restraint, information to and complaints by prisoners, contact with the outside world, religion, retention of prisoners' property, notification of death, illness, transfer and the like, removal of prisoners, institutional personnel, and rules applicable to special categories of prisoners. According to the "Preliminary Observations" of the rules, they

are not intended to describe in detail a model system of penal institutions. They seek only, on the basis of the general consensus of contemporary thought and the essential elements of the most adequate systems of today, to set out what

9. Adopted by United Nations, ECOSOC, Res. 663 (XXIV)C, 1957, amended in 1977 to extend coverage to those arrested or imprisoned without charge ("detained"). Endorsed by the General Assembly in United Nations, General Assembly, Res. 2858, 1971; idem, Res. 3144, 1973.

is generally accepted as being good principle and practice in the treatment of prisoners and the management of institutions.

Nonetheless, the spirit or letter of the rules is often invoked by nongovernmental organizations such as the International League for Human Rights and the International Commission of Jurists in their complaints of human rights violations — invoked usually in the company of the Universal Declaration of Human Rights and the Covenant on Civil and Political Rights. There are those who argue that the rules have entered the corpus of general customary human rights law or that they are binding *qua* treaty law as an authoritative interpretation of the human rights provisions of the U.N. Charter.[10] Moreover, the rules are invoked from time to time in domestic litigation, either as an endeavor to incorporate international standards by way of the common law or in order to give concrete content to abstract domestic constitutional or statutory material.[11]

The torture declaration

The next document to be significantly shaped in the criminal justice part of the U.N. system was the 1975 Declaration on the Protection of All Persons from Being Subjected to Torture and Other Cruel, Inhuman or Degrading Treatment or Punishment.[12] The problem of torture had been before the United Nations General Assembly since 1973, largely in the context of

10. See, for example, Richard B. Lillich and Frank C. Newman, *International Human Rights: Problems of Law and Policy* (Boston: Little, Brown, 1979), pp. 183-261; Albert Blaustein, Roger Clark, and Jay Sigler, *Human Rights Sourcebook* (New York: Paragon, 1987), p. 115.

11. See, for example, *Lareau v. Manson,* 507 F. Supp. 1177, 1187, n. 9 (1980).

12. United Nations, General Assembly, Res. 3452 (XXX), 1975.

Amnesty International's Campaign for the Abolition of Torture, which had been launched at the end of 1972, and the events surrounding the overthrow of the Allende government in Chile in September of 1973. The General Assembly on 6 November 1974 requested the Fifth Congress, which was to take place the following year, to examine "rules for the protection of all persons subjected to any form of detention or imprisonment against torture and other cruel, inhuman or degrading treatment or punishment."[13] The General Assembly's resolution also requested the congress "to give urgent attention to the question of the development of an international code of ethics for police and related law enforcement agencies." It further invited the World Health Organization to draft "an outline of the principles of medical ethics which may be relevant to the protection of persons subjected to any form of detention or imprisonment against torture and other cruel, inhuman or degrading treatment or punishment."

Evidently, some tactical decisions had been made that running the torture and police items through the congress system might be an expeditious way of dealing with them. Amnesty International's legal adviser, Nigel Rodley, has suggested some explanations for this.[14] He notes first that the congress already had on its agenda two related items, one on the implementation of the Standard Minimum Rules and one on "the emerging roles of the police and other law enforcement agencies, with special reference to changing expectations and

13. United Nations, General Assembly, Res. 3218 (XXXIX), 1974.

14. Nigel S. Rodley, *The Treatment of Prisoners under International Law* (New York: Oxford University Press, 1987), pp. 26-27. Rodley's book, which devotes much of its text to analyzing the Crime Committee's work, perhaps unwittingly demonstrates how seriously the major human rights organization for which he works views the Crime Committee.

minimum standards of performance."[15] These items had an obvious relationship with official torture — and one should never underestimate the value of latching on to an existing agenda item!

Second, Rodley notes that the problem of torture is a problem of criminal activity, albeit criminality sometimes committed by those charged with crime prevention.[16] Third, he notes — and I regard this as the most significant argument — that

the participants in the Congress are drawn largely from the ranks of national administrations of justice (judges, prosecutors, senior police officers, and so on) rather than from foreign offices, as is the case with most UN meetings. It might be expected that representatives with this background might want to confirm that torture was the antithesis of their calling.[17]

This aspect of professionalism on the part of those involved with the United Nations' criminal law bodies is, I believe, enormously important to successful development of criminal justice standards.[18] Rodley then argues that since the congress meets only once every five years, deferral of the issue, the traditional tactic of those wishing to obstruct an initiative, was less likely to be successful; I doubt this, however — a five-year delay is not unheard of in the United Nations. Finally, he notes that the First Congress in 1955 had successfully completed and adopted the Standard Minimum Rules; there would be some political momentum for a dramatic landmark twenty years on.

In the event, largely because of efforts by Sweden and the Netherlands, an informal intersessional working group was set up at the congress in early September 1975 to deal with the General Assembly's requests. For the most part, the group's work concentrated on torture, and no text emerged on a code of police ethics[19] or on any amendments to the Standard Minimum Rules. A text on torture was adopted by the congress and, with minor changes, speedily and unanimously approved by the General Assembly on 9 December 1975.[20]

The torture declaration condemns torture and other cruel, inhuman, or degrading treatment or punishment as an offense to human dignity, as a denial of the purposes of the Charter of the United Nations, and as a violation of the human rights and fundamental freedoms proclaimed in the Universal Declaration of Human Rights. States are required to take steps to prevent such practices and to provide for complaint procedures, impartial investigations, criminal proceedings against the guilty, and redress and compensation for victims.

The strategy of using the route of the congress for drafting purposes worked — the instrument was adopted with vast dispatch by U.N. standards.

The Code of Conduct for Law Enforcement Officials

The Code of Conduct for Law Enforcement Officials and the Principles of Medi-

15. See Fifth United Nations Congress on the Prevention of Crime and the Treatment of Offenders, *Report*, U.N. Doc. A/CONF.56/10, 1976, paras. 260, 193.

16. The Crime Committee at its third session described torture as a "major [crime] of transnational concern." Committee on Crime Prevention and Control, 3d sess., *Report* (E/CN.5/516); ibid. (E/AC.57/21/Rev.1), paras. 27, 39 (1974).

17. Rodley, *Treatment of Prisoners*, p. 27.

18. The same considerations apply to efforts to draft standards for doctors, lawyers, and judges, to say nothing of psychiatrists, as witness professional attitudes toward Soviet mental health professionals believed to be involved in the incarceration of dissidents.

19. For discussion of the texts considered but not adopted at the congress, see Rodley, *Treatment of Prisoners*, pp. 279-81.

20. United Nations, General Assembly, Res. 3452 (XXX), 1975.

cal Ethics, which had been contemplated at the same time as the torture declaration, eventually emerged from the General Assembly in 1979 and 1982, respectively.[21] The Committee on Crime Prevention and Control provided the forum for the development of a generally acceptable text for the Code of Conduct for Law Enforcement Officials at its fourth session in June 1976.[22] The draft then found its way through the Commission for Social Development and ECOSOC to the General Assembly.[23]

The main thrust of the code is that officials are to respect the law and basic human rights. Given the realities of who exercises power in some jurisdictions, the commentary that is part of the code notes that "in countries where police powers are exercised by military authorities, whether uniformed or not, or by state security forces, the definition of law enforcement officials shall be regarded as including officers of such forces." Force may be used only when strictly necessary and to the extent required for the performance of an official's duty. The use of firearms is considered as an extreme measure. No law enforcement official may inflict, instigate, or tolerate any act of torture or other cruel, inhuman, or degrading treatment or punishment. Nor

may any law enforcement official invoke superior orders or exceptional circumstances such as a state of war or threat of war, a threat to national security, internal political instability, or any other public emergency as a justification of torture or other cruel, inhuman, or degrading treatment or punishment.

The Caracas Declaration

The Sixth United Nations Congress, of 1980, did not produce any dramatic human rights instruments akin to the Standard Minimum Rules or the torture declaration for adoption by the General Assembly. It did, however, produce the Caracas Declaration, which was duly endorsed by the Assembly[24] and included as an annex to the Assembly's resolution receiving the report of the congress. The congress also, acting in a more formal way than previous congresses, adopted a number of resolutions that may only be located in the report of the congress.[25]

The Caracas Declaration represented in human rights terms a distinct emphasis on the economic, social, and cultural. Its first paragraph, for example, declares that

the success of criminal justice systems and strategies for crime prevention, especially in the light of the growth of new and sophisticated

21. For the Code of Conduct for Law Enforcement Officials, see United Nations, General Assembly, Res. 34/169, 1979; for the Principles of Medical Ethics, see United Nations, General Assembly, Res. 37/194, 1982.

22. United Nations, Committee on Crime Prevention and Control, 4th sess., *Report* (E/CN.5/536), chap. 1A and annex V, 1976; Rodley, *Treatment of Prisoners*, pp. 280-81.

23. The Principles of Medical Ethics, aimed primarily at preventing the involvement of medical personnel in torture and other degrading treatment, were developed under the aegis of the World Health Organization rather than the Crime Committee. See Rodley, *Treatment of Prisoners*, pp. 291-301.

24. United Nations, General Assembly, Res. 35/171, 1980.

25. The human rights resolutions among them deal with such topics as developing minimum standards for juvenile justice; extralegal executions — "a particularly abhorrent crime the eradication of which is a high international priority"; torture and inhuman treatment, encouraging, inter alia, the development of a Convention against Torture, which the Assembly in fact completed in 1984; prevention of abuse of power; specific needs of women prisoners; development of measures for the social resettlement of the imprisoned; transfer of offenders; and exhorting follow-up to previous standard-setting resolutions.

forms of crime and the difficulties encountered in the administration of criminal justice, depends above all on the progress achieved throughout the world in improving social conditions and enhancing the quality of life; it is thus essential to review traditional crime prevention strategies based exclusively on legal criteria.

Its second paragraph insists that "crime prevention and criminal justice should be considered in the context of economic development, political systems, social and cultural values and social change, as well as in the context of the new international economic order."

The capital-punishment safeguards

The abolition of capital punishment has been a controversial item at the United Nations, as elsewhere, and a desultory discussion of the subject at the Sixth Congress, in which both abolition and safeguards in imposition were stressed, failed to produce a resolution that would command a consensus. In 1981, however, the General Assembly referred to the Committee on Crime Prevention and Control a narrower formulation of the issue on which it had by then been possible to obtain some degree of consensus, the need for safeguards in the imposition of the penalty. This resulted in the formulation of the Standards Guaranteeing Protection of the Rights of Those Facing the Death Penalty, which were adopted by ECOSOC in 1984.[26]

ECOSOC's adopting resolution makes the point emphatically that the standards are being accepted "on the understanding

26. United Nations, ECOSOC, Res. 1984/50, 1984, endorsed by the General Assembly in Resolution 39/118, 14 Dec. 1984.

that they shall not be invoked to delay or to prevent the abolition of capital punishment." The safeguards are in a sense both substantive and procedural. They provide that, in countries that have not abolished the death penalty, capital punishment may be imposed only for the most serious crimes, it being understood that their scope should not go beyond intentional crimes with lethal or other extremely grave consequences. It may be imposed only for a crime for which the death penalty was prescribed by law at the time of its commission. If, subsequent to the commission of the crime, provision is made by law for the imposition of a lighter penalty, the offender shall benefit thereby. Persons below 18 years of age at the time of the commission of the crime shall not be sentenced to death, nor shall the sentence be carried out on pregnant women, new mothers, or those who have become insane. The safeguards also impose a standard-of-proof requirement. Capital punishment may be imposed "only when the guilt of the person charged is based upon clear and convincing evidence leaving no room for an alternative explanation of the facts." A fair trial is guaranteed, "including the right of anyone suspected or charged with a crime for which capital punishment may be imposed to adequate legal assistance at all stages of the proceedings." Anyone sentenced to death is entitled to appeal to a court of higher jurisdiction, and steps should be taken to ensure that such appeals become mandatory. Anyone sentenced to death shall have the right to seek pardon or commutation of sentence. The punishment may not be carried out pending any appeal or other recourse procedure or other proceeding relating to pardon or commutation. Where capital punishment occurs, it shall be carried out so as to inflict the minimum possible suffering.

Output of the 1985 congress

The Seventh Congress, held in Milan in 1985, adopted a plethora of substantive resolutions. Three of these, the United Nations Standard Minimum Rules for the Administration of Juvenile Justice (the Beijing Rules), the Declaration of Basic Principles of Justice for Victims of Crime and Abuse of Power, and a resolution on domestic violence, were specifically adopted without substantive change by the General Assembly, and their texts appear among the Assembly's resolutions for the fall of 1985.[27] Each of these is primarily a human rights document. Another resolution of the congress, the Milan Plan of Action, which contains a substantial quantity of human rights language, was approved by name,[28] and the Assembly also "endorse[d] the other resolutions unanimously adopted by the Seventh Congress."[29] Two of these "other resolutions" — the Model Agreement on the Transfer of Foreign Prisoners and Basic Principles on the Independence of the Judiciary — were of particular interest in creating standards of a human rights nature and will be discussed later.[30]

The Beijing Rules aim both at protecting the basic civil liberties of alleged juvenile offenders in the criminal justice sys-

27. Another draft text, forwarded from the Seventh Congress and adopted by the General Assembly as Resolution 40/35, requested the development of standards for the prevention of juvenile delinquency. A draft will be before the Eighth Congress.

28. In United Nations, General Assembly, Res. 40/32, 1985, para. 3. Cf. the Caracas Declaration, which was annexed to the General Assembly's adopting resolution, United Nations, General Assembly, Res. 35/171.

29. General Assembly, Res. 35/171, para. 5.

30. Other of the congress's resolutions, such as those dealing with fair treatment of women by the criminal justice system and with professional standards for prosecutors and other criminal justice per-

tem and at providing for the framework for states to

develop conditions that will ensure for the juvenile a meaningful life in the community, which, during that period in life when she or he is most susceptible to deviant behaviour, will foster a process of personal development and education that is as free from crime and delinquency as possible.

The rules insist that the juvenile justice system should emphasize the well-being of the juvenile and ensure that any reaction to juvenile offenders shall always be in proportion to the circumstances of both the offender and the offense. Juveniles must be guaranteed at all stages basic procedural safeguards, such as the presumption of innocence, the right to be notified of the charges, the right to remain silent, the right to counsel, the right to the presence of a parent or guardian, the right to confront and cross-examine witnesses, and the right to appeal to a higher authority. Nonetheless, the juvenile's right to privacy is to be respected at all stages in order to avoid harm being caused to her or him by undue publicity or by the process of labeling. Deprivation of liberty as a sanction shall be chosen only after careful consideration and "shall be limited to the possible minimum." Indeed, it shall not occur unless the juvenile is "adjudicated of a serious act involving violence against another person or of persistence in committing other serious offences and unless there is no other appropriate response." Capital and corporal punishment are prohibited.

Noninstitutional treatment is thus to be the norm. It is to be accompanied by efforts

sonnel and resolutions concerning extralegal, arbitrary, and summary executions, made a human rights point but were largely derivative of other work in the U.N. system. The two to be discussed here represent a more original contribution.

to provide the necessary assistance, such as lodging, education or vocational training, employment, or any other assistance, in order to facilitate the rehabilitative process. Similar care is, of course, to be provided to those in institutions.

The Declaration of Basic Principles of Justice for Victims of Crime and Abuse of Power contains two parts, one dealing with victims of crime and one with victims of abuse of power.

In the crime section, "victims" is defined to mean persons who, individually or collectively, have suffered harm — including physical or mental injury, emotional suffering, economic loss, or substantial impairment of their fundamental rights — through acts or omissions that are in violation of criminal laws operative within states, including those laws proscribing criminal abuse of power. This definition is broad enough to encompass those who are the victims of such human rights abuses as torture, disappearances, and depredations of the environment that are proscribed under national law. Victims of crime are entitled to a package of rights, including access to justice and fair treatment, restitution from the offender,[31] compensation from the state where full restitution cannot be obtained from the offender, and the necessary health, psychological, and related social services.

In the section on abuse of power, "victims" is defined to mean "persons who, individually or collectively, have suffered

harm, including physical or mental injury, emotional suffering, economic loss or substantial impairment of their fundamental rights, through acts that do not yet constitute violations of national criminal laws but of internationally recognized norms relating to human rights." In this instance, states are exhorted to consider incorporating into the national law norms proscribing such abuses and providing remedies to victims. They are encouraged to develop more multilateral treaty law in the area and to review their domestic legislation periodically. This more precatory part of the declaration aims at the gradual incorporation of provisions on most situations covered in the definition of this section, on the abuse of power — within the regime set up in the first section, on common crime.

The line between the common-crime and abuse-of-power sections of the declaration is not a clean one. Disappearances and other comparable abuses are already caught in the first section. The declaration in fact began its drafting history within the United Nations as a document largely devoted to questions of abuse of power. Ultimately, the ordinary-crime aspects of it came to dominate — a not entirely surprising outcome, given the complexities involved and political sensibilities relating to abuse of power.[32]

The Domestic Violence Resolution[33] invited states to take a range of specific initiatives to deal with violence in the family setting — against spouses, children, and the elderly. Among the principles listed are treating the victim in a sensitive fashion; providing proper training for officials who

31. Para. 11 of the declaration adds: "Where public officials or other agents acting in an official or quasi-official capacity have violated national criminal laws, the victims should receive restitution from the state whose officials or agents were responsible for the harm inflicted. In cases where the Government under whose authority the victimizing act or omission occurred is no longer in existence, the State or Government successor in title shall provide restitution to the victims."

32. On the drafting, see Leroy Lamborn, "The United Nations Declaration on Victims: Incorporating 'Abuse of Power,'" *Rutgers Law Journal*, 19(1):59 (1987).

33. United Nations, General Assembly, Res. 40/36, 1985.

must deal with individual situations; providing temporary solutions such as shelters and other services for the victims; initiating preventive measures, such as providing support and counseling to families, in order to improve their ability to create a nonviolent environment, emphasizing principles of education, equality of rights, and equality of responsibilities between women and men, their partnership, and the peaceful resolution of conflicts.

The Milan Plan of Action lays out both the underlying assumptions of U.N. action and some recommendations about "essential elements" of the strategy that each state should adopt.

The assumptions start with the proposition that crime is a major problem of national and, in some cases, international dimensions that requires a significant amount of multilateral cooperation through the United Nations. Certain forms of crime can hamper the political, economic, social, and cultural development of peoples and threaten human rights and peace, stability and security. Development, the plan goes on to assert, "is not criminogenic *per se,* especially where its fruits are equitably distributed among all the peoples, thus contributing to the improvement of overall social conditions; however, unbalanced or inadequately planned development contributes to an increase in criminality." In such a context, the plan asserts, "The multisectoral and interdisciplinary nature of crime prevention, including their linkages to peace, demands the co-ordinated attention of various agencies and disciplines."

As far as the elements are concerned, the Milan Plan refers to strengthening cooperation, prevention, and research; further exploring the connections between crime and criminality and human rights; and combating terrorism. It also refers to launching a major effort to control and

eventually eradicate the destructive phenomena of illicit drug traffic and abuse and of organized crime and to improve the capacity of the United Nations to expand technical cooperation in the area to developing countries particularly in training, planning, exchange of information and experiences, and reappraisal of legal systems in relation to changing socioeconomic conditions.[34] The plan thus emphasizes economic, social, and cultural rights.

Two other human rights instruments adopted at the Seventh Congress were similarly endorsed by the Assembly but, like the Milan Plan, also do not appear in the form of an Assembly resolution.[35]

The first is the Model Agreement on the Transfer of Foreign Prisoners and its accompanying Recommendations on the Treatment of Foreign Prisoners. These documents recognize the difficulties of foreigners detained in prison abroad owing to differences in language, culture, customs, and religion. The documents proceed on the basis that the aim of social resettlement of prisoners could best be achieved by giving foreign prisoners the opportunity to serve their sentence within their country of nationality or residence. States are there-

34. More detail is spelled out on all of these matters in the Guiding Principles for Crime Prevention and Criminal Justice in the Context of Development and a New International Economic Order, also adopted by the Seventh Congress.

35. They may be found in Seventh U.N. Congress on the Prevention of Crime and the Treatment of Offenders, *Report* (A/CONF. 121/22/Rev.1), 1985. To a degree, this means that the resolutions run the risk of being buried — but note the efforts to publicize at least one of these, mentioned in fn. 36 of the present article. I think that it was mainly because of the techniques used by the individual drafters that the resolutions adopted specifically by the General Assembly achieved the wider exposure that goes with such adoption by virtue of having the text in front of anyone who receives copies of the Assembly resolutions.

fore encouraged to enter into bilateral transfer agreements based on the model provided.

The other instrument is the Basic Principles on the Independence of the Judiciary.[36] This document spells out the fundamental independence of the judiciary and the obligation of all governmental and other institutions to respect it. States are obligated to provide adequate resources to enable the judiciary to perform its functions properly. Judges are to be free to form and join associations of judges or other organizations to represent their interests, to promote their professional training, and to protect their judicial independence. Rules are laid down concerning qualifications, selection and training, conditions of service and tenure, professional secrecy and immunity, and discipline, suspension, and removal. These are a set of standards that are of significant importance to organizations endeavoring to ensure the independence of the judiciary.[37]

Current drafting

The report of the Committee on Crime Prevention and Control on its tenth session — in Vienna, 22-31 August 1988[38] —

suggests that the standard-setting role of the Committee and the Eighth Congress is continuing apace. In conjunction with a series of regional and interregional preparatory meetings, the Committee has been nudging along drafts of a number of major instruments for consideration at the Eighth Congress next year.

In a draft resolution prepared for ECOSOC's May 1989 session, the Committee recommended that the next congress finalize the Draft Standard Minimum Rules for Non-Custodial Measures (the Tokyo Rules), the Draft Bilateral Model Treaty on Mutual Assistance in Criminal Matters, the Draft Guidelines for the Prevention of Juvenile Delinquency (the Guidelines of Riyadh), the Draft Rules for the Protection of Juveniles Deprived of Their Liberty, the Draft Basic Principles on the Use of Force and Firearms by Law Enforcement Officials, the Draft Basic Principles on the Role of Lawyers, the Draft Model Agreement on the Transfer of Proceedings in Criminal Matters, and the Draft Model Agreement on Transfer of Supervision of Offenders Who Have Been Conditionally Sentenced or Conditionally Released. It recommends also that the Eighth Congress make every effort to secure their adoption for the strengthening of regional and international cooperation in the fight against crime. As the titles indicate, a substantial number of these instruments deal with human rights. There is also an interesting mix of the civil and political — instruments such as those on the use of force and the role of lawyers, the latter emphasizing the right to a criminal defense — and the economic, social, and cultural, such as the Riyadh Guidelines for the prevention of juvenile delinquency, which

36. In spite of not being published as a U.N. resolution, these principles have been widely disseminated both by a leading nongovernmental human rights organization, the International Commission of Jurists, which had been actively engaged in the drafting, and by inclusion in the most recent edition of the United Nations' *Human Rights: A Compilation of International Instruments*, 1986.

37. Note, for example, the reliance on these principles by the International Commission of Jurists in a 1988 report. See William Butler, George Edwards, and Michael Kirby, *Palau: A Challenge to the Rule of Law in Micronesia: Report of a Mission on Behalf of the International Commission of Jurists* (New York: International Commission of Jurists, 1988).

38. United Nations, Committee on Crime Prevention and Control, 10th sess., *Report* (E/1988/20),

1988; United Nations, *Economic and Social Council Official Records*, supp. no. 10, 1988.

emphasize creation of a decent society as the major strategy in crime prevention.

IMPLEMENTATION

At the same time, the Committee's report on its tenth session includes a number of draft resolutions for adoption in ECOSOC that indicate another increasing phase of the Committee's work, implementation.[39] Included here are resolutions entitled Implementation of the Declaration of Basic Principles of Justice for Victims of Crime and Abuse of Power, Procedures for the Effective Implementation of the Basic Principles on the Independence of the Judiciary, Guidelines for the Effective Implementation of the Code of Conduct for Law Enforcement Officials, Concerted International Action against the Forms of Crime Identified in the Milan Plan of Action, Implementation of United Nations Standards and Norms in Crime Prevention and Criminal Justice, Implementation of the Safeguards Guaranteeing Protection of the Rights of Those Facing the Death Penalty,[40] Effective Prevention and Investigation of Extra-Legal, Arbitrary and Summary Executions,[41] and United Nations Standard Minimum Rules for the Administration of Juvenile Justice (the Beijing Rules). Also included is the resolution on domestic violence.

39. General discussions of the need to move "from standard-setting to implementation" occurred at least as early as the Sixth Congress. See United Nations, Sixth Cong., *Report* (A/CONF.87/14/Ref.1), 1980, pp. 46-50.

40. See the thoughtful discussion of this resolution in Paul Hoffman, "The U.N. Committee on Crime Prevention and Control," *Newsletter Amnesty International Legal Support Network*, 5(3):1 (Fall-Winter 1988).

41. See discussion by Terri Rosen in *Newsletter Amnesty International Legal Support Network*, 5(3):6 (Fall-Winter 1988).

I have not located any authoritative definition of what "implementation" means in this particular dialect of U.N.-speak. In the general human rights area, it normally refers to the setting up of procedures to monitor state compliance in some systematic way — the work of the Human Rights Committee in dealing with complaints under the Optional Protocol of the Covenant on Civil and Political Rights, or the committee's more general role in examining reports of state parties under the covenant itself. The Committee on Crime Prevention and Control has no such role granted to it by treaty, nor has it been granted such a role under its empowering resolutions from ECOSOC and the General Assembly. It has no power even akin to that of the Commission on Human Rights to consider situations in individual countries in which gross violations of human rights are alleged to be occurring. What then is meant here by "implementation"?

The obvious way to answer the question is to examine one of the typical resolutions to see the kind of approach it takes.

The general resolution on implementation of U.N. norms and standards in fact contains approaches similar to those in the other resolutions, and I will use it as an example. It begins its operative language by inviting governments to adopt in national legislation and in practice, and to implement fully, the U.N. standards. They are also invited to increase, as far as possible, the level of support for technical cooperation and advisory services at all levels for the more effective implementation of standards; support may be increased either directly or through international funding agencies such as the U.N. development program. They are further encouraged to promote the observance of the principles embodied in U.N. instruments, including educational and promotional activities,[42] the support of the mass media, and increased community development. The secretary-general is then requested to prepare a compilation of all existing U.N. standards and norms in crime prevention and criminal justice and publish them in a form similar to that of *Human Rights: A Compilation of International Instruments,* the organization's very useful collection of normative texts. The secretary-general would also be asked to formulate practical proposals for implementation at national, regional, and international levels to be considered at the Eighth Congress.

The resolution would, moreover, encourage the use of the United Nations' advisory services program to assist in the implementation process. The advisory services program consists primarily of the award of fellowships for study to some thirty or so officials a year and some limited technical assistance to states with human rights — including criminal justice — problems. It has come under increasing scrutiny from human rights watchdogs, some of whom fear that it can be used as a fig leaf to avoid holding governments liable for their failings.[43]

Another paragraph in the resolution would encourage participation in the process by the United Nations' regional and interregional institutes in crime prevention and criminal justice.

Finally, the resolution would call for the strengthening of the role of the Committee in the following areas: keeping under review the application of existing standards;[44] assisting other U.N. organs with reports and recommendations relating to their work; and fostering more active involvement of its members, *inter alia,* through the designation from members of resource persons on priority topics. In conjunction with this, the secretary-general would be asked to take appropriate action to establish presessional working groups of the Committee that would prepare items for discussion, oversee the elaboration of questionnaires to be used for reporting, examine replies from governments and other sources of information, and "identify general problems that may impinge on the effective implementation of standards and norms and recommend viable solutions with action-oriented proposals based on the principles of international co-operation and solidarity."

This is all very general, and there is no hint in it of the Crime Committee's reaching into individual countries and trying in an accusatory way to throw the spotlight of public exposure on violations of criminal justice standards. It is very much in the

---

42. A more specific example of this approach appears in the draft resolution on implementation of the Declaration of Basic Principles of Justice for Victims of Crime and Abuse of Power. It recommends that the secretary-general consider, subject to the availability of extrabudgetary funds, the preparation, publication, and dissemination of a guide for criminal justice practitioners and others engaged in similar activities. The challenge in creating such a guide at the global level is to ensure that it is not culture-bound to the requirements of one state or regional group. An excellent nongovernmental draft of such a guide was presented to the Tenth Meeting of the Crime Committee as U.N. Doc. E/AC.57/1988/NGO/1. It is a first-rate basis for further work.

43. See, for example, International League for Human Rights, *In Brief,* no. 7, *Human Rights at the*

United Nations: Using Advisory Services (Oct. 1988); Radda Barren, *UN Assistance for Human Rights* (Stockholm: Radda Barren, 1988).

44. Several of the Committee's resolutions on particular areas call for the submission of reports by governments in an effort to improve upon the Committee's currently haphazard sources of information. The response of governments to requests for survey information and for reports not required as part of a treaty regime is traditionally spotty.

promotional mode that has always characterized much U.N. human rights action. Increasingly, however, with its organs such as the Working Group on Enforced or Involuntary Disappearances and its special rapporteurs on particular countries and its theme rapporteurs who cover such topics as torture and summary or arbitrary execution, the organization as a whole has been showing a much greater disposition to deal with the individual problems of real people in real countries. As it moves further on implementation, the Committee on Crime Prevention and Control cannot be unmoved by such developments and no doubt will make sympathetic responses to them, both in its own functions and in working with other parts of the system. The Committee, the congresses, and the work of the United Nations generally in the criminal justice area have had the advantage over other human rights work of emphasizing technical aspects and of thus avoiding some of the politicization of other human rights organs. The challenge to the Committee as it moves to consider such implementation strategies as the creation of an early-warning system for victims is to maintain its professional integrity.

* * *

QUESTIONS AND ANSWERS

Q: How much have these normative documents served in any national revisions of law?

A: It is difficult to obtain detailed information on that, and what one tends to get is bits and pieces. For example, the declaration on the rights of the victims, it seems to me, has had quite significant influence in the last two or three years on the way a number of states have responded to that particular problem. The Standard Minimum Rules have obviously had some effect on the way people run their prison systems. Surveys sent out to states are not all that helpful, unfortunately, because the states do not give the kind of detail that one needs. I do know from my own experience working with the New Zealand government, for example, that in at least two cases the material was looked at very carefully in relation to their procedures. One was the Standard Minimum Rules. The Justice Department went to great pains to make sure that a new set of prison regulations corresponded to the Standard Minimum Rules.

The other was the Code of Conduct for Law Enforcement Officials. It was very carefully examined, and some of the material was followed up by the police department.

___

Q (Joe Shoemaker, Lambertville, New Jersey): I would like to know if any juvenile has been given the death penalty lately in the United States.

A: It has happened, but I have no detailed statistics on how many such sentences have occurred in recent years. Last year, the Supreme Court of the United States considered a case, *Thompson* v. *Oklahoma,* in which the defendant had been sentenced to death for murder committed when he was 15. The Court noted that 19 states have capital punishment laws that set no minimum age and thus execution of juveniles is apparently possible. Five members of the Court were agreed that Thompson's sentence could not stand, but they could not agree on a rationale. Four took the position that execution of anyone under 16 was always cruel and unusual and thus in violation of the Eighth and Fourteenth Amendments. Justice O'Connor made a fifth vote. She argued that while a national consensus against executing for crimes committed by people younger than 16 probably exists, it was not conclusively found in the evidence presented in this case. Nonetheless, she said that the punishment could not be imposed here, where the legislature may not have fully considered the propriety of such executions. The case leaves open what happens with 16- and 17-year-olds. International instruments like the Geneva Conventions and the Covenant on Civil and Political Rights have an 18-year-old cutoff.

———

Q (David Stivison, Philadelphia, Pennsylvania): In the development of that flat ban on capital punishment for juveniles, was there any consideration given to defining the juvenile as someone under the age of, say, 14 or 15 rather than 18? The practice of treating certain persons under 18 — trying them and punishing them — as adults seems to have a certain amount of justification because in many cases they are acting as adults.

A: The short answer to the question of different treatments for different ages is one on which it is difficult to achieve agreement. Different societies treat people as children for less time than others do. In my own country, New Zealand, compulsory education goes only to age 15, whereas in New Jersey, my children have to go to school for a little longer than that. There are all kinds of differences, and they apply to issues other than capital punishment. I think that even those of us who do not agree on capital punishment could probably agree that children should not be executed,

but then one might have some argument about where to draw the line between child and adult. I do not know if it will ever be feasible to achieve a total international agreement on where the line is for all purposes. That said, the international community debated the issue in the capital punishment area and settled on 18.

———

Q (Gloria Roemer, Cliffton, New Jersey): We are talking about human rights for prisoners, about law enforcement officers doing their jobs, but we do not look at the law enforcement officer's job in terms of the people he has to deal with. He may have respect for the human rights of the prisoners, but the prisoners have no respect for the human rights of the police officers or the correction officers, and I think we lose ourselves in intellectualizing this process.

A: It seems to me that Louis Henkin has addressed this question at least from the point of view of the international documents. There has to be some balancing of police officers' rights with other people's rights. The police are human beings, too. But we have had some discussion as a society that there are certain things we are not going to do and one of them is torturing people. It is just not acceptable in a civilized society to torture people, and this applies to the police as well as to the rest of us.

———

Q (Roy Johnstone, World Constitution and Parliament Association, Lakewood, Colorado): I am very interested in knowing about the condition of people in the jails, whether in the United States or in Jamaica — I come from Jamaica. Many of these people claim they are not getting justice. The reason they do not is that they do not have efficient lawyers to defend them. Therefore, although the system appears to be good, they feel that they are not getting justice. What is the condition of your legal aid system in the United States? Our legal aid system in Jamaica is very bad because we do not have enough lawyers to defend our people. I just want to know what the condition of the legal aid system is in the United States and what we can do about that.

A: One of the things we can do is spend a lot more money on it. But the more difficult question is, What is its condition? There is no easy answer to that. Obviously, it varies from state to state, and in many states it is in a pretty parlous condition. There is just not enough legal aid for the people who need it. The problem is compounded in odd ways by the capital-punishment issue. I think the nightmare of those who have litigated capital-punishment cases in the United States in recent years is that there is the odd prisoner who slips right through the system to execution without a competent lawyer's getting hold of the case. But there is a further problem, one that surprised me. I had not thought about it until a debate in New Jersey four or five years ago on the question of reinstituting the death penalty, which had been struck down as unconstitutional. The strongest argument against reinstitution came from the Public Advocate's Office, which is the body in New Jersey that provides legal aid. Skirting the constitutional issue, the advocate said that the introduction of capital punishment would give his office a lot of new work with no new resources. The problem, though, would be that the best lawyers in the legal aid system would end up working only on the capital cases. I think that one of the side effects of reinstituting capital punishment has been this concentration of legal resources, when they would probably be fruitful in other areas.

COMMENT (Shestack): I would like to address the question of the condition of legal aid. In the United States in 1963 in a case called *Gideon* v. *Wainwright,* the Supreme Court of the United States said that every defendant in a case involving a felony had to have a lawyer. That really gave a boost to the public-defender systems. For criminal cases we have a public-defender system in the United States; most states have a public-defender system, which in most cases is funded by the local or state government. There is also an assigned-counsel system in the courts, especially in the federal court, and in some state courts, lawyers are assigned to criminal defendants. There is a need for more and better talent, but it is not there. On the civil side, there were private voluntary legal aid societies before 1965. The total amount they spent, say, in 1965 was $5 million. President Johnson, under the Office of Economic Opportunity, started a program for legal services, which has grown over the years to the point where Congress now spends $300 million. The program has some 7000 legal-services lawyers around the country giving legal aid in civil cases, and they are supplemented by voluntary help from law firms and others. There is not enough of the legal profession doing what it should, but still, with the possible exception of the United Kingdom, the system in the United States is the best that is available in the world.

Glasnost — The Dawn of Freedom?

By RICHARD SCHIFTER

ABSTRACT: The failure of the Communist economic model brought about in the Soviet Union a crisis of faith in the economic program and the political precepts associated with Leninism. As a result, there have come to the fore, since Gorbachev's accession to power, a group of reformers who, operating within the system, are seeking to create a more open society. The reformers are opposed by hard-line elements whose principal purpose is to maintain their positions of power and privilege. The outcome of the struggle between these two groups is in doubt. The reformist tendencies were not in evidence immediately upon Gorbachev's election to the post of general secretary in February 1985. The first significant indications of change were noted in December 1986. Evidence of profound, systemic changes started to accumulate only as recently as the spring of 1988.

Richard Schifter is assistant secretary of state for human rights and humanitarian affairs. He served as deputy U.S. representative in the U.N. Security Council, with the rank of ambassador, in 1984 and 1985 and was the U.S. member of the U.N. Human Rights Commission from 1983 to 1986. He practiced law in Washington, D.C., from 1951 until his entry into full-time government service.

NOTE: This article was written by the author as a federal employee and is in the public domain.

O N one of my recent trips to Moscow, I joined members of a U.S. delegation in a visit to Lenin's tomb. As we entered the hushed interior, one of my colleagues in the delegation, a high-ranking prelate in the Catholic Church, remarked, "Every society needs its religious symbols."

The appropriateness of this remark was underscored a few months later at a meeting of the Soviet Union's Communist Party Central Committee. Outrage was expressed at the suggestion by a Soviet television personality that the time had come to bury the body of Lenin. The Party chief of the Vladimir region said, "Lingering over such issues is simply immoral." A member from Irkutsk added, "What was said about the most sacred thing—about Lenin—is worse than incomprehensible."

LOSS OF FAITH

In the Soviet Union, communism was over the decades transformed from a political philosophy to a religious faith, with its doctrine, its rituals, its heresies, its expressions of reverence, and, indeed, its symbols. The essence of this religious faith was that history had dictated a course of evolution of humankind that was to lead to a classless society. In that society an ever improving standard of living was to be attained by all through the operations of an economy based on collective ownership of the means of production and distribution. The principal Leninist corollary of this Marxist article of faith was that in order to attain the goal of Communist nirvana, citizens had to surrender their individual freedoms and submit to the dictatorship by a small elite or, perhaps, even a single individual.

It was about ten years ago that the leadership of the world's largest Marxist-Leninist state, the People's Republic of China, began to make it clear that it had concluded that there was something inherently wrong with the underlying precepts of Marxism. Collective ownership of the means of production and distribution did not seem to be the right road to an increased standard of living; on the contrary, it seemed to lead away from that goal.

This heresy then began to spread. Ultimately, not even the Soviet Union and its leadership remained immune from it. After Mikhail Gorbachev began to sweep away the cobwebs of doctrine that had accumulated over the decades, the Soviet Union, too, began to question its underlying articles of Marxist faith. As it began to question its ability to reach its desired goal, it necessarily had to question the Leninist corollary. If the command economy was not the road to an increased standard of living, why the sacrifice of individual rights, why the dictatorship?

So we have, in today's Soviet Union, an increasingly clear recognition of the fact that its traditional economic model has failed, accompanied by a questioning of the political precepts that have guided the country for many decades. Among significant segments of the intelligentsia, there is an increased eagerness to commit the country to principles of individual freedom.

While there seems to be an overwhelming consensus that the economy is not working—after all, the evidence stares one in the face day after day—that consensus is lacking with regard to the abandonment of what I have here referred to as the Leninist corollary. Although the dictatorship was claimed to be a means to an end—namely, that of the socialist millennium—there were a good many adherents of the system who viewed the dictatorship as an end in itself, an arrangement that provided them with the kind of certainty, stability, and order with which they were comfortable and that offered to many of them cushy jobs from which to exercise power. That is the essence of the split in evidence in the Soviet Union today between those who are interested in political reform and those who strongly oppose it.

There is no doubt that the reformers are in the ascendancy, but that does not mean that they have the levers of power securely in their hands, nor does it mean that their ascendancy is assured. Also, as far as the top leadership is concerned, we are not yet dealing with a deep commitment to such principles as those set out in our Declaration of Independence. What seems to motivate the new leadership, above all, is the view that political reform is needed to effect improvements in the economy.

To us this means that, given the Soviet Union's military strength, we should engage in what might appropriately be referred to as a two-track policy: an approach based, on one hand, on the recognition that reformers are in leadership positions in the Soviet Union and, on the other hand, on the realization that these reformers could be replaced by persons who would take us back to the bad old days. In other words, we need to keep our powder dry.

"The evil empire" — that is what Ronald Reagan called the Soviet Union in 1983. There were those in our country who were horrified by this example of what they called cold-war rhetoric. There were others who thought the appellation was just right and applauded it vigorously.

And then, five years later, President Reagan strolled along Red Square with the leader of the Soviet Union, reached agreements with him, and delivered a speech to the students of Moscow State University.

There are those in the general public who remind us of the remark about the evil empire and say, "See, he conceded that he was wrong." There are others, those who once applauded Ronald Reagan's stand on the Soviet Union, who think that he was taken in.

I am sure that President Reagan would not claim to be a scholarly expert on the history of the Soviet Union and the theory of communism. But one of the advantages offered by his age is that he has been around for quite a while. He reached adulthood two generations ago. Though he may not have worked his way through scholarly treatises on totalitarianism, he did follow developments in the world from the 1930s onward in surroundings in which he and his friends and associates paid close attention to public affairs. The rise and fall of Hitler, the creation of the Stalinist dictatorship, and World War II were events that unfolded as he was watching. He did not only watch. He was actively involved. As far as his experience with communism was concerned, he received a thorough education on that subject in Hollywood, particularly as a leader of the Screen Actors Guild. Thus he brought to the job of president of the United States the understanding and thorough distaste of communism that characterized America's antitotalitarian liberals of the 1930s, of which he was one.

Thus, when Ronald Reagan recognized a changed Soviet outlook in his contacts with President Gorbachev, he was not deceived. He knew what communism was all about. When he said that he had noticed change, it was because change was taking place.

As to President Reagan's remark about the Soviet Union as an evil empire and his more recent new assessment, I submit that it was not the case that he was wrong the first time and saw the issue correctly thereafter, as some believe, or vice versa, as others hold. I submit that he was right on the mark both times.

Mikhail Gorbachev's name was surely not a household word as recently as 1983, not in the United States or in the Soviet Union, outside, perhaps, of Stavropol, where he had served as Party leader.

I recall a meeting of the United Nations Human Rights Commission in Geneva in February 1984, when we rose in memory of the late leader of the Soviet Union, Yuri Andropov. A year earlier we had performed the same ceremony for Leonid Brezhnev. A year later we were to go through the ritual for Konstantin Chernenko.

But in 1984, when Chernenko assumed the office of general secretary, perceptive reporters noted that he was in poor health and called attention to the bright new face of a much younger man, who had emerged as the Soviet Union's number two. His name was Mikhail Gorbachev. Therefore, when, at a reception in Geneva I next encountered a member of the Soviet delegation, I asked what he thought of Mikhail Gorbachev. My Soviet colleague furrowed his brow, then suddenly broke into a smile and said, "He is a nice guy." He paused and then added, "I read that in the *International Herald Tribune*." So much for the Soviet Union's traditional process of selecting its leaders.

MINOR COURSE CORRECTION

In the 1960s an extraordinarily well-informed Israeli Sovietologist had told me not to expect any drastic changes in the Soviet Union until the generation that came of age after Stalin rose to the highest level of the Soviet hierarchy. I thought of that remark when Gorbachev was installed as general secretary in 1985, but for quite some time nothing happened. As we are now in the fifth year of the Gorbachev era, I shall try to track developments, as I observed them, year by year.

During the first year of the Gorbachev era, we could indeed have said that the more things change, the more they remain the same. Khrushchev's thaw had been followed by a gradual tightening of the screws. From the middle 1970s on, Soviet repression of dissent had become exceedingly severe. The number of political prisoners reached new post-Stalin highs. Abuse of psychiatry was rampant, religious believers were persecuted. All parts of society were required to toe the rigidly defined party line. A truly imperialist foreign policy remained the order of the day. The program of allowing substantial numbers of Armenians, ethnic Germans, and Jews to emigrate had been brought to an end in 1980.

None of these features of the Soviet system was changed in year one. At a human rights experts' meeting of the signatories to the Helsinki Accord, which took place in Ottawa in 1985, I spent a good deal of time denouncing human rights abuses in the Soviet Union and posed the question to the Soviet delegation as to what Brezhnev had in mind when he affixed his signature to the Helsinki Final Act in 1975, a document that contained extensive promises of respect for human rights. The Soviet delegation's answer was that the Helsinki document stated goals that all participants should strive to reach, that the Soviet Union was working toward those goals but had not yet arrived there. I replied that in the ten years that had elapsed since the Helsinki Final Act had been signed, the Soviet Union had not only failed to approach the act's goals but had, in fact, moved in the opposite direction.

I do recall that the head of the Hungarian delegation told us that the spirit of Gorbachev was hovering over the hall in which we were meeting and would soon be in evidence. Most of us, however, were unable to detect even a whiff of it.

The only signal from Moscow that was truly new in year one was that the leadership was publicly conceding that the economy was in very bad shape, that productivity in the legal sector of the economy had sharply declined, and that, in fact, the only good economic news was that the black market, based on theft, embezzlement, and bribery, was flourishing. The new leadership's answer to this problem was a Stalinist one: cracking the whip harder. During afternoon showings in Moscow movie theaters the lights would be turned on in the middle of the performance to give the police a chance to check whether persons in the movie house were playing hookie from work. The only non-Stalinist innovation was that the new leader was lecturing the Soviet people on the evils of alcohol.

In November 1985 the first Reagan-Gorbachev summit meeting took place in Geneva. There is no doubt that all participants on the U.S. side came away with the impression that a significant change had taken place in the Soviet leadership, that the personality of the new general secretary offered hope of a better relationship.

President Reagan had carefully prepared himself to introduce human rights concerns into the dialogue and did so. Though the response was not hostile, we did not receive any clear assurances either. Nevertheless, there was some hope of early movement on the part of the Soviets regarding human rights, particularly the issue of Jewish emigration, which, because it had minimal internal ramifications,

could be handled easily. Yet, as the months passed, we saw no change in the Soviet Union's policies of repression. The emigration figures, which were the most easily measurable indicator of change, remained at the low levels to which they had dropped in 1982.

Thus year two of the Gorbachev era began, and we were still unable to detect any significant change on the Soviet domestic scene. The first time that I, for one, noted a development affecting human rights in the Soviet Union that startled me was, if I remember correctly, in the fall of 1986, a year and a half after Gorbachev's accession to power. What came across my desk at that time was a summary of the proceedings of a Soviet writers' congress. I noted that the participants in that event were speaking with an openness and expressed criticism of the leaders of their association with a vigor that I most assuredly did not associate with Communist societies. There was something new and refreshing about the way the writers had spoken at that congress. Also, in November 1986 the Soviets announced a new set of emigration regulations, but on close analysis we found them to be excessively restrictive and said so publicly.

Pointing up, by contrast, the continued existence of the gulag, in which many prisoners of conscience continued to languish, Anatoly Marchenko, a long-time dissident, died in prison in December 1986. By then the Vienna Follow-up Meeting under the so-called Helsinki Process had convened and when the news of Marchenko's death reached Vienna, the U.S. delegation led a group of Western representatives in the denunciation of continued repression in the Soviet Union.

I have since then wondered whether the death of Marchenko and the opprobrium heaped upon the Soviet Union thereafter were not causally related to the speed with which the next significant move on the Soviet human rights front was arranged, the granting of permission to Andrei Sakharov and Yelena Bonner to return to Moscow from their place of internal exile in Gorki. This event, too, occurred in December 1986, within days of Marchenko's death.

WINDS OF CHANGE

Toward the end of year two and the beginning of year three of the Gorbachev era we, at last, began to see change in the air as far as the Soviet Union's human rights climate was concerned. The change was most clearly in evidence in the arts and literature. The controls on the theater and on films had been significantly relaxed. Long-suppressed books, we were told, were now to be published. Neither painters nor musicians were any longer required to let the Party *apparatchiks* define the limits of their creativity.

A West European diplomat told me of his experience in Moscow in those days. The Foreign Ministry had provided him with a ticket to a new play, a play highly critical of the Stalinist past. A Soviet diplomat well known to us for his rigid espousal of what has since become known in the Soviet Union as "old thinking" came along as an escort. My West European friend, a man fluent in Russian, told me of the enthusiasm with which the Soviet audience responded to the play, the thunderous applause as the play came to a close. Through it all, my friend's escort sat on his hands. As they walked out, he kept shaking his head and said only, "It's so difficult to understand. It's so difficult to understand."

Early in 1987 we heard the first announcement of the large-scale release of political prisoners. I recall a staff meeting at the State Department at which Secretary Shultz turned to me to ask for my comment on that announcement. I replied that I thought it was significant. He laughed and said that if even I thought so, there must be something to it.

Finally, about this time, we also got the first inkling of a possible genuine change in Soviet emigration policy. In January 1987 quite a number of long-term refuseniks began to receive exit permits. By February the number of departures was up 50 percent; by March the figures were up 370 percent.

We were not aware at that time of another change that had occurred in the Soviet government's human rights policy. Without giving the matter any publicity, the Soviet authorities stopped, either late in 1986 or early in 1987, prosecuting dissidents and religious activists under the articles of the criminal codes that described as felonies such acts as "anti-Soviet agitation and propaganda," "defamation of the Soviet system," and participation in or organization of unauthorized religious groups.

To illustrate how these laws were applied, let me cite the case of Irina Ratushinskaya. In 1983, at the age of 29, this young woman, who had done nothing other than write poetry, was convicted for having written poems that were alleged to constitute anti-Soviet agitation and was sentenced to seven years at hard labor plus five years of internal exile. She was amnestied and released after three years, in year three of the Gorbachev era.

At any rate, only after some time had passed without any prosecutions under the infamous articles 70, 190-1, 142, and 227 of the Russian Criminal Code did we recognize that the Soviets had adopted a policy of no longer enforcing these repressive provisions of law.

GLASNOST AND *PERESTROIKA*

Though we were not yet aware of the implications of this unannounced change in Soviet policy, we did, of course, notice a good many changes that were by 1987 clearly in evidence. I recall making an assessment in the early months of that year of developments in the Soviet Union relating to human rights. The conclusion that I reached then was that the Soviet Union was, for the second time since 1953, engaged in an effort to purge Stalinism from its system. The goal, it seemed, was to return to what was viewed as a purer form of Leninism, the state of affairs that prevailed in the Soviet Union in the early 1920s.

I thought that that would indeed offer an improvement, but that we needed to keep in mind that Lenin conceived the idea of the one-party dictatorship; that he had reestablished the secret police, then known as the Cheka, which had been abolished by Russia's short-lived democratic government; and that the evidence was clear that a Leninist system provided a fertile breeding ground for Stalinism.

Nevertheless, as we entered year three, we were indeed able to observe a new openness in Soviet society, an openness comparable to Khrushchev's thaw and approaching the conditions of the early 1920s. There was even a label for this new development. It was called *"glasnost."*

Glasnost, we thought at the time, was a way of enlisting the help of the Soviet public in what the leadership considered its most important undertaking: *perestroika.* *Perestroika,* the restructuring of the Soviet economy, was clearly necessary to extract the country from its disastrous slump. *Glasnost,* it seemed, would help advance the goals of *perestroika* in that if the citizens were allowed to criticize low-ranking officials for inefficiency, corruption, and drunkenness, this would help the leadership spot these people, who were thought to bear principal responsibility for the country's failures. Once they and their policies were identified, corrective measures could be taken by the leadership. Similarly, if the general public could offer constructive ideas on how to improve the governmental and economic operations that they personally observed, this, too, could help the leadership improve the quality of the work done by governmental agencies and economic enterprises. *Glasnost,* as it was then practiced, required the person willing to speak up to operate within the system, to accept collectivism and the one-party dictatorship as a given, and to offer ideas on what improvements could be effected subject to the understanding that the system as such must be maintained.

But as year three progressed, we saw some changes in Soviet reality beyond the narrow limits that we had assumed had initially been set. The most spectacular of these changes related to the new assertiveness of the Soviet Union's ethnic minorities. In the summer of 1987, Crimean Tatars, members of an ethnic group that had been forcibly relocated in 1944 from its ancestral home in the Crimea to Central Asia, demonstrated for weeks in Moscow to press their case for a return to their homeland. They did not reach their objective and were ultimately detained and returned to their places of residence in Central Asia. That showed the limits of change. But what was nevertheless remarkable was that the demonstrations had been allowed to go on for quite some time and none of the demonstrators had been charged with a felony and sent to Siberia.

Shortly after the Tatar demonstrations had been in the news, we heard of large-scale demonstrations in the Baltic republics. Here, too, the police moved in after a while, but, once again, not with the ferocity that would have characterized police action at another time. That this change was not irreversible, however, was demonstrated in Tbilisi a year and a half later.

As we looked at newspapers and magazines in year three, we found that many writers were no longer limiting themselves to the denunciation of miscreants who had strayed from the path of socialist righteousness. These writers were posing increasingly profound questions about the basic structure of the system and, in this context, also urged a review of past history. Not only was Stalinism denounced, but Brezhnev and the Period of Stagnation for which he was held responsible were subjected to severe criticism. *Glasnost* was beginning to challenge some beliefs that had long been held sacrosanct.

Jewish emigration had now climbed to a level 700 percent above the January 1987 starting point. Armenian and ethnic-German emigration had climbed even faster.

By the fall of 1987, still in year three, we first heard rumors and then saw evidence of the fact that the Soviet leadership was no longer fully united. There appeared to be agreement that the economy was in disastrous shape and that *perestroika* was required, although there may have been differences as to of what it should consist. Beyond that, there seemed to be profound disagreement on the subject of *glasnost.* Yegor Ligachev, presumed to hold the number-two position under Gorbachev, and Viktor Chebrikov, head of the KGB, were heard as sharply disapproving the new trends toward greater openness. This was confirmed by Boris Yeltsin, one of the younger personalities elevated to high rank by Gorbachev, who bluntly denounced Ligachev. Gorbachev then repudiated Yeltsin. He was quickly demoted and was

expected to disappear from the political scene.

By the time year three drew to an end, we had seen the forward spurt toward greater freedom in the early months, the development of opposition to this relaxation of controls, and the creation of an uneasy balance between the two contending forces, which made it difficult to predict the direction in which the country would now move.

Year four began on an ominous note. In our part of the world, it is difficult to appreciate that a mere letter to the editor could shake a country, but in the Soviet Union that is precisely what happened. A newspaper known for its conservative outlook, *Sovietskaya Rossiya,* printed a letter purported to have been written by a Leningrad teacher by the name of Nina Andreyeva. The letter forcefully criticized the new trends toward freedom, defended Stalin, and appealed for a return to the stability and the verities of the recent past. *Sovietskaya Rossiya* would clearly not print such a provocative letter from an unknown schoolteacher without a signal from on high. The letter was assumed to be an authoritative statement of position from ranking personages in the leadership. Were they laying down the new line? Many Soviet citizens, particularly those who belonged to the intelligentsia, were now wondering whether this was the death knell of *glasnost.* Millions of Soviet citizens were figuratively holding their breath. Lest we forget, I am talking about developments in March and April 1988.

Then, after an agonizing wait of about three weeks, came the counterblast, an editorial in *Pravda,* the official newspaper of the Communist Party. It was a ringing endorsement of *glasnost.* The split in the leadership was now undeniable. The decision evidently made by the reformers was to push onward, to accelerate the pace of change. A Party conference was to be called to obtain institutional blessing for the reforms. Both before, during, and after the conference, held in June 1988, a careful examination of the latest articles authored by Soviet reformers suggested a new development regarding doctrine: the reformers were not merely denouncing Stalin's terror state and Brezhnev's stagnation — they were beginning to challenge Lenin's precepts on maintaining power. When I asked one of these reformers whether he was not deviating from Leninism, his truly heretical response was, "Lenin said different things at different times."

MODIFYING DOCTRINE

The deviation from precepts that had long been presumed to be Leninist orthodoxy was not limited to theoretical writings. It was soon reflected in the program adopted by the Party conference and put into practice thereafter through constitutional reform and the initial stab at a relatively free electoral process. The principal new developments deviating from traditional Leninist precepts were that:

— the tendency to concentrate governmental operational authority in the Party, at the expense of the state, was reversed; state agencies were to be reinvigorated;

— the practice of ending debate on an issue on which the Party had reached a decision, euphemistically called "democratic centralism," was abandoned. So-called old thinkers now bitterly complained that their country had turned into a debating society; and

— decision-making power, for long concentrated at the very top, was to be transferred to the general population through the process of real elections.

Another change, minor in doctrinal terms but of symbolic significance, has been the disappearance of such uplifting slogans as "The Communist Party represents the people's will." Lenin, who authored the slogan "All power to the Soviets," believed in demagoguery; Gorbachev seems to abhor it. All over Moscow the Communist Party slogans that once adorned the street scene appear to have been taken down. An effort is being made to appeal to the good sense of the individual citizen rather than to his or her herd instinct.

These changes in doctrine and theory notwithstanding, much of the Soviet Union's day-to-day reality appeared mired in its Stalinist or Brezhnevist past. But there were also changes that transcended the theoretical sphere, such as the transfer of Ligachev and Chebrikov to positions of reduced authority. We also saw, late in 1988, the release of all persons who had been convicted under the political and religious articles of the Soviet criminal codes, an opening toward greater freedom of religion, Jewish emigration at a level thirty times that at the outset, and the beginning of an electoral process of which we can say that, with all its serious shortcomings, it was no longer a complete farce.

There is one other doctrinal change that came clearly into focus in 1988. It had previously appeared in Gorbachev's speech in November 1987 on the seventieth anniversary of the Bolshevik Revolution. It was the concept that the existence of nuclear weapons and the resultant ability of some nations to end the human race made the idea of class warfare on the international scene obsolete. That idea was restated more fully and given practical application in the Soviet Union's evident reconsideration of its theretofore expansionist policies. The withdrawal in Afghanistan, the agreement on Angola, and the expected Vietnamese withdrawal from Cambodia appear to reflect a new approach to foreign policy.

As year four was drawing to an end, the Soviet reformers moved from tinkering with the system to what could conceivably mean profound change. First, the Soviet Constitution was amended to create a new and different legislative body. Second, and more important than this formal change, a foundation was laid for the selection of candidates chosen by the people rather than the *apparat.*

END OF THE MONOLITH

Now we are in year five of the Gorbachev era. Though we cannot say that the election of 26 March was a model of the democratic process, it did constitute a remarkable step forward. It surely was the freest election by far to be held in the Soviet Union since the election of the ill-fated Constituent Assembly on 25 November 1917, an election, by the way, lost by the Bolshevik party, which, by then, had seized power and held on to it, the election results notwithstanding.

Where the people had a real chance to express themselves in the election of 26 March, they voted for reform. The next question, to which we do not as yet have a clear answer, is whether this expression of popular sentiment will spell the end of the authoritarian governmental model that has not only characterized the Soviet state but is the governmental model established by the czars. We now need to watch whether the newly elected deputies will choose a Supreme Soviet in which independent thought will be represented and whether the Supreme Soviet will be allowed to exercise independent authority.

As we await the election of the Supreme Soviet and then begin to examine its performance, we need to keep our eye on the struggle of contending forces in the Soviet Union.

We have in the past been told of sharp divisions in the Soviet leadership, between doves and hawks, when it was likely that these reports were disinformation. But as I have suggested earlier, it does not stand to reason that the divisions of opinion now in evidence are a charade. Criticism of the basic tenets on which the system rests is no longer the province solely of the dissident movement. There are now reformers in the Soviet establishment who have concluded that the doctrines of the past must be put aside and that other standards defining the relationship between the governing and the governed must take their place. Increasingly, they look to the standards that are the product of the Enlightenment of the eighteenth century, the standards to which the Western democracies subscribe. These are the standards, let us remember, that Lenin explicitly repudiated when he formed the Bolshevik faction of the Russian Social Democratic Party.

But we must be careful not to overestimate the extent of the reforms. The Soviet Union remains a one-party state, even though the party is no longer the monolith it once was. The powerful secret police remain as a significant force of intimidation and, where deemed necessary, of repression. Establishment of the rule of law remains a goal. It is not a reality. The entire bureaucracy is studded with old thinkers, who do their very best to undermine the reforms. Severe restrictions on freedom of movement remain in place. Independent groups are harassed.

The April 1988 Central Committee meeting, to which I referred at the beginning, vividly pointed up both the determination of the reformers and the obstacles they face. Once again Mikhail Gorbachev's *perestroika* prevailed. A total of 110 old thinkers — or "dead souls," as they were called, with apologies to Gogol — spontaneously handed in their resignation from the Central Committee. Their thoughts were well expressed in this statement by the first secretary of the Komi Oblast Party Committee:

"Comrades. More elections are ahead. Today secretaries of the city and district party committees are announcing that in such a situation they are not going to take part in these elections because there is a 100 percent guarantee that they will not be elected.

"The impression is such that many difficulties are created almost intentionally. For instance, the well-aimed salvo that the press and television fired at the first secretaries of regional party committees. Did this not influence the outcome of the elections? . . .

"Comrades, look at our movies and our journals. Where's the patriotism, the civic attitude? Where's the labor discipline? How are we going to educate our young? We are educating them in an entirely different vein. Can this really not worry the ideological staff of the Central Committee and Politburo?"[1]

Gorbachev's hard-nosed response was:

"Some have already gone so far as to say that, in a manner of speaking, both democracy and *glasnost* are very nearly a disaster. And the fact that people have begun to act, that they no longer wish to remain silent and insist on their demands, is perceived as a defect of *perestroika*."[2]

But, in spite of these brave words, continuing to lie in wait for Mikhail, as he makes his way through the forest, is the

1. *New York Times*, 28 Apr. 1989.
2. Ibid.

wolf, the opposition to reform. The dead souls are very much alive throughout the *apparat*. There are those who under Gorbachev's reforms would lose jobs, status, and privileges, and they have the support of the millions who simply prefer stability and order and consider democratic trends destabilizing. The Soviet Union, we must keep in mind, is one of the most class-ridden societies now in existence, with its higher aristocracy, its lower aristocracy, and all the hangers-on associated with those who exercise power. Are they willing to accept the new egalitarianism and the meritocracy that the reformers advocate? How hard will they fight to hold on to their positions? What, above all, will be the attitude of the military if sharp budget cuts are ordered?

Let us keep in mind the key role played by the military leadership on two previous occasions, the arrest of Lavrenti Beria in July 1953 and the ouster of Nikita Khrushchev in October 1964. Let us also keep in mind that there is little chance of improving the Soviet economy in the near term unless there is a drastic cut in conventional military spending and foreign adventurism. Will the Soviet military accept the decisions of the present civilian leadership, or will it seek to effect a change? We do not know.

But there is now an institutional basis on which reform can be built. Ironically, it can even be explained in Marxist terms. Marxists, we should note, have spoken of bourgeois revolutions and have identified the bourgeoisie as the foundation on which liberal democracy is built. The question to ponder is whether the Soviet Union's intelligentsia, which is now a significant portion of the population, will in the period immediately ahead provide the foundation for a system of government for which a foundation may have been lacking in February 1917.

Does the reform-minded intelligentsia provide a foundation strong enough to support a new, open, democratic governmental structure in the Soviet Union? Once again, we do not know. Mikhail Gorbachev has been in power for a period about equal to one presidential term. As I have sought to show, it is only as he reached the midterm point that a truly new approach to government and the economy began to emerge. The last major challenge to his policies occurred about a year ago. The great mass of the Soviet public is waiting eagerly for performance in the economic sector, for more goods on the shelves. These goods are not going to be there tomorrow, or next week, or next month. Will Gorbachev have another four years in which to demonstrate the validity of his reform ideas? Will he try to improve on them? Will the reformers be able to open the gates of freedom wider? What role can we of the West play in this context? These are the questions and also the challenges before us.

* * *

QUESTIONS AND ANSWERS

Q: Two or three weeks ago, the Soviet Union used military chemical weapons against the people of Georgia. What is your opinion about this very dangerous situation from the point of view of international law? After all, it is one of the obligations of the Soviet Union not to use chemical weapons. What is the connection between this use and arms control, especially the control of chemical weapons?

A: The Georgia problem goes beyond the question of chemical weapons. As far as the chemical-weapons aspect of it is concerned, this is a matter that is high on our agenda. There is a truly great concern about the spread of chemical weapons, which constitute a far greater danger today than do nuclear weapons, for the simple reason that chemical weapons are now spreading to smaller countries that have irresponsible leadership, more irresponsible than in the larger countries. The risk of chemical weapons' being used is great. As far as the problem in Georgia is concerned, however, let us assume for the moment that nerve gas had not been used. The situation was an example of the old politics. It was recognized in the Soviet Union as such, and we made statements to that effect as well. What is interesting to note is that when Mr. Shevardnadze — both a foreign minister and a Georgian, as well as former head of the Party organization in Georgia — went to Georgia, he fired the entire leadership in Georgia and put in other people and tried to speak to the persons who had been supporters of the demonstrations. One would hope that this matter can be resolved in that particular context. But let me simply say that the situation was another case that demonstrated the vitality of the basic proposition that I have offered here, that there are two major contending forces in the Soviet Union and at this particular point the jury is out — we do not know who will win.

—————

Q: How would you characterize the Soviet reaction to the Baltic communities? Was it the same as toward Georgia?

A: What happened in the Baltic was that when the first demonstrations occurred in 1987, the government's reaction was more heavy-handed than the reaction in Georgia. Since then the government has simply tolerated it.

———

Q (Martin Raven, British Mission to the United Nations, New York City): In the last four or five years in the Soviet Union, there has been one event, it seems to me, that is not necessarily part of the human rights fare but that could have dominated the whole trend in the Soviet Union: the explosion at Chernobyl. Chernobyl is an example of the Soviet people's being forced to take up an issue that in another political system would have been handled very differently. Do you think that Chernobyl had an effect not only on nuclear energy and science but also on human rights?

A: That is a valid point. Chernobyl is one of the settings in which Gorbachev and, I think, people on his side of the leadership struggle believe that the deficiencies in the system were serious. The problems were, first of all, problems of management: inadequate management, inadequate controls, and failure on the part of people at local levels to exercise independent judgment in dealing with the issue. The way the Soviets handled the disaster demonstrated these problems; it also showed that people wait around too long for orders from the top before they begin to function and there are situations in which they cannot wait that long. The other aspect of it was, I think, that the leadership recognized that it was a serious mistake to try to hide the issue by delaying the release of information on it and by taking inappropriate safeguards.

ANNALS, *AAPSS,* **506,** November 1989

Perestroika, Socialism,
and the Constitution

By VALERY CHALIDZE

ABSTRACT: This article takes a general view of *perestroika* and analyzes certain possible changes in the Soviet Constitution. The recent struggle in Soviet society is viewed as competition between a previous tendency to unify social relations and recent demands for democratic pluralism in society. Further, the author discusses possible changes in the Soviet Constitution that could be brought about by *perestroika.* The Soviet Constitution must provide a juridical definition of socialism if the Soviet Union is to continue development of a socialist democracy. Finally, the author formulates a model juridical definition of socialism, which sets forth a socialism of rights and not a socialism of restrictions.

Valery Chalidze is editor in chief of the Khronika Press *and editor of* Internal Contradictions in the USSR. *Born in Moscow, he was educated at Moscow University and Tbilisi University in physics and was chief of the polymer research unit at the Institute of Plastics in Moscow. He is the author of several books and numerous articles and reports.*

NOTE: Thanks to my wife, Lisa, and to Aron Katsenelinboigen, of the University of Pennsylvania, for discussions on constitutional law and *perestroika.*

A VIEW ON *PERESTROIKA*

President Reagan played a rather peculiar trick on me. All my life I had been in opposition to governments, first in the USSR and later, for different reasons, in the United States. Then, in 1980, a man who called for reduction of government interference in the life of the country came to the White House. Ultimately, by calling for the reduction of federal programs, he called for the reduction of his own authority. Of course, I liked that. He did not manage to fulfill his program completely, because of the resistance of a Democratic Congress—somehow those who declare themselves advocates of the people's interests very often want a stronger government. Reagan's presidency allowed me to experience what it is like not to be in the opposition, even though before then I had always considered that bad manners.

One can observe that, usually, politicians and bureaucrats want to increase the scope of their authority and want their positions to become more important, not less so. That is why it is interesting and commendable when a leader does not behave in this fashion. In Russia least of all would one expect a leader to shrink his authority or the authority of his position, but Gorbachev tries to limit his Party's interference in the life of the Soviet Union. Whether he will succeed is unclear; the Party is very strong and fully accustomed to controlling everything in the country. Retraining the Party is a difficult task. The very attempt to do so is remarkable, and the architect of the attempt deserves respect for that alone.

It might be said that Gorbachev's efforts to reduce Party control of the economic and cultural life of the country are not really efforts to decrease his own authority. After all, he became head of state as well as leader of the Party, and most likely he does not plan to leave this post; but this may be explained by something other than a personal desire for power. If Gorbachev wants the Party to share its power with the people, it is rather natural—and tactically understandable—that he would try to retain control over this process of power sharing. In this manner, he could guarantee the gradual nature of the process and make it less frightening to Party bureaucrats. This same tactical consideration may underlie the combining of the posts of Party secretary and chairman of the Soviets. Such a plan may also have served as a concession to the conservatives. I myself like to maintain positions of principle, but I will not blame a politician for reaching stabilizing compromises, especially in such a difficult situation. Society can achieve internal peace only by utilizing compromises and deals, and Russia still has to learn this art.

There are many people in the USSR and in the West who do not see in Gorbachev a leader who wants, or is able, to make changes. It is obvious to me that this is an unjust evaluation, and we see that his attempt to change the country has already brought results. Many people in Russia already view themselves and their roles in the life of the country differently. There is not yet democracy; there is not yet a real civic dignity in the people. But something has already changed, and now it will be harder to force people back into silent slavery.

The basis for such gloomy skepticism about Gorbachev is a traditional disbelief in the internal potential for development in the Soviet system. This disbelief is unjustified in general, because the Soviet system has always been changing, although the relative stability of Soviet phraseology has deceived many people. This phraseology was more or less the same in Lenin's time, when the Party tried to achieve a quick transition to communism. It was the same during the New Economic Policy, when concessions were made to capitalism, as was then believed; and it was also the same in the Stalin era, when an extreme right-wing dictatorship was built using the same socialist slogans.

Soviet phraseology has continued to be practically the same during the last 35 years, while the country was gradually trying to modify the previously constructed right-wing dictatorship. This last 35 years, regardless of the imagined stability of ideology, has not been less revolutionary than any *perestroika*. Although people did not learn to express their opinions, they learned very well not to accept the opinions pressed on them by the authorities.

After Stalin, people also learned to resist the pressure of the authorities in all areas of life. Let us remember that Stalin built his system of government on the constant use of violence. When he died, the system remained the same, but his successors hardly utilized violence, except in relatively rare political cases. On the one hand, this decline in violence permitted an enormous liberalization in comparison to Stalin's time. On the other hand, it brought the system to a crisis: when the violence was removed, the system could not function as it was built to. I think Gorbachev is the first Soviet leader to understand that the system itself must be changed, recognizing that Stalin's system minus the violence just will not work.

MULTIPLICITY VERSUS CENTRALIZATION

For the last 35 years, the intelligentsia, including human rights activists, have energetically worked to find alternative ways to build the system. Now it is time to apply

that intellectual potential and the ability of people to have their own opinions. This will be impossible without struggle, patience, and retreats. The results will be even more valuable as a result, however, because freedom given by decree will never become a true part of a society's life if the society is not ready for it. The struggle for freedom, then, serves not only to bring freedom closer but is at the same time a process of ripening, so that the consequences will be harder to undo.

One cannot, by the way, attribute all the problems in this process to the fact that not everyone is ripe for freedom. There are many philosophical issues to consider — for example, the question of the scope of authority of the leader, which I have already mentioned. This is very much connected to the question of centralization of power. One can be a great lover of freedom and still not understand that the contemporary, very complex public life is not compatible with strict centralization, even if this centralization does not limit fundamental human rights. Centralization can be successful and useful in a society with primitive social relations. The more complicated the social relations, however, the more difficult it is to manage them through a centralized structure. That is why the increasing complexity of social and economic relations throughout the development of civilization has brought, and will continue to bring, crises when those in power do not take steps to ease centralization. Failure to decentralize will automatically result in pressure to simplify social relations in society and to unify social processes; it will result in leadership unable to cope with the inevitable growth of multiplicity in society.

The Soviet Union, therefore, now finds itself facing a choice. Its society can have either multiplicity and self-regulation or unification and centralization.

Gorbachev and many of his colleagues probably understand this dilemma, but they have met very strong opposition from those in the USSR who are afraid of multiplicity and do not believe in the possibility of self-regulation of society. These opponents are afraid of the enormous speed with which the human mind can be liberated, and they try to maintain stability, as they understand it. One should not blame these people for stupidity or cowardice. They are simply acting within the limits of the world as it was when they first learned to understand it: a simple, centralized, and, one might say, attractively constructed world. These people are not concerned with ethical evaluations of their current positions; if order in the world were achieved by Stalin and his repressions, they would justify Stalin and repression. Any sacrifice seems acceptable to them, if it can save the world from an earthquake.

One should therefore be very careful in evaluating contemporary Stalinism and should even show some understanding. The problem is not love of Stalin or barbed wire; contemporary Stalinism is the unavoidable resistance on the part of people whose simple and attractive world might be destroyed in the name of a scary and unknown multiplicity. Stalin, as a symbol of this attractive simplicity, pops up accidentally. Anything or anyone can be a symbol of the world that is being lost. For example, extreme nationalism or anti-Semitism could be the same type of symbol.

This is a very old conflict. It is certainly not the first time Russia has resisted multiplicity. The West, the intelligentsia, and Jews, as providers of ideas for multiplicity, were as much enemies to the nineteenth-century Stalinists as they are now. At the end of the nineteenth century, one could see that multiplicity was close to winning. It was a slow process. Social relations were becoming increasingly complex and growing slowly inside a simple world, transforming gradually the consciousness of new generations. As we know now, however, in 1917 those who wanted a simple, unified, and centralized world were triumphant. It does not make any difference, for purposes of this discussion, which political color the winners were. In nearly any political group, one can see both those who want to simplify the world and those who accept multiplicity.

A centralized authority that does not wish to deny the complexity of society finds itself in a difficult position in the struggle between the champions of simplicity and the champions of complexity. Gorbachev has now found himself in a complicated situation. Although he wants to clear the way for self-regulating mechanisms in society, he finds himself in conflict with his own desire to keep control of the process. This conflict must result in some contradictions in the behavior of the authorities, which we now can see. For instance, a call for increased democratization was followed by a law restricting demonstrations; demands for a more active role of cooperatives was succeeded by a decree on stricter control over cooperatives. Such contradictions can be criticized but are nonetheless unavoidable and do not necessarily represent unfriendly maneuvers by the opponents of *perestroika.*

My goal in this article is to discuss a few principles that need to be reflected in the Soviet Constitution and to offer a more precise definition of socialism. I think that those who write the new Soviet Constitution must understand and remember the unavoidable struggle between unification and multiplicity. The Constitution will not be able to identify, in advance, all possible forms of multiplicity in society. Nonetheless, it must be formulated in a way that does not inhibit the development of multiplicity in society. The new Constitution must not be an instrument for providing future unification, as were previous Soviet constitutions.

GOALS OF THE CONSTITUTION

I assume that the development of *perestroika* will demand the writing of a new Constitution. All the recent changes in Soviet society were possible only because no one cared what the existing Constitution permitted. The program of the Nineteenth Party Conference can be regarded as contradictory to the existing Constitution, and I find myself in a rather uncomfortable position. On the one hand, I support society's carrying on its activities within the framework of constitutional limitations. On the other hand, I oppose the limits imposed by the existing Soviet Constitution. One must characterize the recent *perestroika* as a revolution in order to justify the disregard of the current Constitution.

I hope, though, that *perestroika* will bring about a more serious and less propagandistic document than the current Constitution. Whether this will happen within the current *perestroika,* or one that will commence in the future, I do not know; nor do I know how successful the present reforms will be or how often and to what extent there will be retreats. The main point, however, is that I believe in the internal potential of the Soviet system to develop. I believed in it even in the dismal Brezhnev years, which are now usually referred to as stagnant, and will continue to believe in it even if the present *perestroika* is followed quickly by another period of stagnation.

My general topic here is the constitutional formulation of the main principles of socialism. A bit later, I will try to show that juridical formulation of these principles is possible and does not require the previous Soviet practice of mixing in ideology and propaganda. I am writing this with the Soviet Union in mind, but this analysis may be utilized by any country that wants to choose socialism of rights over socialism of restrictions. Before I get to specific formulations, however, I would like to discuss the general goals of a constitution.

Unfortunately, the authors of previous Soviet constitutions focused more on the supposed ideological superiority of the Soviet regime than on the creation of a realistic, working document whose principles could successfully regulate social activity. It is very important that the new Soviet Constitution be free from propagandistic elements and that it be a serious legal document.

The Constitution must be functional. That is, its guarantees must be used in legal practice, whether or not the guarantees appear in other legal, nonconstitutional documents. Until now, constitutional guarantees were taken seriously only if they also appeared in the form of other laws. What is more, even if a given guarantee did so appear, often it would not be used in practice until bureaucratic instructions—often secret—explained whether and how the law should be applied. For example, Article 58 of the Constitution of 1977, regarding appeal of a bureaucratic decision to the courts, was long unused because there was no law on how to appeal. Now there is a law on the appeal procedure, but it limits the cases considered appealable much more than the Constitution does.

Another example of the ineffectiveness of the Constitution alone is drawn from my personal experience. In 1970 I brought before a Moscow district judge a complaint regarding the exclusion of a student from college because she signed a human rights petition. The complaint was naturally based on the constitutional right to education. After hearing the complaint, the judge immediately said to me, "The right to education is a constitutional right. The court does not defend it."

It is very important that courts will defend and enforce constitutional rights; that the quoting of the Constitution be permitted in legal proceedings; and that courts base their decisions on the Constitution, even in the face of a contradictory statute or decree. A hierarchy of legislation is unavoidable in a society with complex social relations, and it is very important that the Constitution be superior to other types of laws, in practice as well as in theory.

There are four groups of principles that, in my opinion, must be formulated in the Soviet Constitution. They are

— principles of federation, establishing the legal basis on which the republics are united in the Soviet Union and the limitations on the power of the union;
— principles of democracy, defining the legal bases of the creation of the government, and the limitations of power at each level of the government;
— principles of fundamental human rights, common to civilized countries; and
— principles of socialism, specific to socialist countries, meaning the guarantees of social and economic rights, and the degree of implementation required.

It must be understood clearly that these are four separate groups of principles. There have been democracies without human rights; federations without democracy or socialism; and democracies without federation or socialism. It is still debatable, however, whether socialism can exist without democracy, and many think that socialism has already been established in the Soviet Union and that it only needs to be improved with democratic principles.

Much depends on definition. A major failing in previous Soviet constitutions is that there was no clear definition of socialism, yet that is precisely what a socialist constitution must provide. Sad experience testifies to this requirement. Soviet history has demonstrated that those who exercise power without consulting the people exploit the vagueness of the concept of socialism in order to falsify the real meaning of federation and democracy. Empty phrases like "socialist democracy" and "socialist federation" were used. The absence of democracy, the violation of human rights, and the violation of the rights of republics were justified by reference to socialism, apparently on the assumption that socialism was of such a great value that mere reference to it justified the distortion of all other values. Therefore socialism must be clearly defined, and the foregoing four groups of principles must be treated independently of each other.

In my opinion, then, the goal of a socialist Soviet constitution must be the declaration of a legal definition of the principles of federation, democracy, human rights, and socialism, in such a manner that the expression of one principle would not distort the others. I cannot discuss all of these topics within the limits of this article but instead have opted to discuss in detail the principles and definition of socialism.

SOCIALISM

My writing on socialism is intended to be impartial. I am not a socialist. I love free competition and the free market, even when I lose money on the stock market. My personal sympathy to democratic capitalism, however, does not prevent me from understanding that socialist ideas in society are unavoidable and even necessary. One could say that it is thanks to capitalist ideas that contemporary Western civilization was built, but that it is the ideas of socialism, if not extreme, that made this civilization more humane. The competition of ideas, including opposing ideas, is a tested and successful way for humankind to develop.

The Soviet Union wants to be a socialist country, and not a country with free competition between capitalism and socialist ideas. This requires a clear understanding of what socialism is. In Russia we were taught, from childhood, that socialism is a government monopoly on everything that can be monopolized. I was about 12 years old when, following the excitement of the grown-ups, I studied Stalin's book on the economic problems of socialism. Unlike the grown-ups, though, I did not understand why the role of the government in the economy had to grow even more.

Only now have people begun to understand that instead of socialism, Stalin gave the people a right-wing dictatorship with a governmental economic monopoly. The majority is still far from understanding this. The opinion of Yuri Afanasiev that there is no socialism in the contemporary Soviet Union was quickly rejected by *Pravda.*

So let us try to imagine the place of socialism in the multidimensional space of social possibilities. I will start with one axis. Let us imagine the most extreme point on the left of this axis, which would be theoretical communism: a society of absolute material equality. This condition of society was described by Lenin in one sentence that says more than many volumes: everyone must work equally and everyone will receive equally. Now let us imagine that on the extreme right of our axis is an area representing theoretical capitalism: a system with free participation in production, with no artificial limitations on income received. On this axis, then, there is a wide spectrum of social conditions between the point of communism on the left and capitalism on the right that one could call socialism, that is, a society in which active people have limited but reasonable opportunities to demonstrate their activity and passive people are defended from the greediness and pressure of active people.

What we need to do is locate on this axis the point at which not just socialism but working socialism is found. We must find a balance between the desire of the passive people for material equality and the desire of active people for inequality, so that the initiative of the active will not be suppressed and the frustration of the passive, resulting from inequality, will not disturb the social peace. The experience of humanity shows that we had better look for such a point closer to the right end of the axis, because economic success depends on the active. Most likely it will be not simply a point but some range on the axis, in which the desire for material equality and inequality exist in proportions such that both social peace and a working economy are provided.

The location of this area on our axis will depend on many factors, so, of course, a one-dimensional approach is not enough. Let the second dimension characterize the role of government. A government that is economically monopolistic is probably not socialist at all. Judging by the Soviet experience in such presumed socialism, it is definitely not the kind of society for which millions struggled and died. We can also see from the Soviet experience that total state monopoly does not result in a working economy. So what degree of government interference should one suggest as acceptable?

The Soviet Union and other countries that choose socialism must find an answer to this question through many years of trial and error. In my opinion, the role of the government should be minimized. Give land to the peasants, give workers or stockholders the factories, and develop as many cooperatives as possible. Such a system, sooner or later, will work; but it will probably work later and not sooner. The transition period will inevitably be painful for social relations and will jeopardize investment in the future of the country and economy.

Investment in the future is where the role of government is most important, especially in the transition period. I refer now to investments in scientific and technological progress, ecology, and so on. What is more, participation of the government is probably unavoidable in redistributing national wealth. These needs will probably prevent speedy limitation of the role of government, but any steps in this direction are steps toward a working socialism.

Of course, two dimensions are still not enough. For example, the two axes I discussed do not take into account the level of confidence of those people who are willing to take the initiative. The people who are capable of contributing much to the economy and to society must have confidence that they will be rewarded for their activity. That is, they must be provided with some motivation for exercising their capabilities. So we need to add one more dimension: the confidence of the active part of society. Neither slogans nor bank credits will utilize to the fullest the initiative of active people, unless there are strong legislative measures to help these people rid themselves of their suspicion. The government fooled the Soviet people for many decades. It is not easy now to rebuild social trust in the government.

The government must finally understand that people engage in activity to achieve their own goals and not because they want to please Uncle Gorbachev or any other uncle. Soviet propaganda must put aside talk about the primacy of the public interest over personal interests. In a well-organized society, people usually follow their own personal interests, and in so doing they serve the interest of society. This will not be easily understood by people who were raised on the romanticism of serving the government, but the time has come to understand it. The thesis of the primacy of the public interest was invented precisely to suppress the population, to unify the multiplicity and richness of the personal interests of individuals. There is no doubt that society in general suffered from this thesis.

Another aspect of this problem is the need for the government to defend those who are active and successful from those who are jealous of their success and also from ideologists. Last spring there was a small but very significant revolution in the USSR: a new law on cooperatives was passed that removed the upper limits on salaries in cooperatives, thereby allowing great differences in salary within the same cooperative. Although I usually defend economy in legislative technique, this time I understood why such an important part of the law was buried in several pages of propagandistic text.

DEFINITION OF SOCIALISM

I am trying to provide a fairly precise definition of socialism, because if socialism cannot be expressed in terms of certain human rights, there is no reason to struggle for it.

In the last century much has been said about socialism, and many people have declared themselves socialists. Very often, the building of socialism has been the justification for the violation of human rights, including the most intolerable violations. We saw it in the Soviet Union, in Hitler's Germany, and in China. The ideas of socialism, which are basically clear, very often were drowned in ideological nonsense, with the obvious goal of deceiving people and of justifying dictatorship, poverty, and slavery.

But if one were to put aside the ideological garbage and formulate the ideas of socialism clearly, in a manner that would allow the results to be easily tested, we would see that socialism is not anything other than guarantees and implementation of social and economic rights achieved via redistribution of public wealth. What is more, the limits of this redistribution must be defined not by ideological fantasies but by consideration of what the economy can tolerate, that is, by the necessity of leaving enough motivation for economic development.

I mentioned formulations, the results of which can be easily tested. I think this is the key point in the ideological fog surrounding socialism. Unclear formulations, foggy promises, mean that their consequences cannot be tested. There is no way to determine whether such promises have been kept. This is very convenient for dictators who are unsuccessful at providing a working economy and implementing social and economic rights. This convenience accounts for so many decades of fuzzy phraseology; so much falsification of, and secrecy over, statistics; so many ideological struggles against so-called formalism, even struggles against formalism in such fields as mathematics, not to mention law.

Briefly speaking, there has been too much dishonest talk about socialism. I do not think circumstances are good for the continuation of such dishonesty. People in the Soviet Union are smarter now. The historical experience has helped them to ask more questions. It is time to become formalists and guarantee in the Constitution only what can be verified and implemented. The following is my attempt to define socialism juridically and can be viewed as a suggested model for one article of any socialist constitution. This article would contain four paragraphs.

Paragraph 1: Socialism is a social order in which the state guarantees to its citizens social and economic rights and implements those rights as much as possible, depending on the economic potential of the country.

This paragraph is as precise as possible assuming, however, that the Constitution in other articles will give a relatively complete list of the social and economic rights referred to in paragraph 1, and assuming further that there will be democratic procedures established for the determination of the appropriate degree of implementation of those rights. The main point that this paragraph expresses, however, is an honest admission that there will be no streets of gold or rivers of honey, because society cannot give more than it has. If citizens are not given enough in terms of social and economic rights, let them look for the reason. Let them work better, or choose better bosses, or create new economic mechanisms. If this does not help, let them understand that they have achieved the maximum possible from redistribution of existing wealth and that they must reduce redistribution and invest more in the economy.

There is, of course, a question as to the procedure for making decisions to limit redistribution. In a capitalist system, such decisions, theoretically, are made automatically by the market, in the form of modification of salaries, prime rates, and prices. I said "theoretically" because government and unions distort the role of the market considerably. In a socialist society, the role of state democratic mechanisms probably must be much bigger than in a capitalist system, if we accept that implementation of social and economic rights is the obligation of the state. But even if the market itself is not allowed to govern redistribution automatically, it must be regarded as an important indicator, giving signals to the state on how to redistribute.

Paragraph 2: To achieve the goal of better implementation of the social and economic rights of citizens, the union and the republics must implement measures for development of the economy, including support of economic activity of citizens and cooperatives, and the creation of new forms of economic activity.

Obviously, there would be no need for such a paragraph if, historically, economic activity and the search for new forms of such activity had not been forbidden by the state.

Paragraph 3: For implementation of the social and economic rights of citizens, the union and republics may impose a tax on the income of citizens and associations. No tax may be imposed in a manner that will suppress the economic activity of people.

As vague as it is, this paragraph is needed to prevent the government from using the taxing power to suppress cooperative enterprises, as has happened in Soviet history. Ideally, without any government enterprises, taxing can provide enough revenue for a reasonable level of implementation of social and economic rights. Right now, of course, the biggest source of revenue for the Soviet government is profit

from government enterprises, but the Constitution should not take that into account, because it can be used to prevent society from freeing itself from government monopoly in the economy.

Paragraph 4: Within the limits defined by law, the union and republics may regulate the degree of implementation of social and economic rights, depending on the needs of citizens and on the citizens' level of participation in the economy.

If a democratic society forbids forced labor, and I hope that the Soviet Union will do so, there must be economic methods to defend society from those who do not want to do anything. This paragraph takes that need into account. At the same time, it is natural for society to consider that some members of society have greater needs for assistance, regardless of the level of their participation in the economy. This also is reflected in this paragraph.

The goal of the model presented in this article was to give an example of the general principles of socialism, leaving society room to search for a working model of socialism. I did not include in my model definition any of the usual ideological phrases about a planned economy, public ownership of the means of production, or the character of use of the land. All this may have a place in books on ideology, but not in the Constitution. They are principles of economic organization and must be accepted or rejected depending on the needs of the economy.

For Soviet society, there are decades of searching ahead, including the search for a working model for the economy. There will therefore be a great need for a constitution that provides sufficient flexibility and a socialism of rights instead of a socialism of restrictions.

* * *

QUESTIONS AND ANSWERS

Q (Ilkka Heiskanen, Embassy of Finland, Washington, D.C.): One of the parts of the Constitution, of course, should be the right to national self-determination. How would you see that right in the Soviet Union? How should that right be organized in the Soviet Union with respect to the rights and duties of the union versus those of the republics?

A: I was concentrating on only one model article expressing socialist principles. The Constitution obviously has to have four groups of principles: the principle of federation, the principle of democracy, the principle of human rights, and that of socialism. I did not touch on the right to national self-determination, but that does not mean that I do not want it. There must be a principle of federation, but whether there will be a right to secede or not is up to the will of the Soviet people. The right currently exists, but for seventy years one could very easily find oneself in prison for mentioning it. I do not know how the Soviet people will decide. A natural thing for a federation is to have this right, but, at the same time, there was a lot of trouble in the United States in the mid-1800s because some states wanted to secede and other states did not want them to secede. So some federations do not have these rights. Because there is talk in the Soviet Union about national minorities, most likely there will be a lot of defense for the right to secede. On the other hand, the democratization of the Soviet Union may be held up if the separatists' movement gains in strength. Such gains will be made as the Soviet Union becomes more liberated and as the nationality problems grow.

ANNALS, *AAPSS*, **506**, November 1989

Civil Rights in the Soviet Union

By ARKADY I. VAXBERG

ABSTRACT: Civil rights in the Soviet Union are discussed against the backdrop of changes occurring in the Soviet legal system. The Soviet Union is set on a course to create a law-based state. With the signing of the Vienna Concluding Document, the Soviet Union recognized the priority of international law over domestic Soviet law, with the consequence that efforts are being made to bring domestic Soviet legislation into conformity with international law. Now permitted, even encouraged, is the creation of voluntary organizations that monitor the implementation of the Helsinki Accord. Furthermore, a program is being carried out to educate the public on the international agreements on human rights that the USSR has signed. Immense changes are taking place in the public's legal consciousness, and these will guarantee that the defense of civil rights will become a reality.

Arkady I. Vaxberg is a distinguished Soviet journalist, lawyer, and long-time leading advocate of progressive reform of the Soviet legal system. In addition to legal reform, he has written on police brutality, the plight of the victims of Stalin's show trials, and the corruption of the Brezhnev era. He is a regular contributor of articles to the influential Soviet journal Literaturnaia gazeta.

I approach this discussion about the status of civil rights in the Soviet Union at a time when great changes are taking place in the country, at a time when immense social processes are occurring that, on the one hand, have given birth to these changes but, on the other hand, have been provoked by them. Among the changes that have drawn the attention today of, truly, the entire world community are the changes in the legal system. It was not so long ago that the question of law was on the periphery of society's interests, and the very profession of the lawyer and the practice of the law in various spheres and in various systems were not considered prestigious in the eyes of the population at large. These circumstances arose because nowhere were the tragic consequences of the decades of Stalinist dictatorship more obvious than in the area of law and the violation of civil rights.

A LAW-BASED STATE

We have embarked on the creation of a law-based state without, unfortunately, having a clear strategy for creating that state or even having exactly defined what content we are putting into this concept of a law-based state. This is a sad state of affairs with which we must come to terms, but I think that it is understandable. Given the decades of having a shattered legal system and such tragic lawlessness, it would be strange if the concept of a law-based state would have been formulated otherwise.

This confusion appeared quite vividly at the very onset of this task. In the very first official document in which this task facing society was proclaimed, it was said that we were confronted with completing the construction of a law-based state. But the question immediately arose, Can we complete

what has not yet been begun? The confusion was immediately reflected in the fact that, having taken on the creation of a plan to realize legal reforms, legal scholars right away conflated two concepts: *pravo* and *zakon*, right and law, *jus* and *lex*. This is not a purely terminological misunderstanding, and it is hardly a purely theoretical or academic dispute; rather, it has the most direct, concrete, and practical significance.

It was seen, then, that at the very beginning we should have defined the strategic task, defined which conception of the law we wanted to create in our society, and then drafted a system of legislation that would correspond to that ideal. Of course, it is now obvious that, first of all, we should have begun with changing the fundamental legal basis, we should have begun with changing the Constitution. This task was postponed, however, in order to push through as quickly as possible legislative changes in specific areas of the law. I do not mention this to condemn anyone in particular but in order to illustrate the difficulties that are faced by those who have taken on the resolution of this problem. In some sense, I can understand the impatience of those who want to push through changes that are more important, that concern the more painful problems of our legislation, which affect people directly.

HUMAN RIGHTS

It was not until quite recently that the very concept of human rights was relegated by official propaganda to the category of institutions of bourgeois law that are absolutely alien to socialist law. A whole generation was raised on such primitive Stalinist formulas. People were taught that while the bourgeois government defines the freedom of each person as a guarantee for the freedom of all, the socialist government guarantees the freedom of everyone as a guarantee for the freedom of each individual. Our attitude toward civil liberties was based on this illiterate and absurd formulation for many years. But it would be a mistake to consider that, during all those years, the struggle for civil rights in the Soviet Union was being waged only by those who were called dissidents and not also by honest lawyers, the press, and official agencies. These lawyers never called it a struggle for human rights, but only so that the fight over terminology would not take the place of the fight for the fate of humanity.

The basic rights and freedoms of citizens have been laid down in all the Soviet constitutions. The problem is that under Soviet law, it is not possible to appeal to any judicial or other agency in order to defend one's rights by referring only to the norms of the Constitution. In order to have such a lawsuit, complaint, or appeal accepted — even accepted for review — one must refer to specific legislative acts and not to constitutional norms. In the absence of such norms, the rights and liberties laid down in the Constitution frequently become mere decorations.

The situation now is changing substantially. In January 1989, after the Vienna Concluding Document was signed — signed with unbelievable speed, in light of our traditions — a principle received recognition that was long ago very common to the legislation of the democratic countries. This was the notion of the priority of international law over domestic legislation — in this case, over domestic Soviet law. In this way, all those international rights agreements signed by the Soviet Union would become recognized as binding in the territory of the Soviet Union itself, which would mean that all the domestic legislation would have to be changed in light of the statutes of international agreements. If we conducted a comparative analysis of these international legal agreements and domestic Soviet legislation, we would see that to this day there is a very large discrepancy between the two.

In recent years, the attention of the whole world has been focused on only one inalienable right violated in the Soviet Union: the right to emigrate. I am not going to discuss now the de facto changes that have taken place with respect to that issue in our country. These facts are all very widely known and have been very widely covered in the press.

Despite the importance of such an inalienable human right as the right to emigration, not all civil rights can be reduced merely to this one. The 280 million people who live in the Soviet Union are not all planning to emigrate, but they very much want to have the civil rights and freedoms that every person in a civilized world should possess. The attention of the world community, however, has been focused to a far lesser extent on problems associated with these latter rights. For example, we have a statute existing to this day on the system of *propiska,* or residence permits. It is a product of the Stalin era. The residence-permit system has nothing in common with the norms laid down in international agreements signed by the Soviet Union; this violates both the guarantees of international agreements and the Soviet constitutional guarantees on freedom of movement. Unfortunately, all the efforts to curb this system, for the time being, have foundered due to the obstacles created by the security agencies.

Both the Helsinki Accord and the Vienna Concluding Document guarantee complete access to information and the freedom of each citizen to express his or her thoughts publicly. Unfortunately, there are no authentic guarantees of freedom of speech in Soviet legislation or practice.

The list of what is absent but ought to be contained in Soviet law according to international law could be extended, but the real issue is not a question of a list. The problem is that the Vienna Concluding Document, among other things, does not establish any period by which the countries that signed the document must bring their international legislation into conformity with the statutes contained in the document. Thus this process of bringing about compliance with international law may be dragged out. The very tendency, the very effort to bring domestic law into conformity with international law is evident to me. But the tempo of this process is still under question. Moreover, the Soviet Union has now officially declared its readiness to submit itself to the jurisdiction of the International Court of Justice in the Hague. But as is well known, a private individual cannot appeal to the International Court in order to defend his or her rights, and there is no other procedure established for defending a right at the international level as opposed to the national level. In the coming years, as we approach the convening of the Moscow Human Rights Conference in 1991, legal scholars of various countries should think about an international legal procedure to defend civil rights.

INDEPENDENT ASSOCIATIONS

I would like to touch upon one other very important aspect signifying changes in the human rights situation in the Soviet Union. If, in recent years, voluntary organizations, or self-organized groups, or independent public associations that attempted to monitor the implementation of the Helsinki Accord were looked upon by our courts as having committed criminal offenses, now the creation of such social institutions is no longer inhibited but is encouraged. In fact, there are quite a few of these groups already founded in various individual Soviet republics as well as in Leningrad, Moscow, and other cities. In particular, this mission has been taken on by a public organization that has immediately become authoritative, the Moscow Tribune, headed by Professor Yuri Afanasyev. Among the leaders of the Moscow Tribune are Academician Andrei Sakharov and Academician Roald Sagdeyev. An exceptionally important initiative on this question has been launched by an organization that is completely new but that immediately and authoritatively announced itself; the organization is formally called the Soviet-American Cultural Initiative, widely known in our country as the Soros Foundation.

It has been noted that very many Soviet citizens – if we are to speak accurately, almost all Soviet citizens, particularly the representatives of the younger generation – have almost no concept of the international agreements signed by the USSR on human rights. Moreover, efforts to produce mass editions of these agreements encountered the traditional objection: that there was a shortage of paper in the country. With the assistance of the Soros Foundation, then, we decided to help our country. Using a grant from the Soros Foundation, we purchased the necessary paper abroad. Now one of the well-known publishers in Moscow has taken on the obligation of publishing half a million brochures by the fall of 1989 that will include the texts of the basic international rights agreements. An arrangement was made with us whereby the distribution will be under our control.

We will distribute the brochure mainly to university students and elementary and high school students, upon whom all our hope rests. In large type on the cover of this brochure will be written that all the articles of these agreements are obligatory for implementation in the territory of the Soviet Union.

Some might find this action of ours quite naive, but we have such a situation in our country that without these elementary steps, we cannot go any further. I think that this effort to launch a program of legal education is one of the most important concrete tasks facing those who really want to attain the defense of civil rights in the country.

If one were to ask me what the most significant result of the *perestroika* processes going on in the country is, I would answer thus: the political activity that has been awakened in millions, and the awareness of many, many people of themselves as a subject and not an object of the law. Before our very eyes, immense changes are taking place in the legal consciousness, and that is a guarantee that the defense of civil rights will turn from a mere declaration into a reality.

* * *

QUESTIONS AND ANSWERS

COMMENT (Clark): There is indeed an individual complaint procedure that is available to the Soviet Union: the procedure under the Optional Protocol to the International Covenant on Civil and Political Rights. That procedure would permit Soviet citizens to complain to the Human Rights Committee. I have seen some literature that suggests that it is not entirely inconceivable that the Soviet Union will become a party to that procedure in the next year or two.

Q (Vaxberg): But is the decision that the committee or court would make binding for the given legal institutions of a certain country?

A (Clark): Any decision rendered by an international body as an obligatory decision is a little difficult to enforce. The Human Rights Committee issues what are described as views, and for the most part decent governments comply with those views. On the other hand, the decisions of the International Court of Justice are obligatory, but not everybody follows them.

COMMENT (Vaxberg): The other point is that the Soviet Union never signed the Optional Protocol.

COMMENT (Clark): But it can, that is my point. The Soviet Union has to do it!

———

Q (John Ratnaswamy, Chicago, Illinois): In America, in truth, the protection of rights is dependent less on the understanding of the general populace than on professionals in the legal profession and others defending those rights. Are the latter sort of person in the Soviet Union — lawyers, judges, police — capable of making the transition to a system in which legality is taken much more seriously?

A: Virtually for decades, the legal scholars who are working today were raised in a completely different spirit and on the basis of a completely different school. These educators, representatives of the old concepts, in turn have trained the new, young generation. An immense change has to take place in their consciousness as well, and I think that this is a very lengthy process. But I am absolutely convinced that as applied to our society, which, with regard to the sphere about which we were talking, found itself in a condition of lethargy for many years, the awakening of popular legal consciousness is a guarantee for the awakening of legal consciousness among legal scholars. I cannot envision changes in the legal consciousness of, say, judges or procurators without demands to defend rights that would come from those whose rights have been violated. Only mounting massive and prolonged pressure could lead to a situation in which there would be some serious movement in the positions of judges and procurators.

Q (Ilkka Heiskanen, Embassy of Finland, Washington, D.C.): This was the first time, Mr. Vaxberg, that I heard anybody mention the question of only concentrating on the right to emigrate. Of course, the right to emigrate, the right to move, to leave one's country, is important, but I have always thought that it is even more important to arrange the rest of the rights in the country in a way that one need not use one's right to emigrate. Furthermore, there is a danger that, if the Soviet Union grants the right to emigrate to the people who want to leave, at least two old cultures will be destroyed, the Russian Jewish and the Russian German, if the Russian Jews and Russian Germans all leave.

A (Chalidze): I think there is a misunderstanding. Dr. Vaxberg did not say that the right of emigration is the main thing. He said that in the West there is too much of a focus on it. In fact, this is not the case, but in Russia they have heard that people in the West pay more attention to emigration.

A (Vaxberg): I want to be understood correctly, and I want to reiterate that the significance of the right to emigration is not being questioned here at all. It is just my opinion that world public opinion has perhaps somewhat confused the scale of these rights, to the detriment of domestic civil rights. The world press has devoted tens of thousands of lines to the unjust sentences of those who have suffered for political reasons. But so many lines never appeared in the world press about those unlawful sentences that affect the fates of millions and millions tried for so-called economic crimes, which in general are not crimes at all in a normal legal sense. I had only wanted to draw attention to the correct balance of attitudes toward various areas of violations of human rights.

Q (Roy Johnstone, World Constitution and Parliament Association, Lakewood, Colorado): I was very pleased to hear about the Moscow Tribune and its involvement in examining individual rights and its advocacy of a cultural initiative.

A: I am very glad that you have so warmly welcomed the appearance of these two initiatives about which I spoke, the Moscow Tribune and the Soros Legal Culture Initiative. To be frank, I devoted some attention to them because I am personally involved in the work of both. I should say, however, that there are many such organizations, and, to my great regret, I am not even aware of them all. They are created spontaneously; they are very active, but they are not always covered in the press. We would very much like to have contact with all the nongovernmental organizations, with all the organizations concerned with the same issues with which we are involved.

ANNALS, *AAPSS*, **506**, November 1989

Assessing Israel's Record on
Human Rights

By RITA J. SIMON

ABSTRACT: Using public opinion data, this article examines Israeli Jewish and Arab attitudes toward and support for various aspects of civil liberties, such as the right to express unpopular beliefs and to engage in acts of protest. It also contrasts public attitudes with the Israeli system of law and justice and with Israeli responses to the uprising in the occupied territories of the West Bank and Gaza. The public opinion data show Israelis to be similar to Americans in their attitudes toward many civil liberty issues. The data also show differences between Jewish and Arab responses in their satisfaction with the way democracy works in Israel. Current Israeli practices on the West Bank and in Gaza involving violations of human rights such as the destruction of Arab homes, sending writers and intellectuals into exile, and invoking censorship and curfews are juxtaposed with the public opinion data. The author concludes that due process, adherence to the rule of law, and tolerance for unpopular ideas are not usually honored when a society believes it must respond to external threats to its security.

Rita J. Simon is a University Professor at the American University, Washington, D.C. From 1983 to 1988, she was the dean of the School of Justice at the American University. Earlier, from 1963 to 1983, she was on the faculty of the University of Illinois, where she was a professor of sociology, law, and communications research. She has been editor and consulting editor of several journals and has written and edited many books, articles, and monographs.

NOTE: Funds for this project came from the Ford Foundation, whose support is gratefully acknowledged.

T HERE is a paradoxical bias involved in the investigation of human rights violations in societies that are relatively open and that have democratic institutions. Violations, whatever their proportions, are more likely to be documented and publicized in such societies. The more open the society, the more likely it is to be scrutinized.

How does one go about making a fair and accurate assessment of human rights violations? Are comparisons with other societies at the same point in time and in the same part of the world useful and meaningful? Are comparisons over time with societies that share similar values and institutions and that have faced comparable problems better measures? Are there absolute, objective criteria that one should apply in evaluating a society's record on human rights? These are the issues one must confront in considering the Israeli record.

Examination of the record involves going back to the founding of the state 41 years ago, when some allege the first violations occurred. The specific acts were the swift and dramatic switch in majority-minority statuses that occurred between Arabs and Jews as a result of the war for independence in 1948. Prior to the war, prepartition Palestine had a population of 1.95 million, of whom 1.3 million were Arabs and 650,000 were Jews. Of those 1.3 million Arabs, about 700,000 lived in that part of Palestine that was to become Israel as a result of the U.N. resolution and vote. But by the time a cease fire had been declared and the fighting had stopped, Jews made up 87 percent of the population. Estimates are that about 550,000 of the 700,000 Arab inhabitants fled the Jewish state.

The Jews explain the diminution of the Arab population largely as a result of Arab residents' following the instructions of the invading Arab armies to leave their land temporarily so as to make it easier for the advancing Arab military forces to defeat the Jewish army. Arabs fled their homeland in the expectation that they would return after the armies of Jordan, Egypt, Iraq, and Syria had defeated the Israeli forces and had destroyed Jewish hopes of establishing a country of their own in the Middle East.

The Arabs have a different version. They claim that as the Jewish forces advanced and occupied Arab neighborhoods in Jerusalem, and in Arab towns and land in the Galilee and other parts of the country, they forced the indigenous Arab population to vacate their homes, farms, and lands and flee. Those who were unable to make their way across the borders into various neighboring Arab states became the first generation of Arab refugees; and many of them became the founders of the Palestine Liberation Organization and other Palestinian movements that today still seek a national homeland.

The next major event in the chronology of possible human rights violations occurred in the aftermath of the Six Day War, in 1967, in which Israel won a quick and dramatic military victory over Jordan, Syria, Egypt, and other Arab states and thereby acquired more than twice the land that it had previously held and increased the Arab population under its control by 1.3 million. It is the activities of the people living under that occupation for 22 years that provide the basis for the current focus on Israel as a violator of human rights. In the area known as the "West Bank," because it comprises the western provinces of the Kingdom of Jordan as a result of the 1947 U.N. partition, and the Gaza Strip, which before 1967 had been under Egyptian rule, an uprising called the *"intifada"* began in December 1987. Thus far, it has cost the lives of some 500 Palestinians – 50 of whom have been killed by Palestinians because they were believed to be informers — and 17 Israelis. Israelis' reactions to the *intifada* are the immediate and direct source of the allegations about Israel's violations of human rights. The specific charges have included beatings, killings, burying people alive, destroying homes, and deporting persons who have actively protested the Israeli occupation.

THE CONTEXT

Unlike what occurs in many societies that have been the subject of sanctions or even strong verbal criticism for their policies vis-à-vis dissidents, the Israelis themselves have been among the most vocal and visible of the critics of their government's policy, and the Israeli military forces, as well as the government, have allowed greater access by the media to the areas in which the antigovernment activities are occurring. News clips showing Israeli soldiers chasing, holding, and beating dissidents appear regularly on television in the United States and major cities around the world. How much, one should stop and ask, do these pictures tell us about human rights violations? Let us first examine the statement "The camera doesn't lie." While the camera depicts what is happening at any point in time, it does not provide what may be crucial background and follow-up information on any specific event. If, for example, we see film clips of soldiers chasing school-aged children in the market areas of Hebron and Nablus, the camera does not tell us what events or activities precipitated the chase. Was someone badly hurt or even killed before the soldiers gave chase? When police are shown on camera taking women into custody, the camera does not show the stone throwing and the taunts that have been directed at the police prior to the roundup, nor does the camera stay around long enough to show the women being

released after only a brief time in custody.

Two points are thus worth emphasizing. Israel has been open about reporting the public debate that has gone on within its own borders concerning the policies it should pursue vis-à-vis the *intifada*. Interviews with soldiers, many of whom say, "What we are doing in the West Bank has nothing to do with being in the army"; results of public opinion polls; and views expressed by leading public officials have been widely aired by the Israeli press and television. Second, on most occasions, even when the Israeli defense forces realize that what will be shown on television all over the world will place Israel in an extraordinarily negative light, they have not barred television cameras. They grant entry knowing full well that under almost any circumstances, the electronic media favor civilians over the military. A predictable aftermath of such policies is distortion and bias about the extensiveness of the uprising and the severity of the responses. Two or three deaths or beatings inflicted by Israeli soldiers — serious and powerful as these acts are — take on the same or even greater notoriety than accounts reported in the press of hundreds of Tibetans, Kurds, Bahais, Armenians, or others being killed by soldiers and police in countries in which cameras and direct news reporting are much more limited or forbidden.

Another result is a distortion of the strength and extent of the uprising. The camera photographs specific events that are limited as to time and place. But their appearance night after night on the television screens suggests that the protests are ongoing and continuous occurrences; that there are no periods of quiet; that ordinary day-to-day activities have ceased to occur. We know that is not the case.

Are these remarks meant to exonerate Israel and give it a clean bill of health on the matter of human rights violations? No, they are not. They are meant to place Israel's responses to the uprising and the protests into a larger context. One aspect of this context is to consider how societies that have less respect for the rule of law and democratic institutions behave in the face of such activities. Another is to compare Israel's conduct with that of societies that have a history of democracy and support for the rule of law and to examine how they have behaved when their authority has been under attack. Let us look, for example, at the behavior of the British when they were under attack from the Indians or the Irish, or examine the French responses to uprisings in Algeria and Southeast Asia. We might also compare the U.S. decision to round up and intern American citizens of Japanese heritage during World War II. Have the Israelis behaved with less respect for human rights than the British, the French, and the Americans? Have the Israelis responded with the same ferocity to dissident activities as the Soviets vis-à-vis the Georgians, the Armenians, and the Uzbekians; as the Iranians vis-à-vis the Bahai community; as the Iraqis vis-à-vis the Kurds; as the Chinese vis-à-vis the Tibetans? In light of such comparisons, the Israelis seem better than many other societies. Perhaps they have acted with even more restraint than the British and French when faced with comparable problems.

Frankly put, part of what is involved has to do with expectation levels. The world — even Israel's enemies — expects better of Israel than is expected of most other countries. In truth, Israel is partly responsible for those expectations. It has projected itself as a society with higher moral standards, as a country and a people that would act as a "beacon of light" to the rest of the world. Perhaps it has been taken at its word. It is now being judged by those standards and has fallen short. We have all seen film clips of Israeli soldiers chasing, clubbing, rounding up adolescents, even young children and their mothers. We have seen and read of Arab journalists, writers, and intellectuals being led out of their homes into exile. We have watched the destruction of Arab houses by tanks and bulldozers because the owners have provided shelter to dissidents. Less often have we witnessed and read about the complaints and reservations expressed by Israeli soldiers assigned to duty in Gaza and on the West Bank, of the public meetings held in Israel proper by persons who are against the occupation, of the debates in the Parliament attacking government policies vis-à-vis the occupied territories; nor have we often read the newspaper editorials that have denounced military and government actions with the same vehemence that outside human rights observers have directed at those activities.

In the remaining sections of this article, I shall bring evidence of a different sort to bear on the issue of Israel's human rights record. Admittedly, the evidence will be indirect, but I believe it is relevant and perhaps more reliable than the impressions gained from the media. The source of the data is public opinion polls conducted in Israel proper of Jews and Arabs about their assessment of the extent to which civil liberties and the right to express unpopular beliefs and to engage in acts of protest are protected by Israeli law and honored by Israeli institutions and law enforcement officials. The last of these surveys were conducted just prior to the onset of the *intifada*. They do not focus on activities on the West Bank and in Gaza. Nevertheless, it is reasonable to assume that public attitudes and support for such basic issues are not so ephemeral or subject to such sharp swings that the responses obtained in 1986 and then again in 1987 would not provide useful guidance for assessment of public support of those values less than two years later. In addition, if one has an understanding of the structure of Israeli society, it is also reasonable to assume that public opinion reflects government policies to a considerable degree, just as it would in the United States or Great Britain. To be sure that this point is clearly understood, a brief description of the structure and organization of the Israeli political and judicial system follows.

The closest comparison is Great Britain, which Israel, in establishing its government, clearly used as a model. Except for the fact that, in addition to the House of Commons, Britain also has a House of Lords, the executive, legislative, and judicial branches of the Israeli government are similar in organization and function to the British Parliament, Prime Minister's Office, and Supreme Court. The Israeli Parliament, or Knesset, consists of 120 members who are elected for four-year terms through a system of proportional representation. The cabinet is the executive branch, headed by the prime minister, who may select members of his cabinet from within or outside of the Knesset. The cabinet, or the government, is responsible to the Knesset. A government cannot be formed without majority support in the Knesset and must resign when it fails to maintain the confidence of the Knesset.

Like Great Britain, Israel does not have a constitution and the Israeli Supreme Court does not have the power of judicial review. It can invalidate administrative actions or interpretations of statutes that it regards as contrary to the rule of law, but it cannot declare a law passed by the Knesset unconstitutional.

The absence of a constitution or of any similar authoritative declaration of individual civil liberties has produced recurrent public and parliamentary debate about how to establish a stronger legal basis for the protection of such liberties. Attempts were made at drafting a constitution or bill of rights in 1962 and again in 1964. Unsuccessful attempts were also made to repeal legislation still in force from the British mandatory period — particularly the Defense Emergency Regulation of 1945 — that permits arrests, searches, seizures, and censorship in a broadly discretionary manner.

As of the spring of 1989, the draft of a Basic Law: Fundamental Human Rights had been approved by the cabinet and awaited passage by the Knesset. The rights protected under this law include the right to equality, life, and human dignity; freedom of the individual; and freedom of movement, expression, religion, association, and assembly. The bill states, "Human rights may not be curtailed, save by a statute that is fitting in a democratic society, and provided that the curtailment does not exceed the degree necessary." The bill itself will be entrenched so that it cannot be amended without a two-thirds majority in the Knesset.

It is important to point out that the bill would not be applicable in those areas, the West Bank and Gaza, in which the major issues concerning human rights have been raised. Israeli law does not apply in those areas that are under military occupation.

RESEARCH DESIGN AND
SURVEY DATA

The source of the Jewish Israeli opinions are two national surveys conducted in the summers of 1986 and 1987 by the Israel Institute of Applied Social Research, a major survey agency comparable to the Harris or Gallup polls in the United States. Israeli Arab opinions are derived from two smaller surveys, using the same instrument, conducted in the two Muslim Arab villages of Baqa El Garbiya and Jat. The Arab survey was supervised and administered by Israeli Arabs.

The first national survey had 1174 Jewish respondents who were located in the major urban areas plus smaller cities and rural areas. The second had 573 respondents, all of whom were located in major urban areas in which over 85 percent of the population lives. Each of the two surveys of Arab opinions contained 200 respondents. They were conducted at approximately the same time as the national polls. The current surveys included items that had been asked in a 1975 poll of Israeli attitudes toward civil liberties and that have also appeared on recent surveys of U.S. public opinion.

Freedom of expression

Jewish and Arab Israelis agreed on many of the free-speech items included in the survey, but they disagreed on "how things are run in Israel." In 1986 and 1987, 37 and 42 percent of the Arab respondents said that "people are too restricted in what they are allowed to think and do," compared to 12 percent and 11 percent of the Jewish respondents. Most of the Arab respondents — 49 percent and 60 percent — believe it is "never justified" to refuse to hire a professor because of his political beliefs as opposed to 30 percent and 38 percent of the Jewish respondents. Along the same lines, Arabs are more likely to believe that the government never has the right to fire a person because of disloyalty to the country: 19 and 35 percent as opposed to 3 and 4 percent of the Jewish respondents. About half of the Arab respondents, in contrast to a third of the Jewish ones, believe the government "never

has the right to punish someone for a particular speech."

Each of these disagreements consistently places the Arab community on the side of greater freedom and greater support for the right of dissent than the Jewish community. Of course, these opinions must be seen in the context of the position that Israeli Arabs occupy in the state. Formerly the majority community, they now occupy a minority status within a Jewish state, but they hold ethnic, religious, and political ties to Israel's enemies in the surrounding area. Thus, for example, the political beliefs that a professor is likely to hold that would make hiring him a questionable decision are likely to be beliefs sympathetic to the Arab cause. But these differences of opinion should be seen in light of the shared views that are held on related items such as the following.

In 1986 and 1987, respectively, 45.9 and 53.4 percent of the Jewish respondents, compared to 49.5 and 65.8 percent of the Arab respondents, agreed that "books that preach the overthrow of the government should be made available by the library just like any other book." The statement "Freedom to worship as one pleases applies to all religious groups regardless of how extreme their beliefs are" was agreeable to 49.6 and 38.4 percent of the Jewish respondents and to 32.0 and 37.6 percent of the Arab respondents. The statement "Free speech should be granted to everyone regardless of how intolerant they are of other people's opinions" was agreed to by 58.7 and 57.9 percent of the Jewish respondents and by 54.5 and 45.5 percent of the Arab respondents.

Items pertaining to book censorship, freedom of worship, a professor's political beliefs, and granting free speech to intolerant people had been included in a national survey conducted in the United States in

1979.[1] Only on the freedom-to-worship item did the American public express stronger support for civil liberties than did Jewish or Arab Israelis. Of the U.S. respondents, 69 percent said it should apply to all groups. Only 18 percent of the Americans polled believed that refusal to hire a professor because of his or her political views is never justified, and 32 percent believed that books that preach the overthrow of the government should be available in the library. American public opinion matched Jewish Israeli views on the item that stated that "free speech should be granted to everyone regardless of how intolerant they are of other people's opinion"; 59 percent of Americans agreed with the statement.

Police interference

The role and power of the police are significant measures of the amount of restriction a society places on its citizenry. Initially in 1975, and again in 1986 and 1987, we included a series of questions about various forms of police surveillance and intrusion into the activities and movements of the populace. The format for the specific items reads as follows:

How strongly do you support or oppose the police listening to telephone conversations, reading mail, maintaining surveillance, limiting freedom of movement, and forbidding demonstrations on the part of a wide range of political groups in Israeli society, including leftists (Racah) and rightists (Kach, Jewish underground movements) and religious groups that oppose the state (Netora Karta)?

The figures in Table 1 report the respondents who supported, opposed, or had no opinion about police intervention for all the political and religious movements just cited. On the whole, and especially in 1987, the Arab respondents showed less opposition to police intervention than did the Jews.

Contrary to expectations that might have developed from stories in the popular media, Jewish Israeli opposition to police interference vis-à-vis all of the groups tended to increase or remain at about the same level from 1975 to 1986-87 on all of the activities shown in Table 1.

The same issues, with different political groups as illustrations, were included in a national U.S. poll in 1975.[2] Unlike in the United States, where constitutional guarantees forbid most of these activities, in Israel legislation exists that provides a legal basis for the execution of each of these activities by administrative bodies that are essentially free from judicial review. The American responses differed from the Israelis' on three issues. Americans were more opposed than Israelis to direct invasions of privacy — for example, 69 percent opposed tapping telephones, and 80 percent opposed opening mail — and forbidding demonstrations was opposed by 70 percent. But they expressed less opposition than Israelis to placing persons under surveillance — only 17 percent were opposed. On placing limitations on internal movements, the American public shared views similar to those of the Jewish Israelis — 53 percent were opposed compared to 50 percent.

So, once again, we have a basis of comparison between Israeli and American support for civil liberties. We found that while the American public demonstrated greater

1. Herbert McClosky and Alida Brill, *Dimensions of Tolerance* (New York: Russell Sage Foundation, 1983).

2. Rita J. Simon and David Barnum, "Comparative Assessment of Public Support for Civil Liberties in the United States and Israel," *Research in Law and Sociology,* 1:81-100 (1978).

TABLE 1
OPINIONS SUPPORTING AND OPPOSING POLICE INTERVENTION
(Percentage of respondents)

	Jews			Arabs	
Activities	1975	1986	1987	1986	1987
Listening to telephone conversations					
Support*	20.0	28.9	24.6	5.5	10.4
Oppose†	43.0	48.2	50.1	56.5	37.1
No opinion	11.0	5.8	6.6	4.5	15.3
Opening mail					
Support*	20.0	23.8	22.2	6.5	9.4
Oppose†	45.0	54.4	53.8	51.0	40.6
No opinion	12.0	6.0	6.6	3.5	15.3
Surveillance					
Support*	31.0	35.1	30.2	6.0	10.4
Oppose†	26.0	37.6	40.1	44.5	27.7
No opinion	11.0	6.0	5.9	6.0	19.8
Limiting movement					
Support*	15.0	20.2	21.3	4.5	9.9
Oppose†	50.0	53.8	52.9	44.0	33.2
No opinion	9.0	6.3	6.6	6.5	17.3
Forbidding demonstrations					
Support*	14.0	26.1	19.2	9.0	8.4
Oppose†	56.0	48.8	58.6	40.5	36.1
No opinion	7.0	6.1	5.6	8.5	15.3

*Proportion of respondents who approve of the activity for all groups.
†Proportion of respondents who disapprove of the activity for any group.

support for the personal rights of privacy — namely via telephone and mail — a majority of the Israelis also demonstrated their respect for privacy and a concern for limiting police interference in public as well as personal activities, even though in Israel such activities are legally mandated.

Confidence in
public institutions

In two national surveys conducted in Israel in January and July 1987, Israeli sociologists Ephraim Yuchtman Yaar, Yohanan Peres, and Mira Freund of Tel Aviv University reported responses to items that asked about the extent of trust in central institutions in Israeli society. In discussing the implications of their study, they observed:

The amount of trust felt by the public toward the institutions of a society based upon democratic principles constitutes one of the most important indicators of the vigor of that type of society and of its prospects for persevering in its democratic character. Indeed, the existence and stability of democracy, more than any other type of political regime, depend upon the degree of support and legitimacy which governmental and other central social institutions receive from the public.[3]

3. Ephraim Yuchtman Yaar, "Public Trust in Social Institutions," *Israeli Democracy,* 1(3):31-34 (1987).

In our second survey, we included items that also asked about trust in many of the same institutions. The Jewish responses on our survey match closely those reported by Yaar and his colleagues.[4] For example, they found, as we did, that the military was the institution that received the highest degree of support: 76 percent in January 1987 and 66 percent in July answered "a great deal of confidence" on their surveys, and 73 percent of our respondents answered the same. In their surveys and ours, the courts ranked second, with 56 and 57 percent on theirs and 52 percent on ours answering "a great deal of confidence."

The question we raise now is, How similar are the Arab and Jewish respondents? The answer, as shown in Table 2, is that except for the military, in which only 1 percent of the Arab respondents expressed a great deal of confidence, Jewish and Arab ratings matched closely on important institutions that were not directly political, for example, the courts, the universities, the trade unions, banks and financial institutions, and small businesses. They disagreed in their confidence in the police, the government, and the Likud Party. Unlike the Jewish respondents, the Arabs expressed much more confidence in the Labor Party than they did in the right-of-center Likud Party.

Issues that revealed much greater disagreement between Jews and Arabs and much greater disaffection on the part of the Israeli Arabs were revealed in their responses to the following questions. When asked, "How satisfied are you with the way democracy works in Israel?" 21 percent of the Arab respondents compared to 46 percent of the Jews answered "extremely" satisfied and "very satisfied." When asked, "Do you believe you will remain faithful to

the state of Israel under any conditions?" 27 percent of the Arabs answered positively compared to 75 percent of the Jews. To the question, "To what extent are Arab citizens' rights in Israel safeguarded today?" 77 percent of the Arabs answered "hardly" or "not at all" compared to 23 percent of the Jews. Finally, when asked the more general question, "To what extent are civil liberties observed in Israel today?" 62 percent of the Arabs answered "hardly" or "not at all" compared to 19 percent of the Jews.

These Arab responses may well reflect the Arabs' views of life both in Israel proper and on the West Bank. They may also reveal a much closer sense of identity and loyalty with the Arabs in the occupied territories and with Palestinians generally than Israeli Arabs have had in the past forty years. These attitudes and shared identities may give rise to acts of civil disobedience and confrontations with Israeli police on a scale not heretofore engaged in by the Israeli Arab community.

CONCLUDING REMARKS

I return to the issue posed initially about Israel's violations of human rights on the West Bank and in Gaza. The death of some 500 Palestinians is a harsh indictment. The continued enforcement of the Emergency Regulation of 1945 that limits movement and expression in the occupied territories involves violations of human rights. Some, many of whom are Israelis, claim that the continued occupation of the West Bank and Gaza is, by itself, a violation of human rights. The survey data that show that Israelis have high regard for fundamental civil liberties and the rule of law should be viewed in the context of those events. How does one understand Israel's behavior on the West Bank and Israel's simultaneous

---

4. Yaar, "Public Trust in Social Institutions."

TABLE 2
DEGREE OF CONFIDENCE IN ISRAELI INSTITUTIONS, 1987
(Percentage of respondents)

Institutions	Jews	Arabs
Military		
A great deal	73.1	1.0
Some	18.2	10.9
Only a little	4.9	33.7
Almost none	1.7	19.8
None at all	1.7	32.7
No answer	0.3	2.0
Courts		
A great deal	52.2	39.6
Some	25.8	25.7
Only a little	12.9	18.8
Almost none	3.0	8.9
None at all	3.8	6.4
No answer	2.3	0.5
Universities		
A great deal	21.1	24.3
Some	34.6	36.6
Only a little	27.4	19.8
Almost none	5.2	9.4
None at all	5.9	9.4
No answer	5.8	0.5
Police		
A great deal	15.7	4.5
Some	25.1	10.4
Only a little	32.5	41.1
Almost none	13.1	23.8
None at all	11.9	18.8
No answer	1.7	1.5
Government		
A great deal	4.9	1.0
Some	17.6	5.4
Only a little	43.5	26.2
Almost none	20.2	41.1
None at all	13.1	25.2
No answer	0.7	1.0
Trade unions		
A great deal	9.6	12.4
Some	19.7	19.8
Only a little	32.8	34.2
Almost none	17.6	16.3
None at all	17.6	15.3
No answer	2.6	2.0

TABLE 2 continued

Institutions	Jews	Arabs
Religious parties		
A great deal	6.1	3.5
Some	9.4	5.9
Only a little	24.8	17.3
Almost none	22.9	33.2
None at all	34.7	39.6
No answer	2.1	0.5
Banks and financial institutions		
A great deal	7.0	9.9
Some	23.7	24.8
Only a little	38.7	32.2
Almost none	15.9	18.3
None at all	14.3	13.4
No answer	0.3	1.5
Small businesses		
A great deal	3.1	2.0
Some	17.5	15.3
Only a little	41.9	40.6
Almost none	21.1	30.2
None at all	12.6	9.9
No answer	3.8	2.0
Likud Party		
A great deal	10.1	2.0
Some	18.0	3.0
Only a little	25.3	16.8
Almost none	20.6	23.8
None at all	23.4	54.0
No answer	2.6	0.5
Labor Party		
A great deal	12.7	5.9
Some	20.6	23.3
Only a little	27.7	34.2
Almost none	16.1	18.8
None at all	20.6	17.3
No answer	2.3	0.5

respect for civil liberties? Part of the answer must stem from the similarity that Israelis have to the British, the American, the French, and other peoples who have a history of tolerance and respect for due process. That similarity is the adherence to the idea that the same rules do not always apply to outsiders.

Thus, while the Israeli security forces may be violating due process in their treatment of suspects, in placing severe limitations on movement, in invoking censorship and curfews, at the same time those rights may still be honored within the body politic and among those who are an integral part of the society. History and national comparisons have demonstrated many times that there need be no carryover from the way a government responds to external threats to its response to internal threats, or to the protests of persons or groups it believes to have a legitimate status in the society. Thus, because most Israelis believe that the Arab nations do not seek peace, that the danger from terrorists' activities is great, and that the army is its most important source of protection and security, they condone, or at least do not actively oppose, the harsh treatments and violations of civil liberties meted out to the Palestinians living on the West Bank and in Gaza. It is possible for the Jewish Israeli public to condone those activities, while believing in and actively protecting and supporting individual freedom and civil liberties within its own borders. The Israelis may be able to do it as well as the British, French, and U.S. publics have when the occasion has required it.

It is possible that Israel is behaving as well as any occupying power could, under the circumstances. But that is not good enough to avoid human rights violations. With every day that the *intifada* goes on, the likelihood that the Israeli Arab community will join it increases. Should the growing allegiance that Israeli Arabs claim to feel toward the Arab community on the West Bank result in acts of violence within Israel proper, the danger to Israel's democratic institutions will be greater than they have ever faced. The not unrealistic probability that the *intifada* will spread into Israel proper is one of several good reasons why Israel should agree to withdraw its troops and cease its role as an occupying power.

* * *

QUESTIONS AND ANSWERS

Q: I do not understand that there is any way that the camera makes any difference. There is no allegation that the Palestinians of the *intifada* have firearms. They are being shot for throwing stones.

A: Have you been there?

Q: No, I haven't been there; so what?

A: Do you think they only throw stones? That is not true. They do not only throw stones.

Q: They do not have firearms.

A: They have grenades.

Q: Grenades have been used on occasion. There have been 17 Israelis killed. But how is it possible to justify the Israeli response along the lines that you are arguing?

A: I am not justifying it, but one must look at it in context. To say that the Palestinians just throw stones is a terrible distortion.

———

Q (Marvin Wolfgang): You made comparisons, or allusions of comparability, with the English and the French. Are you willing to put any quantitative weight on those differences or similarities? Is one of those examples worse than what the Israelis are doing?

A: I lived in India for a year in the mid-1950s and I spent a lot of time talking with Indians who had been there under the British and who were involved in the movement for independence. One of the things that a lot of them said was that living under the British was terrible and that many Indians were wounded. Some were grateful that the British were not the Germans. Comparisons between various situations in which human rights are violated must be made. There will be differences between the situations, and making the comparisons is not to say that being beaten does not hurt and is not a violation. But not making the comparisons leaves us in a make-believe world.

————

Q: During the 41 years that Israel has existed, there has been a change of political power. What differences does your survey show between the Ashkenazi and Sephardic communities?

A: There will be many articles coming out that look at these differences. By and large, Sephardic Jews are less supportive of civil rights. If social class is not held constant, the differences are very great and Sephardic Jews are much less supportive of civil liberties and civil rights than Ashkenazi Jews. When education and other variables are held constant, there are still differences, though not as great. The differences are real.

————

Q: I was very much interested in the interview conducted among the Arabs and the Jews. Did the fact that you were an American tend to bias the responses in any way?

A: I did not do the interviews with the Israelis. They were done by the Israel Institute of Applied Social Research. They are national polls, like the Gallup polls. Neither did I do the interviews with the Arabs. Ever since 1968, however, when I started

doing research in Israel, I had very close contact with a few Arab families in Baqa El Garbiya. Several of the family members are trained in social science, and they have worked with me on other projects. When I found that the Institute of Applied Social Research had never in the forty years of its existence interviewed Arabs in its national polls, I was astonished and I encouraged my Arab friends to conduct the interviews. I gave them my questionnaire translated into Arabic, and I promised to work with them and train any of the Arabic interviewers so that the data could be collected. So America was not involved; I was invisible.

————

Q: I am a little disturbed about the comparison between Israel now and, say, England. It seems to me that we always must compare similar situations across time, and I have a strong faith that we can solve almost everything by communicating, by exchanging views. England has had bad times, and it is certainly an empire. But England asserted its Magna Carta, it has had its Bill of Rights, it has had its religious struggles to change the level of toleration, and one can see that almost all sources of opinions are tolerated in England today. I wonder whether it would not be a good thing if Israel started its law almost from scratch from 1941. I am not quite sure if Israel has accepted the conventions that have developed in England. While England does not have a written constitution, certainly there is a nonwritten constitution that is embodied in so many of the things that we need to see today.

A: The Israeli Declaration of Independence is a magnificent document. It talks about equality, freedom, and so forth, but it does not have the power of a constitution. Recently, in April, Israel did pass, after over twenty years of trying, its basic law on fundamental human rights, and there is every expectation that it will be adopted by the Knesset once the cabinet has approved it. But there again, how much will it affect activities on the West Bank and in Gaza? Not very much. It is, however, a major step in terms of the kinds of legal protections that we were talking about.

ANNALS, *AAPSS,* **506,** November 1989

The Role of Science and Scientists
in Human Rights

By CAROL CORILLON

ABSTRACT: The topic of science and human rights encompasses dozens of issues and involves scientists and scientific organizations in all corners of the globe. This article examines four of these issues and touches on the specific activities of scientists and scientific organizations in a number of geographic areas. The article is divided into four sections: the scientist as human rights activist, the scientist as human rights victim, the scientist as human rights abuser, and the application of science to human rights work.

Carol Corillon is director of the Committee on Human Rights, National Academy of Sciences, and the Committee on Health and Human Rights, Institute of Medicine, Washington, D.C. She organized and led Academy human rights missions to Chile and Somalia and was awarded the Academy's 1988 Professional Staff Award for Distinguished Service. From 1980 to 1984 she was professional associate on the Advisory Committee on the Sahel, National Research Council. From 1976 to 1980 she was a print and broadcast journalist in Kinshasa, Zaire, for the BBC and Reuters, among others.

NOTE: This article is based on my experience as director of the human rights committees of the National Academy of Sciences and the Institute of Medicine; however, the views expressed herein do not necessarily represent the views of these institutions.

O N 15 March 1989, 12 scientists were released from prison in Somalia, after spending more than seven years in solitary confinement. Some had been severely tortured. In mid-April, at the National Academy of Sciences, we received a letter from one of those scientists, a mathematician.

In it he said that he had been very moved on learning, after his release from prison, of the Academy's activity in behalf of him and the other imprisoned scientists. He said he felt that our persistence was a key factor in obtaining his freedom and also comforted his "family and friends." He wrote that although the physical and psychological injuries he received during his imprisonment would remain for a while and although "some of them [might last] forever . . . learning about multidimensional pressure and its effects [had] already" begun to heal him. Following his signature are the words "ex-prisoner of conscience" in parentheses.

This article is about the relationship between human rights and the world scientific community. Although I will focus on the natural scientists, all scientists — and individuals in every field of endeavor — have a responsibility as human beings to protect and defend human rights. Although I am addressing many scientific issues, the underlying theme is the individual victim of abuse.

I began this article by referring to a letter from a Somali scientist because, ultimately, the questions of science and human rights are about the fate of individuals, as that letter so poignantly reflects.

What do scientific organizations have to do with human rights? The short answer, which is only the beginning of the whole answer, is that science must have a conscience, it only flourishes in freedom, and its goal is truth. When scientists are oppressed, when freedom is denied, and when the truth is subverted, science suffers.

One of the greatest scientists and humanitarians of our time, Albert Einstein, spoke often of the relationship between science and human rights in many of his innumerable musings during his lifetime. To Einstein, freedom and concern for one's fellow human being were inalienable parts of one's being as a scientist. Einstein said it is not enough for a scientist to "understand about applied science. Concern for man himself and his fate must always form the chief interest of all technical endeavors. . . . Everything that is really great and inspiring is created by the individual who can labor in freedom."[1]

The success of a scientist's work is dependent on free inquiry and communication and the ability to know and speak the truth. It is this approach to science — and to life — that makes so many scientists the world over abhor oppression. It is this mind-set that leads many of them to speak out against such oppression and that, in speaking out, sometimes leads to the abrogation of their own rights. That is the short answer to the question.

THE RELATIONSHIP BETWEEN SCIENCE AND HUMAN RIGHTS

The beginning of the long answer to the question about what science has to do with human rights is that the topic of science and human rights encompasses dozens of issues and involves scientists and scientific organizations in all corners of the globe.

I want to focus on four parts of this topic: the scientist as human rights activist, the scientist as human rights victim, the scientist as human rights abuser, and the

1. Albert Einstein, Speech delivered at the California Institute of Technology, Pasadena, 1931.

application of science to human rights work.

The scientist as human rights activist

It has been my experience that American scientists generally become involved in human rights issues as a matter of conscience. They may learn that a scientific colleague in one country or another has been arrested for expressing his or her views — be they scientific or political — that he or she has disappeared while working in a rural clinic, or that a colleague has been denied scientific work on religious or political grounds.

At the National Academy of Sciences, some of the members are emigrants who fled their countries of origin because of repression and have become America's most distinguished scientists. These scientists in particular, because they have experienced human rights abuses firsthand, often feel a strong obligation to help their less fortunate colleagues.

In addition, because science knows no geographic or political boundaries and speaks a universal language, scientists consider themselves part of a world scientific community. When their colleagues face repression, they come quickly to their defense.

Many of these individuals have encouraged scientific institutions with which they are affiliated to create human rights committees that are empowered to act in behalf of their colleagues around the world. In the United States, the American Association for the Advancement of Science (AAAS), the American Mathematical Society, the American Psychiatric Association, the American Physical Society, the Association for Computing Machinery, and the American Society of Civil Engineers are among the scientific organizations that include human rights components. There are also scientific groups that have been established to deal specifically with human rights issues, such as the Committee of Concerned Scientists and Physicians for Human Rights.

Through these organizations, members are exposed and become sensitized to human rights concerns. Soon they begin speaking out, and governments tend to listen. It has been my experience that, often, foreign governments listen more closely and more willingly to scientists because their appeals are so obviously based on humanitarian concern. The question of possible political motivations is rarely an issue. This was quite obvious prior to, during, and following the National Academy of Sciences mission to Chile in 1985[2] and the joint mission by the Academy and the Institute of Medicine to Somalia in 1987.[3] The delegates were told by the officials with whom they met how impressed they were that such prestigious institutions and respected scientists took the time to travel to their countries and to appeal for their colleagues.

A number of academies of sciences abroad also have human rights committees. A few of them, with whom we work most closely, include the Accademia nazionale dei lincei in Rome, the Académie des sciences de l'institut de France in Paris, and the Royal Society of Canada in Toronto.

In addition, many medical groups and associations around the world are actively involved in the defense of human rights and medical ethics. They include the Medical College of Chile, the Voice against

2. *Scientists and Human Rights in Chile: Report of a Delegation* (Washington, DC: National Academy Press, 1985).
3. Carol Corillon, ed., *Scientists and Human Rights in Somalia: Report of a Delegation* (Washington, DC: National Academy Press, 1988).

Torture in Pakistan, the Turkish Medical Association, and the National Medical and Dental Association in South Africa.

Many such groups function in countries in which human rights activities can be considered crimes against the state and their members risk becoming human rights victims themselves for their outspoken objection to abuses of human rights and medical ethics. In Iran, according to health professionals who have emigrated to the West, the Iranian Medical Council was abolished after the Islamic regime abrogated the outcome of independent elections of board members and arrested the new members and physicians who supported them. In Syria some 100 doctors who were members of the Syrian Medical Association were detained in 1980 following a strike protesting human rights abuses under the state of emergency.[4] These doctors reportedly are still in detention. The Syrian Engineers Union also suffered severe repression.[5]

*The scientist as
human rights victim*

Many scientists become victims of human rights abuse simply because they carry out their professional and ethical responsibilities. In recent decades, hundreds of health professionals in Latin America have been arrested or abducted and killed while working in areas of conflict. Doctors have also become victims for opposing torture or refusing to participate in it or conceal evidence of it.

Another well-known example of a victim of repression is that of Dr. Anatoly

4. *Violations of Human Rights in Syria: How Medical Professionals Can Help* (Washington, DC: Amnesty International, USA, 1983).

5. *Violations of Human Rights in Syria: Imprisonment of Engineers* (Washington, DC: Amnesty International, USA, 1983).

Koryagin, the Soviet psychiatrist who documented and publicized abuses of psychiatry for political purposes. Dr. Koryagin was the chief psychiatric consultant to the Working Commission to Investigate the Use of Psychiatry for Political Purposes, a human rights group in the Soviet Union. During a four-year period just before his arrest in 1981, he and another psychiatrist examined several dozen dissidents who were released from psychiatric hospitals or threatened with detention. None of the individuals examined was found to be in need of psychiatric treatment or confinement. Dr. Koryagin spent six years in a Soviet labor camp as a consequence of his actions.

Dr. Ramiro Olivares, the physician for the Vicaria de la solidaridad in Santiago, Chile, a respected human rights organization that operates under the auspices of the Roman Catholic Church, spent more than 16 months in detention, without trial, after having examined an individual with a gunshot wound and not reporting it to the authorities. It was subsequently learned that the injured man had been involved in a shoot-out with the police. Dr. Olivares's detention, far longer than the 60 days stipulated for having failed to report examining a victim of a gunshot wound, was seen by many human rights groups as an attempt by the Chilean government to discredit the work of the Vicaria.

Two economists in Nicaragua were sentenced in September 1988 to 16-year jail terms for possession of state secrets. According to an article in the *New York Times,* "The secrets are economic projections, estimates of grain production, export figures and other data that are public information in most countries." The article went on to say that the case "has political overtones because one of the economists . . . worked for a business group opposed to Sandinista rule. His lawyers say he was singled out for prosecution as part of a political campaign aimed at intimidating the opposition."[6]

In late 1987 a number of scientists involved in environmental preservation projects and public welfare issues in Malaysia were arrested after criticizing the government's environmental and social policies. They were given two-year detention orders and became the object of an international outcry. Most were released within a year. All are now free.

Many scientists suffer repression as a result of their humanitarian or political activities. We are all well aware of the courageous and outspoken leadership of Soviet physicist Andrei Sakharov for more than two decades against abuses of human rights. Sakharov was forced to spend seven lonely, frustrating years in internal exile in Gorki as punishment. Merely three years ago, no one, except perhaps the most starry-eyed optimists, would have dared hope, let alone predict, that Sakharov would be allowed to return to Moscow, would be elected to the presidium of the Soviet Academy of Sciences, and would travel to the United States and elsewhere and speak frankly about some of his continuing concerns about human rights, peace, and environmental problems.

During his visit to the U.S. National Academy of Sciences in November 1988, Dr. Sakharov told the American scientists who gathered to honor him of how much he appreciated the support he received over the years from the Academy and its leadership. Sakharov also said that, while he was denounced by many Soviet scientists, "at the same time, the American academy sup-

6. Stephen Kinzer, "Managua Jails 2 Economists, Stirring Fears," *New York Times*, 2 Oct. 1988. Copyright © 1988 by The New York Times Company. Reprinted by permission.

ported me unequivocally, and this is a fact that I can never permit myself to forget."

No one would have believed, just a few years ago, that Sakharov would twice ask Secretary Gorbachev to amnesty all prisoners of conscience and would run for and be elected to a seat in the Congress of Deputies. It is a delightful and encouraging turn of events.

Unfortunately, a little further to the east, in China, another renowned physicist and outspoken human rights activist, Dr. Fang Lizhi, is traveling a similar road of unpopular dissent against the Chinese government. Dr. Fang has been openly critical of his government's policies and of human rights abuses. In early 1987, after participating in a demonstration for greater democracy, he was expelled from the Chinese Communist Party and fired from his position as vice-chancellor at the Science and Technology University of Hefei in eastern China. In October 1988 he was denied permission to travel to the United States to visit and work in several academic institutions. Many scientists, including Dr. Frank Press, the president of the National Academy of Sciences, and Dr. Sakharov — who was not permitted to travel outside the Soviet Union until 1988 — have appealed to the Chinese government to lift the travel ban on Dr. Fang.

As we work our way around the globe, we find hundreds of scientists, engineers, and health professionals in every geographic region who have spoken out against oppressive government policies or in defense of human rights and who are languishing in prison or unable to pursue their work. Unlike Sakharov and Fang, most of these individuals are relatively unknown outside their own countries.

In South Africa, Professor Ismail Mohamed, an associate professor of mathematics at the University of Witwatersrand

and an outspoken opponent of apartheid, has been subjected on several occasions to detention without trial for political reasons. In 1985 he spent more than 10 months in detention on charges of high treason, a capital offense, but later all charges against him were dropped. Dr. Mohamed was a founding member of the Detainees' Parents Support Committee and vice-president of the Transvaal United Democratic Front. Both organizations, along with 15 others, were placed under severe restrictions by the government of South Africa in early 1988.

In Somalia more than a dozen physicians and scientists, including the mathematician mentioned at the beginning of this article, were arrested after they organized a group of citizens in the northern town of Hargeisa. They merely formed a group to help improve conditions in the local hospital and schools. These scientists were released only recently, after spending more than seven years in prison. Many, like the man whose letter I described, were severely tortured and kept in solitary confinement.

The list continues. The Israeli government has detained a number of scientists from West Bank universities and continued their detention orders without bringing them to an open trial. In Poland in the mid-1980s dozens of scientists were detained after campaigning for human rights and criticizing the policies of the Polish government. The Iranian government has executed dozens of scientists for their political and religious beliefs. And the list goes on.

The scientist as human rights abuser

Physicians are dedicated to preserving life and must, above all, do no harm. Although scientists are most often human rights victims, they are sometimes human rights abusers. Naturally, the perversion of medical and scientific knowledge and techniques is a matter of grave concern to the scientific community.

I have already mentioned the abuse of psychiatry for political purposes that was exposed by psychiatrist Anatoly Koryagin and others in the Soviet Union. It should be pointed out that psychiatry is abused for political ends in other countries as well, although the abuse does not appear to be systematic.

The Soviet government has never formally admitted that healthy individuals who opposed government policies — or who simply asked to emigrate or continued religious observances — were consequently incarcerated by psychiatrists in psychiatric hospitals and that many were administered psychotropic drugs.

A few years after its All-Union Society of Psychiatrists and Neuropathologists was condemned by the World Psychiatric Association, the Soviet Union withdrew from the association because of fear of expulsion. In the past two years the practice of abusing psychiatry for political purposes has been sharply reduced. In addition, many forcibly institutionalized individuals have been released, there has been criticism of Soviet psychiatry in the official press, and new mental health laws have been passed. But according to the International Association on the Political Use of Psychiatry, which is based in the Netherlands, many of the psychiatrists most responsible for the abuses remain active in Soviet psychiatry.[7]

Another extremely serious issue is the participation or collusion of health professionals in torture and its concealment. In-

7. *Soviet Psychiatric Leaders* (Amsterdam: International Association on the Political Use of Psychiatry, n.d.).

volvement ranges from falsification of death certificates to the use of medical knowledge and techniques in torture, from observing a torture session in order to ensure that the victim does not die to treating the victims so that torture can be continued.

It has been reliably reported that in Argentina, during the self-proclaimed dirty war, health professionals systematically colluded with torturers in the Argentine military. Dr. Jorge Antonio Berges, a former police doctor, although convicted and imprisoned in Argentina in 1986 for his involvement in torture, was subsequently released under the law of due obedience.

In Brazil in 1988 the medical society of Rio de Janeiro suspended Dr. Amilicar Lobo from the society for reportedly participating in torture conducted in military facilities between 1969 and 1974.

The medical college in Chile has publicly condemned the practice of torture and has reported that over eighty physicians were directly or indirectly involved in "acts of ill-treatment, humiliation, or torture; the great majority of these physicians belonged to the armed forces and were attached to the security agencies."[8] The medical college has suspended some of those physicians from its organization and has expelled others.

In Pakistan, according to a Pakistani doctor, Mahboob Mehdi, who is a member of an organization called Voice against Torture, "the participation of doctors in the process of torture is usually legal and has been made part of the duties of the doctor." Dr. Mehdi has interviewed numerous torture victims, including a doctor who faced his former medical school classmate in the torture chamber. According to Dr. Mehdi,

information that he obtained from these torture victims indicated that the doctors usually "advise the torturers about the actual condition of the victim's health and revive the victims sufficiently to undergo further torture."[9]

According to Dr. Mehdi, physicians in Pakistan are required to medically examine individuals sentenced to floggings to ensure that they will not die as a result of the punishment. The flogging is carried out in the presence of the authorized medical officer and, if after the punishment has begun the medical officer believes that the individual could die, the punishment is postponed until the individual is certified by the physician to be physically fit to undergo the remainder of the punishment.

Doctors and other health professionals are also called upon to participate in executions. According to Amnesty International, doctors can be asked to determine the mental and physical fitness of an individual for execution, to give technical advice, to prescribe, prepare, administer, and supervise doses of poison, and to perform medical examinations during executions so that an execution can continue if the prisoner is not yet dead. The World Medical Association has resolved that "it is unethical for physicians to participate in capital punishment, although this does not preclude physicians certifying death."[10]

In Pakistan, Iran, the Sudan, Mauritania, and a number of other countries, medical professionals have participated in amputations of hands, feet, and fingers as pun-

8. Francisco Rivas Larrain, "Doctor Torturers Penalized by Their Professional Body in a Country Where Torture Is Practised," *Danish Medical Bulletin*, 34(4):191 (Aug. 1987).

9. Mahboob Mehdi, "Torture in the Medical Scene of Pakistan" (Paper delivered at "Medicine at Risk," Amnesty International Seminar, Paris, France, 19-21 Jan. 1989).

10. Resolution on Physician Participation in Capital Punishment, adopted by the Thirty-fourth World Medical Assembly of the World Medical Association, Lisbon, Portugal, 29 Sept. 1981.

ishment. In Iran health workers have helped develop a machine to perform these punitive amputations, and they have been forced to remove blood from prisoners before their executions for future use in treating injured members of the revolutionary guard.

The application of science to human rights

While the distressing fact exists that science is sometimes perverted and scientists do become involved in unethical practices, to a much greater extent scientists apply their science to document and deter human rights abuses. For example, forensic anthropologists have applied their skills in a number of countries to identify and determine the cause of death of individuals who have disappeared under repressive regimes. These efforts not only serve to bring those responsible to justice but can also have a significant deterrent effect.

In the last few years the AAAS has taken forensic anthropologists and others to Argentina and the Philippines to help train local scientists and medical and anthropology students in techniques for exhuming and examining the bodies of individuals who disappeared during the self-proclaimed dirty war in Argentina and during the Marcos regime in the Philippines.

In Argentina between 1973 and 1985 at least 9000 people vanished. Many were picked up by paramilitary groups, then tortured and killed. Some bodies have been found in unmarked graves. Scientists who disappeared in the late 1970s and whose cases have never been resolved include four physicists: Dr. Federico Alvarez Rojas, Dr. Gabriela Carabelli, Dr. Antonio Misetich, and Dr. Eduardo Pasquini.

During his work for the Argentine National Commission on Disappeared Persons, Dr. Clyde Snow, a forensic anthropologist from the Cook County Medical Examiner's Office in Chicago, helped the Argentines collect enough evidence on individuals who disappeared to convict a number of high-ranking military and police officers, including seven junta members.

Snow has described the case of three young people who were abducted, killed, and buried in an unmarked grave. "'Each of them had four or five closely spaced bullet wounds in the upper chest—the signature . . . of an automatic weapon. Two also had wounds on their arms from bullets that had entered behind the elbow and exited from the forearm.'" According to Dr. Snow, "'That means they were conscious when they were shot. When a gun was pointed at them, they naturally raised their arm.'" [11] This is important scientific evidence when such a case is brought to trial.

According to Dr. Snow, "'If you have a colonel who ran a detention center where maybe five hundred people were killed, you don't have to nail him with five hundred deaths. Just one or two should be sufficient to get him convicted.'"[12] Forensic evidence can "help authenticate the last moments of the victim's life and bring a dimension of reality to the judges and jury."[13]

Another AAAS effort in Argentina uses scientific techniques to reunite the offspring of the disappeared with their biological families. Many of the parents were abducted and killed and their children were adopted, sometimes by their parents' torturers or members of the military. In Argentina 200 infant kidnappings have been documented. Epidemiologist Mary-Claire King "has joined immunologists at the

11. Patrick Huyghe, "No Bone Unturned," *Discover,* Dec. 1988, p. 45.
12. Ibid., p. 45.
13. Ibid.

Durand Hospital in Buenos Aires to compare genetically determined markers in people's white blood cells with markers in the blood of their putative relatives."[14] Dr. King applied these molecular biology and genetics techniques to help the grandparents identify their long-lost biological grandchildren. The identity of about sixty children has been proven so far.

Forensic pathologists also have a responsibility to help document and prevent arbitrary killing by performing thorough autopsies. To this end, the Minnesota Lawyers International Human Rights Committee has developed the Minnesota Protocol.[15] This protocol includes a model autopsy protocol that assists experienced forensic pathologists "to ensure a systematic examination and to facilitate meaningful positive or negative criticism by later observers." In potentially controversial cases, "a systematic and comprehensive examination and report is required to prevent the omission or loss of important details." For "general pathologists or other physicians who have not been trained in forensic pathology but are familiar with basic postmortem examination techniques, . . . the protocol may also alert them to situations in which they should seek consultation, as written material cannot replace the knowledge gained through experience."[16]

Health professionals also apply their skills toward the rehabilitation of torture victims. It is a sad comment on the extent of torture in the world that during the past few years we have seen the establishment of torture treatment centers, in Denmark, Pakistan, Canada, France, the United States, and elsewhere.

CONCLUSION

I have described only a few of the many aspects of science that relate to human rights. The underlying issue here is the victim and the responsibility that each and every one of us shares, no matter what our professional calling, in coming to his or her assistance. As Elie Wiesel said when he accepted the 1986 Nobel Peace Prize, "What all these victims need, above all, is to know that they are not alone: that we are not forgetting them, that when their voices are stifled, we shall lend them ours, that while their freedom depends on ours, the quality of our freedom depends on theirs."[17]

* * *

QUESTIONS AND ANSWERS

COMMENT (Marvin Wolfgang): Carol, you have enlightened me. I was not aware of the extent to which the National Academy Committee has been involved around the world. As a criminologist, I sometimes teach a course on the history of penology. In the archives in Paris, there were elaborate rules and regulations for physicians to keep a tortured victim alive. Under what was called the Ordinary and

14. "At the AAAS," *New Scientist,* 28 Jan. 1989, p. 29.

15. "The Minnesota Protocol: Preventing Arbitrary Killing through an Adequate Death Investigation and Autopsy" (Report, Minnesota Lawyers International Human Rights Committee, Subcommittee on Inquiry Procedures, June 1987).

16. Ibid., p. 15.

17. Elie Wiesel, Speech delivered at the Nobel ceremony, Oslo, Norway, 10 Dec. 1986, quoted in "Wiesel's Speech at Nobel Ceremony," *New York Times,* 11 Dec. 1986.

Extraordinary Questioning Period, torture was not used as punishment but as an interrogation procedure. It was extremely important to keep the prisoner alive. That was in the fourteenth century, and to hear, in your remarks, that the same kind of thing is going on today is incredible.

COMMENT (Gerald Porter, Committee of Concerned Scientists, New York City): I would like to commend Ms. Corillon for making us aware today of the important fact that, while we rejoice in the achievements that have taken place over the last ten years, we still have a long way to go in human rights. As a national board member of the Committee of Concerned Scientists, I feel that I would be remiss at this time if I did not express our appreciation of and gratitude for the work that the National Academy has done over the last half dozen or ten years under Ms. Corillon's leadership and that of my colleague, Eliot Stellar, and, before him, Lipman Bers. It has been important for us at the Committee of Concerned Scientists to feel that the National Academy of Sciences was working with us in promoting the rights of scientists as opposed to working against us. As recently as a dozen years ago, the National Academy advised a colleague of mine who was going to visit the Soviet Union that he should not visit refuseniks; the reason given was that scientists should not meddle in the internal politics of other countries. That that situation has changed — and changed as dramatically as it has — is very important and something for which we should express our gratitude to those who caused it to happen.

Q (John Ratnaswamy, Chicago, Illinois): While the allure of the national security state may be waning, perhaps an increasing number of persons, including some scientists, argue for greater state power to deal with ecological problems such as population pressure. Perhaps both Professor Shelley and Ms. Corillon could address whether a nation that respects individual autonomy and human rights has an advantage or a disadvantage in dealing with environmental problems and whether there is a possibility that environmentalism and the human rights movement are to some extent on a collision course.

A (Shelley): I do not think there is a simple answer to that question. Sometimes the two are mutually exclusive and sometimes they are not. In the Soviet Union, for instance, some of the protests in Armenia arose out of the Karabagh Committee's pressing ecological issues. These issues were seen as so threatening in some respects that they were subject to repression. Independent voluntary movements are arising in many parts of the country over ecological questions; there is a growing awareness that ecology needs to be addressed, and it is something that is being encouraged by the state. The extent to which national issues are linked to the environment determines how threatening environmentalism is perceived to be to the viability of the state. On the contrary, environmentalism could be seen as a renewal of individual interest in the preservation of the state. Moreover, it is too simple to say that human rights and environmentalism are on a collision course. There are costs that an economy has to pay to preserve the environment, but if the whole society wants to pursue that course, then the costs are worth paying.

A (Corillon): I cannot exactly answer the question either, but we have seen some examples of collision between environmentalists and their governments. For example, in Malaysia, some environmental activists who were working on issues of deforestation on Borneo protested government policies on logging and radioactive waste and were arrested. We have run into the same problem in Brazil, with the rubber tappers and environmental activists in that country defending tropical forests against developers and suffering repression as a result.

Q (Lenora Wolfgang, Lehigh University, Bethlehem, Pennsylvania): Could you share with us some of the specific charges against these scientists, perhaps some of the language of the charges?

A: Generally, the charges are related to national security, and they are usually not more specific than that. Underlying the charges is the objection that the individuals were opposed to government policy. In Somalia, the charges were more related to the fact that the individuals were from the wrong clan. They were Isaaqs from the north and President Siad Barre is a Marehan from the south, and in Somalia, such a difference practically leads to being viewed as a criminal. One case had to do with funding. Funding tends to go to the capital city, Mogadishu, so Hargeisa was being neglected and some of the scientists in that area decided to take things into their own hands, collect money, and try to improve the local services themselves. This action was seen as very threatening by the government. In other countries, individuals who are charged are simply involved in carrying out their professional activities. The physicians who are working in rural clinics are caught in military conflicts. They treat anyone who comes to them for medical attention, and sometimes these people are guerrillas, sometimes they are members of the military. The groups in conflict are upset that a physician has treated a member of an opposition party.

Q (Solomon Alber, Committee of Concerned Scientists, New York City): First, I want to stress the importance of the support of the world scientific community to refusenik scientists in Moscow. Every week or two, one hears of a group of scientists or physicians coming to Moscow and sometimes visiting. They participate with us in scientific seminars, thereby keeping us up to date professionally. They support our right to emigrate from the Soviet Union, and they have saved us in very difficult situations. My second comment is about human rights for scientists and the matter of secrecy and state security. Secrecy and state security are special in the Soviet Union. In many cases they are not connected with real secrecy and real state security; they are used as excuses for punitive and sometimes political purposes. I know that almost all scientists must sign special documents about their so-called clearance. They work in very strange situations, and as a result they do not have any right, for example, to give a speech at a meeting or to have any contact with foreigners who come to the Soviet Union. They have no right to go abroad or to have any scientific contacts with colleagues abroad or sometimes to take part in conferences in the Soviet Union. I can give one example of this secrecy. If you want to read the notices of the American Medical Association, you must have special permission from a special department, and after this you must have a clearance and you are alleged to be involved in secret work, because notices of an American society are secret papers in the Soviet Union. According to the Committee of Concerned Scientists, there are now in Moscow about 400 scientists and engineers who have not been allowed to emigrate as a result of this secrecy. I know a lot of cases in which secrecy has punitive or political meaning. What is your opinion about this situation in the Soviet Union?

A: I think you expressed the problem very accurately and very well. It is an issue that our committee has examined. We have secrecy issues here in the United States, as well. We have classified scientific information, but we also have the First Amendment and we do not try to lock up people based on the knowledge they have. They simply pledge that they will not reveal that information. It has been announced by a Soviet official that there will be a new law put into effect that a secrecy clearance would be lifted after seven years. That would certainly be an improvement over what has been happening. We wonder if it will actually go into effect. We also wonder whether the continued use of clearances will have an effect on Soviet science if individuals decide that they do not want to have clearances because of the implications for the rest of their lives and as a result go into other areas of work.

COMMENT (Eliot Stellar, American Philosophical Society, Philadelphia, Pennsylvania): The National Academy of Sciences has been very active in dealing with its colleagues in the Soviet Academy, discussing the issue of secrecy every year that we have had a scientific exchange. Such discussion is part of the charter of the exchange program. The charter specifies that issues of this sort will be brought to the attention of the Soviet counterparts, so the issue is very much alive. I think that the potential change in the law can be helpful. I think that the continued pressure from Frank Press, the president of the National Academy of Sciences, and Bill Gordon, the foreign secretary, not only in meetings with members of the Soviet Academy but also in meetings with the refuseniks themselves is also helpful.

ANNALS, *AAPSS*, **506**, November 1989

Homeless Children:
Philadelphia as a Case Study

By ELAINE R. FOX and LISA ROTH

ABSTRACT: Homeless children are rapidly emerging as a new segment of the nation's underclass. This article describes the origins and implications of this phenomenon, using Philadelphia as a case study. The recent rise in the number of homeless families is due to a decrease in the amount of affordable housing and a simultaneous increase in the number of families living in poverty and its attendant social problems. As a result, homeless children in Philadelphia and the nation experience severe disruptions in family life that can have devastating, and possibly permanent, effects on them. These effects include poor health, limited access to a source of continuing health care, developmental delays, emotional disturbance, and poor school performance. We must address both the children's immediate needs for comprehensive social services and the systemic causes of family homelessness in order to prevent future generations of homeless children.

Elaine R. Fox, M.A., is director of homeless programs at Philadelphia Health Management Corporation. She currently directs the Health Care for the Homeless Project for Philadelphia. She is the author of Homelessness in Philadelphia: People, Needs, Services *and numerous other articles related to homelessness.*

Lisa Roth, J.D., M.S.S., is a research associate with the Philadelphia Health Management Corporation. She is currently evaluation manager for the Homeless Families Initiative of the United Way of Southeastern Pennsylvania and for the Emergency Room Aging Connection Project.

T HIS article describes a new and growing phenomenon in Philadelphia and
other urban areas in the United States: the
emergence of a new segment of the
nation's underclass — homeless children.

Homeless families — consisting of a single female and her children — are the most
rapidly growing segment of the homeless
population. It is estimated that as many as
1 million children across the nation are
homeless. Currently, in Philadelphia, there
are 900 homeless families and over 2200
homeless children; 60 percent of these children are under the age of five.

In Philadelphia, these children and their
parents do not live on the street as do some
homeless adults; they live in public and
private emergency shelters for the homeless. These family shelters were intended
only a few years ago to be temporary residences for the emergency placement of
families in crisis, but they have now become, in effect, transitional or even permanent residences for families who have no
other place to live. For the first time in this
country's history, large numbers of children are being born and raised without
roots and without a place of their own.
They are growing up in large institutional
settings because their parents have no other
place to go or because their parents cannot
maintain a stable residence.

CONTEXT OF HOMELESSNESS
IN PHILADELPHIA

As have other cities, Philadelphia has
experienced recent dramatic changes in its
homeless population. These changes reflect both the increased number of people
who are homeless and the changing com-
position of the population.

A 1985 report by Philadelphia Health
Management Corporation (PHMC), *Homelessness in Philadelphia: People, Needs,*

Services,[1] synthesized the findings of a
two-year foundation-funded project, the
Emergency Shelter Monitoring Project.
The project had a number of objectives,
including the collection of data on the characteristics and needs of Philadelphia's
homeless population, the identification of
gaps in the system, and the development of
recommendations for further services.

While the earliest descriptions of the
homeless were of a largely skid-row population living in the fringe areas of the city,
PHMC's 1985 report described a more pervasive, nationwide problem, at its most
visible in large urban centers. While recognizing the basic heterogeneity of Philadelphia's 10,000 to 13,000 homeless people and the difficulty of using a single
factor to classify these individuals — most
of whom almost always have multiple
problems — the 1985 report classified the
homeless into three major subgroups.

The first subgroup is the chronically
mentally ill. These are the individuals most
visible on the street, individuals with serious mental illness. They include older,
deinstitutionalized individuals and younger, more violent individuals who, because
of more restrictive civil rights laws regarding institutionalization, may never have
been hospitalized. In 1985, PHMC estimated this group to represent 10-15 percent
of the homeless in Philadelphia, a percentage that has remained constant through the
present time.

Substance abusers constitute the second
subgroup. PHMC's 1985 report classified
the vast majority of the 1200-1500 homeless substance abusers as chronic alcoholics. Drug abusers appeared as a relatively
rare occurrence in shelters. Since PHMC's

    1. Philadelphia Health Management Corporation,
*Homelessness in Philadelphia: People, Needs, Ser-
vices* (Philadelphia: Philadelphia Health Management
Corporation, 1985).

report was written, there has been a dramatic increase in the number of homeless individuals who use illicit drugs, especially crack. Crack is a highly concentrated, highly addictive form of freebase cocaine, sold in small crystalline chunks that are smoked in a water pipe. It produces a short-lived euphoria. Because of its low cost and its easy availability, its use is particularly appealing. The effects of cocaine use are dramatic and insidious. Recent statistics from a group of hospitals in Philadelphia show that one of every six women delivering babies in Philadelphia hospitals showed evidence of cocaine use. Infants born to cocaine-addicted mothers often suffer from cocaine addiction themselves, low birth weight, and/or a wide variety of congenital and developmental problems. Cocaine use is also linked to higher rates of sexually transmitted diseases and poor prenatal care.[2]

The third subgroup is composed of the economically disadvantaged. PHMC's 1985 report classified the largest category of the homeless — estimated at the time to be 8000 to 11,000 — as economically disadvantaged so-called marginal individuals, with chronic employment problems and limited education and job skills. Until recently, this group mostly comprised single men who had exhausted their eligibility for public benefits, especially since the reduction in the Pennsylvania General Assistance Program in 1983. Since the report was written, this group has swelled with large numbers of families who are now homeless; this trend has occurred not only in Philadelphia but across the nation. In Philadelphia the number of families with

children requesting emergency shelter rose 30 percent between 1986 and 1987, until between one-third and one-half of the city's shelter population consisted of families. This trend is not unique to Philadelphia; in 1986, the U.S. Conference of Mayors reported an increase in the number of homeless families in 85 percent of the cities in the nation.[3]

WHO ARE
HOMELESS FAMILIES?

Last year in Philadelphia, homeless families made up one-third of the homeless population. As mentioned earlier, these families reside in Philadelphia's 200 shelter residences — both boarding homes and large converted warehouses — that provide a place to sleep and three meals a day. Many homeless families share a single room with another family. Refrigerators, food, and cooking facilities are usually not allowed in the rooms. Bathrooms are often communal, and recreational space is scarce. Many children must confine their play to shelter halls.

The cost of homelessness has increased dramatically with the increase in the number of persons in shelters. In Philadelphia, the cost of the city's programs for the homeless rose from $18.1 million in fiscal year 1985 to $30.2 million in fiscal year 1988. It costs the city an average of $10,800 to shelter a family of three for a year, or an average of $10 per person per day. The average length of a family's stay in a shelter is nine months.[4]

2. City of Philadelphia, Coordinating Office for Drug and Alcohol Abuse Programs, "Comprehensive Plan for Drug and Alcohol Abuse Treatment and Prevention, FY 1991-1993" (Draft, 15 May 1989), pp. 15-16.

3. U.S. Congress, House, Select Committee on Children, Youth and Families, *Homeless Families, A Neglected Crisis: Hearing,* 99th Cong., 2d sess., 1986, p. 8.

4. Vernon Loeb, "The Shelter Fiasco," *The Inquirer* (magazine of the *Philadelphia Inquirer*) 6 Mar. 1988, p. 18.

Homeless families in Philadelphia do not differ significantly from other urban homeless families or from other urban low-income families. The vast majority of Philadelphia's homeless families are headed by young single minority women with larger than average families.

The sole source of income for many shelter families is Aid to Families with Dependent Children (AFDC). In Pennsylvania, AFDC payments for a family of four are $474 per month, or $5688 annually. This amount is approximately 70 percent of the 1987 federal poverty threshold for a family of four.

The overwhelming majority of homeless mothers are unemployed. For these women, lack of affordable child care and marketable skills has resulted in unemployment or short-term, poorly paid jobs that are insufficient to support a family in independent housing. As a result, many homeless mothers have little experience living independently. For example, in one 1988 study of homeless families receiving case-management services in Philadelphia, over 85 percent of the families shared housing at least once in the past five years. Three of five, or 60.0 percent, of the families had shared housing immediately before their shelter stay: 20.8 percent had lived with relatives, 20.8 percent with friends, and 20.0 percent with others.[5]

ECONOMIC CAUSES OF
FAMILY HOMELESSNESS

Why have the numbers of homeless families increased so dramatically in recent years? Family homelessness is caused by an increase in the number of low-income families and a decrease in available, af-

fordable permanent housing.[6] Both of these trends are the result of a failure of society to provide for its most vulnerable members.

Poverty

The number of people living in poverty fell to 11.1 percent in 1973, and until the early 1980s the number of people living in poverty remained virtually static, rising to only 12.7 percent in 1979. Beginning in the late 1970s, however, the gains that low-income families had made during the War on Poverty began to be eroded by high unemployment and high inflation rates. Between 1979 and 1983 the number of people living below the poverty level increased by 49 percent due to two recessions and Reagan administration cuts in eligibility and benefit levels for AFDC families. By 1984, the percentage of families living below the poverty level had risen to 17.4 percent. During the same time period, the average income of the poorest 20 percent of all families dropped by 34 percent, while the income of the highest fifth fell by only 2 percent.

Black female-headed families were hardest hit by these trends. In the past twenty years, the number of households headed by single women has increased dramatically among both white and black women. This feminization of poverty has resulted in an increase in the number of children who grow up in poverty in single-parent households. By 1980, single-mother families accounted for more than 48 percent of all black families with children, and 56 percent of black single-mother families had incomes below the official poverty threshold. Black single-mother households had approximately 30 percent less income

5. Philadelphia Health Management Corporation, Homeless Families Initiative of the United Way of Southeastern Pennsylvania, unpublished data, 1988.

6. Kay Young McChesney, "Families: The New Homeless," *Family Professional*, 1:13-14 (1986).

than their white counterparts. Black mothers on average are younger, have more children, and have younger children than white mothers. As a result, a black child in a poor female-headed family faces an average of 12 years of poverty.[7]

Housing

While the number of low-income families was increasing, the supply of available affordable housing was decreasing due to economic forces in the private sector and cuts in federal funding for public housing. High interest rates and recessions in the late 1970s and early 1980s resulted in fewer housing starts and higher housing costs. Many families who could not find affordable housing doubled up, creating overcrowded conditions. From 1978 to 1983, the number of families living two to a dwelling unit doubled, reversing a thirty-year trend.[8]

At the same time, the Reagan administration began to retreat from funding public housing. Since 1980, the federal budget for low-income housing has been cut by over 60 percent. In addition, the Department of Housing and Urban Development increased the amount a low-income family was required to pay for rent from 25 to 30 percent of their income. As a result, by 1985 there were twice as many poor households as there were available low-income housing units.[9]

Economic trends in Philadelphia

In Philadelphia, homelessness has escalated with the increasing poverty. The poor in Pennsylvania were especially hard hit by then Governor Richard Thornburgh's 30 percent reduction of the general assistance rolls by limiting benefits for single able-bodied individuals without children to 90 days in the calendar year.

Housing costs in Philadelphia rose at the same time that the income of poor families dropped. The amount of money a low-income family has left after paying the rent has decreased steadily since 1970. In 1970, black renters paid an average of 22 percent of their incomes for rent. By 1988, black families were spending more than half — 53 percent — of their monthly incomes on rent. While median rents for black renters rose from $111 in 1975 to $278 in 1988, black renters' median annual income increased only marginally above $5000. Real renter incomes, in constant 1988 dollars, fell by 8 percent, real rents rose by 9 percent, and public assistance allowances fell by almost 50 percent. Today for a family of three the median monthly rent, which is $384, is $50 more than the total AFDC allowance, which is $334.[10]

Public housing in Philadelphia cannot meet the overwhelming demands. Currently, there are 34,000 subsidized housing units in the city and an estimated 129,000 renters and 66,000 owners who need housing assistance. The waiting time for a Philadelphia Housing Authority unit is nine years.[11]

SOCIAL PROBLEMS

Most studies of homeless families in the United States point out that although lack

7. Ann M. Nichols-Casebolt, "Black Families Headed by Single Mothers: Growing Numbers and Increasing Poverty," *Social Work*, 33(4):308 (July-Aug. 1988).

8. McChesney, "Families: The New Homeless."

9. Ibid.; Cushing N. Dolbeare, *Housing in Philadelphia: A Report for the Public Interest Law Center of Philadelphia* (Philadelphia: Public Interest Law Center of Philadelphia, 1988), pp. 24-26.

10. Dolbeare, *Housing in Philadelphia*, pp. 24-26.

11. Ibid., p. 20.

of affordable housing is the underlying cause of family homelessness, most homeless families have multiple problems that cannot be solved by housing. Bassuk and her colleagues suggested that, in addition to external factors,

psychosocial factors, particularly family breakdown, play an important role as well. There can be little doubt that the constellation of economics, subsistence-living, family breakdown, psychological deprivation and impoverished self-esteem contribute to the downward cycle of poverty, disruption, stress and violence. With the unavailability of affordable housing, the most emotionally vulnerable and marginal members of society will be the first to fall through the "safety net."[12]

In a study of homeless families in Los Angeles, McChesney identified two precipitants of family homelessness: economic events, which accounted for 75 percent of cases, and relationship events, accounting for 25 percent. She described a population of families who

were poor long before they became homeless; they had often been barely "making it" for some time before their episode of homelessness began. Then, on top of all the usual strains of poverty, an additional adverse event occurred that upset their already precarious economic balance and eventually led to homelessness.[13]

Local trends

Data on homeless families in Philadelphia from PHMC's United Way Homeless Families Initiative, a research demonstration project for 100 families, indicate the same pattern of homelessness. The over-

whelming majority of families in the initiative are single-mother-headed households that are poor and have been poor for a long time. The families have moved from one overcrowded living situation to another an average of 5.7 times in the past five years. Three of five families, or 60.0 percent, had lived with others immediately before entering the shelter. Eventually, they exhausted their resources. One-quarter of the mothers could not name anyone who would help them if they needed it.

Although poverty was the underlying cause of homelessness for all of the families in the initiative, multiple personal problems often interacted with poverty to produce homelessness. Battering by a spouse and substance abuse were the two most frequent noneconomic precipitants of homelessness. Nearly one-third of the mothers, or 31.3 percent, reported that they left home to avoid an abusive spouse and one-quarter left due to the end of a relationship with a man. More than half of the women, 58.4 percent, left in part because a spouse or someone in a shared living arrangement was abusing alcohol or drugs. There is currently no accurate count of the number of parents in family shelters who abuse drugs, but anecdotal evidence indicates it is very high.

Other events that precipitated homelessness included disputes with others in shared housing, accounting for 22.9 percent of the cases, and overcrowded housing, accounting for 20.8 percent. It is important to note that more than one-third of the families listed more than one cause of their homelessness.

Like the homeless mothers studied by Bassuk and her colleagues,[14] the homeless women in the Homeless Families Initiative

12. Ellen Bassuk, Lenore Rubin, and Alison Lauriat, "Characteristics of Sheltered Homeless Families," American Journal of Public Health, 76(9):1100 (1986).

13. Kay Young McChesney, "New Findings on Homeless Families," Family Professional, 1(2) (1986).

14. Bassuk, Rubin, and Lauriat, "Characteristics of Sheltered Homeless Families."

had experienced troubled childhoods. Nearly one-quarter — 22.9 percent — reported being abused as a child and two of five — 41.7 percent — were children of alcoholics.

Obviously, the solution to family homelessness must include the alleviation of poverty and its attendant social problems. Affordable housing can decrease the shelter population but will not stop the growth of a permanent urban underclass. Unfortunately, the chief victims of this cycle of poverty and homelessness are the children.

EFFECTS OF HOMELESSNESS ON CHILDREN

While homeless women do not appear to differ significantly from other poor women, homeless children face severe disruptions that have devastating and possibly permanent effects on their lives. Homelessness affects children's physical and mental health, their ability to learn in a school setting, and their psychological and social development.

Health

Homeless children are in poorer health than children who are not homeless. Chronic physical disorders are nearly twice as common among homeless children as among nonhomeless children. Lack of ongoing health care and the problems of growing up in an institutional setting are the primary factors that negatively affect the health and well-being of homeless children.

Homeless children are often born to women who have no prenatal care or good nutrition, placing them at greater risk for higher infant mortality rates and low-birth-weight babies. Cocaine abuse — now highly prevalent in Philadelphia, as in other urban areas — is related to higher rates of nonexistent or poor prenatal care, sexually transmitted diseases, premature deliveries, and lower birth weights. Further, nearly one-third of the cocaine-using mothers require cesarean deliveries and 28 percent of the babies are admitted to intensive-care nurseries, compared to 10 percent of nonusers' babies.[15]

Although homeless children are more in need of health services than other children, their access to care is limited. Because of frequent moves, the chaotic state of their mothers' lives, and the lack of services in shelters, homeless children lack basic health services and have no source of continuing health care. As a result, these children are behind in normal immunizations, placing them at risk for measles, mumps, and whooping cough — diseases that are preventable and were thought to have been eradicated. Delayed immunizations also prevent homeless children from enrolling in school.

The lack of ongoing care also means that problems that may be observed and monitored in nonhomeless children are often overlooked. Of course, children who receive episodic care rarely receive routine health assessments — vision, dental, and hearing — that are essential to good preventive care.

Additionally, the problems of living in an institutional setting are marked by poor diet, overcrowding, and poor hygiene, and they result in frequent colds, skin rashes, and bouts of diarrhea. The recent rise in hepatitis in shelters is also linked to these conditions. The lack of refrigeration in many shelters and the frequent switching from one infant formula to another or the

15. City of Philadelphia, Coordinating Office for Drug and Alcohol Abuse Programs, "Comprehensive Plan for Drug and Alcohol Abuse Treatment and Prevention," pp. 15-16.

use of powdered milk raises serious nutritional concerns.

Developmental delays

Current work conducted by PHMC and other research as well suggest that homeless children are highly vulnerable to developmental delays and emotional disturbance. In a survey of homeless children living in Massachusetts shelters, Bassuk and Rubin found that nearly one-half — 47 percent — of 81 homeless children manifested developmental delays in at least one major area of the Denver Developmental Screening Test. Language skills and personal and social development were particularly problematic.[16]

The results of a study of a group of homeless children aged 3 to 12 years in Philadelphia shelters confirm these observations made by Bassuk and Rubin. A school psychologist who assessed children aged 3 to 6 from homeless families participating in the Homeless Families Initiative of the United Way of Southeastern Pennsylvania concluded that many of the children exhibited significant delays in the development of language skills. Developmental delays and emotional problems in homeless children may have their roots in the stresses of shelter life and homelessness and/or long-standing family problems.[17]

Education

It is no wonder, given this constellation of problems, that homeless children do poorly in school. Numerous researchers cite the serious problems children have in maintaining satisfactory school performance. Faced with schooling that has been delayed or disrupted by frequent moves or by long waits while school records are transferred and faced also with the stigma of being identified as homeless by schoolmates, the children fall behind and often fail. A recent Massachusetts study of school-aged children indicated that of 52 homeless children of school age residing in shelters, 53 percent were failing or doing below-average work, 43 percent had already repeated a grade, and 25 percent were in a special class.[18]

CONCLUSION

The large and continually growing number of homeless children in Philadelphia and throughout the country is nothing short of a national disgrace. That children are born — often abused and neglected — into multiproblem families and that they are growing up in institutional settings — which are often dirty, impersonal, and overcrowded — is a violation of children's human rights. It is no wonder that these children suffer from feelings of shame, that they show serious signs of depression and anxiety, and that they are failing in school. Our children are entitled to a healthy and secure home, with at least the possibility of a bright future.

In Philadelphia, service providers are seeing the second and even third generation of families being raised in shelters. We are seeing young pregnant teenagers returning to the same shelter where they themselves were raised as homeless children only a few years ago.

What will solve the problem? First and foremost, addressing the needs of homeless children must be made a national priority.

16. Ellen Bassuk and Lenore Rubin, "Homeless Children: A Neglected Population," *American Journal of Orthopsychiatry,* 57(2):281 (1987).

17. Ibid., p. 285.

18. Ibid., p. 283.

A start must be made by, first, addressing the root cause of homelessness, poverty. Federal support for low-income housing and drug and alcohol programs must be brought up to needed levels.

In Philadelphia, ending family homelessness means closing the gap between the income of poor families and the cost of permanent housing. The number of subsidized housing units in Philadelphia must be substantially increased to meet the needs of the 195,000 owners and renters in the city who are competing for 34,000 subsidized units. Dolbeare estimates that the total costs of closing the housing affordability gap for these owners and renters would be $500 million annually and that a comprehensive housing program for Philadelphia would cost a total of $1 billion annually over the next ten years. This includes increases in the amount of welfare payments, which have failed to keep pace with increases in the cost of living.[19] Current welfare allowances for households of three or fewer persons are now lower than the Department of Housing and Urban Development's approved fair-market rents for the Philadelphia area. In other words, the 70,000 AFDC families in the city must spend more than their welfare allowance for housing. Raising welfare allowances should be a top priority at the state level.

Second, Philadelphia's substance-abuse epidemic, another factor in family homelessness, must be addressed at the same time as affordable housing and increased AFDC benefits. Women and children are frequent victims of the city's cocaine epidemic. The City Coordinating Office of Drug and Alcohol Programs reports an increase of over 150 percent in the number of females admitted for treatment to city-funded programs between 1986 and 1987.

19. Dolbeare, *Housing in Philadelphia,* p. 96.

The current publicly funded treatment programs are inadequate to meet the needs of drug-addicted women with children. Women who enter most residential treatment programs are forced to leave their children with relatives or in foster care. At the present time, there are only 44 beds at residential treatment programs in the city for women with children. More federal, state, and local funding for drug treatment programs for women and children—and men as well—is desperately needed.

Third, from the discussion of the multiple problems faced by homeless families it is apparent that reducing the growing number of homeless families lies not in building more emergency shelters or even in building low-income housing alone but in providing access to permanent housing and a full range of services that address the multiple needs of the families.

Attention must be focused on the needs of homeless mothers for a full range of services, which will help them lead independent lives. Mothers need a coordinated array of services aimed at addressing serious gaps in parenting skills, self-esteem, and—since most women have never lived independently—life skills. For example, budgeting and household skills need to be taught. Access to ongoing prenatal care and ongoing health care is essential.

Fourth, immediate and intensive interventions to treat the serious deficits that homeless children face in the area of developmental delays, educational delays, and psychological trauma, all of which are the direct result of living as a homeless child, must be addressed.

Fifth, even with attention focused on the problem, we know that the need for facilities that serve the homeless will not disappear within the immediate future. We need to ensure that children living in shelters in Philadelphia—and in welfare hotels in

New York — are safe and protected and that these facilities are decent and safe places.

Last, we need to pay close attention to the marginally homeless, that population of women and children currently living in housing projects or doubling up in residences in Philadelphia and elsewhere who are in danger of becoming homeless. We need to act now to prevent future generations of homeless children.

* * *

QUESTIONS AND ANSWERS

Q (Ruth Leventhol, American Association of State Colleges and Universities, Washington, D.C.): You have touched on a very important aspect of some human rights problems that are certainly not peculiar to Philadelphia and are certainly not indigenous just to the United States. In light of the global statistics on some of the economic and social rights issues, it seems to me very apparent that women and children are universally deprived of that set of human rights to a much greater degree than the adult male segment of the population. I do not know if the reason is poverty, religious fundamentalism, or benign neglect on the part of the governments, or outright sexism, but it is very clear that women and children have much less access to education, health care benefits, and food and housing.

COMMENT (Fox): I agree with your observation. It is a problem for women to obtain education and job training. Sexism certainly exists for the homeless population in their exercise of human rights.

———

Q: Are there more homeless men than homeless women?

A (Fox): Until 1985, 75 percent of the homeless in the city of Philadelphia were men. There are still significant numbers of men, but the number of homeless has grown, and grown mostly through the addition of women and children. Families now represent a third of Philadelphia's homeless.

———

Q (Marcelino C. Martinez, Fremont, California): You claim there are 17,000 or more homeless individuals in this city. How many of them are actually residents of the city as opposed to people who have come from the surrounding areas?

A (Fox): We have heard a lot of stories in which social workers tell people in Philadelphia's neighboring counties to come to Philadelphia so that they will be able to obtain a bed, several meals a day, and social services. Most of the people who are homeless in Philadelphia, however, are Philadelphians, although there are people from surrounding counties. Philadelphia does not see, as do some of the Sun Belt cities, large migrations of people from other parts of the country. There are a number of moves in Philadelphia to pull back from the unlimited-shelter policy; it will be interesting to see what will happen in the years to come in terms of who is homeless and who has access to beds. One of the major changes has to do with the mayor and the Task Force on Homelessness. The feeling is that people should have some responsibility in pursuing their own lives and becoming accountable for what happens to them. People will be expected to resolve some of their problems, particularly drug abuse, in order to receive shelter.

COMMENT (David Stiveson, Philadelphia, Pennsylvania): I wondered how Ms. Fox's paper and Judge Zaffaroni's would relate to each other. Now I think I understand that better. The same kind of policies that produce the massive murders in South and Central America, that produce the start of the drug trade are worked out to their conclusion in the maternity wards in Washington and Philadelphia.

Q (Gerald Porter, Committee of Concerned Scientists, New York City): What do you think the effect of the epidemic of acquired immune deficiency syndrome (AIDS) has been so far and will be on homelessness?

A (Fox): I think AIDS will be devastating but not because the homeless are a pool of potential human immune deficiency virus. The interface between AIDS and homelessness takes the form of intravenous drug abusers. In some of the shelters in Philadelphia, 80 percent of the people are using drugs. Many are using them intravenously, and many of these are using intravenously for the first time in a few years and will not use condoms. We are doing our best to educate them about safer sex and how to bleach needles, but I think AIDS will be a massive problem and not only in Philadelphia but in all of the cities.

CORRECTION

The article "DoD, Social Science, and International Studies," published in the March 1989 issue of *The Annals*, contained an error. The negative reaction to funding under the Defense Academic Research Support Program of a project in African studies based at the University of California at Los Angeles arose not on that campus, as stated in the article, but in the African Studies Association, and the subject was a political science bibliography, not a foreign language project. This project, as well as several other projects funded by the Defense Intelligence Agency there and elsewhere, is now proceeding successfully with amicable relations on both sides.

Book Department

PAGE

INTERNATIONAL RELATIONS AND POLITICS 152
AFRICA, ASIA, AND LATIN AMERICA 154
EUROPE 157
UNITED STATES 164
SOCIOLOGY 171
ECONOMICS 177

INTERNATIONAL RELATIONS AND POLITICS

CARVER, LORD. *Twentieth Century Warriors: The Development of the Armed Forces of the Major Military Nations in the Twentieth Century.* Pp. vii, 468. New York: Weidenfeld & Nicolson, 1987. $24.95.

Field Marshal Lord Carver announces his intentions crisply: "In this book I have set out to trace the development of the armed forces of the major military nations in this century. I have restricted my study to Britain, France, Germany, Russia and the Soviet Union, the United States of America, Japan and China." He carries through with considerable narrative aplomb, despite the mass of historic detail and necessary proliferation of empirical data on casualties of various engagements as compared to number of soldiers fielded; tanks lost to tanks built; tactical air sorties to traceable battlefield effects; strategic bombardment tonnage to disruption, or not, of one's opponent's wartime production; and so on.

Carver is refreshingly free of cant. He avoids excessive moralizing. The effect on the reader, when Carver does pronounce judgment, is all the more powerful as a result. For example,

in discussing the many ways Hitler outmaneuvered the Wehrmacht, divided it, and brought it under his sway, Carver is decisive. Although the army was not directly implicated in the notorious Night of the Long Knives on 30 June 1934, in "its silent acceptance of a blatantly illegal and inhuman act, the army gravely weakened its position, both politically and morally." Because Carver's admiration for the skill, courage, resolution, and improvisational acumen of the German army and soldier is clear, this and similar indictments are devastating, more devastating by far than anathemas that dehumanize all German soldiers, turning them into zombies or monsters.

A second strong feature of this enormously helpful work is Carver's modesty. He appreciates the bewildering scale of the events he unpacks, and he has the wisdom to realize that the many wars he surveys cannot be reduced, after the fact, to tidy models of clear-cut causation. None of these wars was inevitable, he insists, but all were the result of the complex and often ambiguous policies adopted by the governments involved. He rightly sees the state of the armed forces of each country he studies as the product of political events. He also worries that the "sheer size," technological wizardry, and run-amok fascination of the current American defense establishment may have turned into the tail that wags the dog. Rather than concentrating on the study of war and "the art of training," and keeping the military in a proper subsidiary relationship to political policy, heavy American reliance on technical advances "aggravates the rivalry between the armed forces, which is itself partly a cause of the [arms] race." That is, as the Army, Air Force, and Navy vie, Clausewitzian wisdom withers. This can only bode ill, Carver insists, and the weight of historical evidence supports his concern.

Carver emerges as a cautious proponent of limited deterrence. Given his assessment of the Soviet armed forces at present as "undoubtedly . . . the most formidable war machine the world has ever known," the United States labors under various compulsions to counter Soviet strength or to tip the balance in its favor. Although he does not say so directly, Carver appreciates the exigencies in the minds of American policymakers who understand that Soviet military doctrine holds that the Soviets will not commit themselves to war unless "the correlation of forces" is in their favor. This sustains a precarious superpower situation, but it is hoped that it is one that can be kept in balance and perspective.

For it is clear, Carver concludes, that "theories and possible scenarios of limited nuclear war" all fail and all have about them "an air of unreality" that suggests it is not possible, in a nuclear situation, "to conduct operations which could meet Clausewitz's definition of war as the continuation of state policy by other means." All students of international relations, diplomacy, and twentieth-century history will appreciate Carver's enormous good sense, whether or not they accept the doctrine of deterrence. Carter's is but one of several recent works reviving Clausewitz or, perhaps better said, reminding us of what Clausewitz knew that twentieth-century practitioners and theorists of total-war or nuclear-war gaming so consistently forget.

JEAN BETHKE ELSHTAIN

Vanderbilt University
Nashville
Tennessee

SHERR, ALAN B. *The Other Side of Arms Control: Soviet Objectives in the Gorbachev Era.* Pp. xviii, 325. Boston: Unwin Hyman, 1988. $44.95. Paperbound, $17.95.

This book aims to set forth Soviet views of the costs and benefits of nuclear arms control, obviously a vital issue for us in the United States as well.

Nine chapters, a bibliography, and an index make up the corpus of the work. The chapters range from presentation of Soviet foreign policy before and under "Gorbachev's new concepts" to technical discussions of "strategic defensive nuclear arms control" and "verification." Sherr concludes that "the Soviets want and need Western cooperation." Hence now is the time for significant progress to be made in nuclear arms control. The United States is thus practically admonished to get busy and get its act together! But why, it may well be asked, does the United States have to make available extensive economic aid and technological expertise to the Soviet Union in order to reach agreement on nuclear arms control with that country if such a goal is agreed to be mutually desirable?

Sherr, who was president from 1980 to 1987 of the Lawyers Alliance for Nuclear Arms Control, through which he "was introduced to the Soviet Union," presents the Soviet viewpoints, as he understands them, in an earnest and seemingly dispassionate way. There is, however, occasional emphasis or de-emphasis or use of terminology that can signal danger to this country.

More than once we are told that even under Gorbachev's liberalizing sway the ultimate goal of "leading the world to a classless society under communism . . . has certainly not been abandoned."

What are we to make of a set of sentences such as the following? "However, if as a practical matter the continued long-term existence of the capitalist system is assumed, then a fundamental reorientation of Soviet foreign policy has also been assumed. The USSR's new role in international relations is now principally goading and guiding the capitalist world into a nondestructive and cooperative direction, rather than also aspiring to replacing it in the forseeable future." Does the United States really need such "goading and guiding" from, in Sherr's view, the altruistic Soviet Union?

If read with care, this book is an informative study. But the writing tends to be heavy-handed, and the discussion of the different elements of nuclear weaponry threatens to swamp the reader in the absence of an accompanying glossary of terms.

DAVID HECHT

Pace University
New York City

AFRICA, ASIA, AND
LATIN AMERICA

BRANNON, JEFFREY and ERIC N. BAKLANOFF. *Agrarian Reform and Public Enterprise in Mexico: The Political Economy of Yucatán's Henequen Industry.* Pp. xv, 237. Tuscaloosa: University of Alabama Press, 1987. $31.95.

In *Agrarian Reform and Public Enterprise in Mexico,* Brannon and Baklanoff examine postrevolutionary economic policy, offering the henequen industry of Yucatán as a case study. They focus principally on the impact of land tenure reforms in the 1930s that redistributed land to *ejidos,* or agricultural collectives, and on the consequences of the nationalization of cordage manufacturing under Cordemex in 1964. They argue that federal intervention has been a disaster. By the early 1980s, the industry was near collapse, plagued by inefficient production, corrupt management, and irresponsible fiscal policy as well as by foreign competition and the expanded use of synthetic fibers. In their concluding chapters, Brannon and Baklanoff examine the prospects for regional economic diversification; they end by calling for the privatization of henequen production and cordage manufacturing and for the promotion of new export agricultural enterprises and *maquiladora* industries to provide jobs for displaced *ejidatarios.*

Theirs is a familiar story, but it is told well. Since Cordemex, after its initial success in modernizing production and developing new do-

mestic markets, was once considered a model for progressive federal intervention, its failures since 1970 are particularly impressive. Brannon and Baklanoff's analysis is lucid, systematic, and well documented.

The authors are especially critical of the willingness of federal authorities to sacrifice sound economic policy to the political imperatives of the Partido Revolucionario Institucional (PRI). For example, they show how the *ejidos,* designed to fulfill the promise of land redistribution and mobilize rural support for the party and the postrevolutionary state, quickly became dependent on federal subsidies. The subsidies, in the form of unrecovered loans from the Banco Agrario, increased to well over a billion pesos a year by the late 1970s, even though — in fact, because — productivity was declining sharply and the collectives were losing money.

Cordemex also labored under constraints imposed by politics. The necessity of accepting high wage costs for its own workers, and its inability to negotiate lower prices for raw fiber produced by the *ejidatarios* limited its opportunities to economize. Brannon and Baklanoff show very convincingly how together, Cordemex and the Banco Agrario came essentially to operate a costly welfare system that rewarded inefficiency and obstructed rational planning.

Their prescription for reform is much less convincing. Privatization seems unlikely to be the panacea that they envision. Diversification, they concede, is a slow process, with no promise that new enterprises will be able to absorb large numbers of unemployed. Finally, there seems even less likelihood that any fundamental reorganization can be accomplished without serious political and social unrest. Brannon and Baklanoff's answer to this is a direct subsidy to individual families, a temporary political necessity to support the displaced while they look for new work. They do not say how much this would cost or what the alternatives would be if jobs failed to materialize.

KEVIN GOSNER

University of Arizona
Tucson

MITTELBERG, DAVID. *Strangers in Paradise: The Israeli Kibbutz Experience.* Pp. xx, 223. New Brunswick, NJ: Transaction Books, 1988. $34.95.

This volume was originally conceived as a Ph.D. dissertation, but David Mittelberg expanded it to a full publishable study. The setting is Kibbutz Yizreel, a single cooperative collective community, but Mittelberg's goal is more ambitious. It is an attempt to develop a theoretical framework for a sociological theory of strangeness that ultimately might lead to the sociology of travel. The utilized methodology formulates theoretical concepts that are applied to the analysis of the problems.

The introductory chapter describes briefly some background of the kibbutz movement. The early founders were imbued with ideals of creating a utopian community guided by the principles of socialism and Zionism. This perfect life is labeled as a paradise in Israel. A major change occurred in 1967, following the Six-Day War, with the arrival of an overwhelming number of men and women from the United States, Canada, and many European and other countries. These newcomers offered to work in the kibbutz without remuneration. The study divides these people into two groups. The first is ulpan students who were Jewish and between the ages of 18 and 20; they worked for four hours a day and devoted the other four hours to studies. The second group, non-Jewish, were in their thirties and worked all day. Both groups were recruited because of the existing labor shortage and because they offered free labor. But the underlying purpose in enlisting these workers was stated more euphemistically: "the kibbutz experience heightened the Jewish, Zionist, and Socialist identity of Young Jews from abroad." Evidently this led to the desire to test the real meaning of the kibbutz experience.

An interesting chapter is devoted to the structuring of a theoretical framework about the phenomenology of strangeness. Many theoretical principles were distilled from the classical works of Simmel, Berger, Luckman, Goffman, Weber, and others. The discussion of strangeness and familiarity culminates with a stated need for a sociology of travel.

The tested population sample is rather limited: 93 ulpan students and 33 adult volunteers. The methodology involves the use of three questionnaires and some interviewing. Mittelberg admits that the sample is not representative of the vast number of volunteers working in the many kibbutzim. His statistical analysis provides many tables appropriate to the study. The last chapter dovetails the findings of the study to the theoretical framework originally structured.

What is missing is the linkage of the tested experience to the impact that it had on the total life of the kibbutz. The question that puzzles me is, In what way did the kibbutz change because of the impact of all ulpaniks and volunteers who came to Kibbutz Yizreel during the course of a number of years?

Furthermore, Mittelberg maintains that kibbutz life develops a greater interest in Jewish fulfillment. He does not clarify what is specifically Jewish in the kibbutz. For example, acquiring a knowledge of Hebrew is undoubtedly helpful in communication, but does a non-Jewish volunteer who learns Hebrew become a dedicated Jewish Zionist?

Moreover, some areas of cultural conflict are completely overlooked. For example, the possible conflict between the young ulpaniks' home orientation to traditional Jewish religious practices and the absence of such Jewishness in the kibbutz is simply dismissed as "not the same aspect of cultural shock but . . . an ill-conceived cultural distance on site." Not dealing with the reality of the tested population is unfortunately a lost opportunity and sounds like sweeping it under the rug to hide it.

In conclusion, the framework, based upon the classical sociological and social-psychological writers and researchers, is well conceived and structured. The utilization of this knowledge by applying it to the findings of the study may, it is hoped, pave the way for the launching of a new sociology of travel. Mittelberg's hypothesis that the short-lived experience in the kibbutz resulted in a major cultural and psychological change in the young ulpaniks requires more in-depth study to furnish verifiable proof. On the whole, the study is lucidly conceived and well written and adds to the currently expanding literature about life in the kibbutz.

MARTIN E. DANZIG

City University of New York

SCHATZBERG, MICHAEL G. *The Dialectics of Oppression in Zaire.* Pp. x, 193. Blooming-ton: Indiana University Press, 1988. $25.00.

Michael Schatzberg argues that the Zairian state creates and exacerbates a pervasive dialec-tic of oppression as it tries to cope with the conditions of insecurity and scarcity. Initially, measures adopted by the Mobutu regime to end the turbulent conditions in Zaire's early years of independence were to blame. As personal, political, and economic insecurity increased, people in power accumulated wealth as rapidly as possible by extracting resources from the citizenry, creating new sources of insecurity and scarcity in the process. According to Schatzberg, pervasive insecurity interacted with general economic scarcity that resulted from "the fall in the price of copper, a badly managed economy, and a thoroughly corrupt polity."

The Mobutu regime has endured by co-opting or suppressing opposition political parties; by using the state's coercive arms — political po-lice, the armed forces, and the magistracy — to terrorize and intimidate the population; and by the clever manipulation of symbols, images, and metaphors. Schatzberg develops these argu-ments with detailed empirical data that demon-strate the complex ways in which the govern-ment and the citizens of Zaire are trapped in a web of insecurity and scarcity that results in the continued oppression of the vast majority of the people by the politically powerful few.

This study is a detailed micropolitical anal-ysis of interrelationships of the Zairian state and its citizens that is based largely on field research conducted in 1973-74 in Lisala, capital of the Equateur Region. As viewed by the citizens of this hinterland, the state is a fragmentary, often contradictory set of institutions that is only loosely bound to the authority of the central government. The boundaries between the state and its citizens are ill defined and quite fluid, a situation that contributes significantly to the urgency of the politically empowered to accumulate as much wealth and power as they can today lest they lose their opportunities tomorrow.

Schatzberg's study is rich in empirical data, and the analysis and the conclusions are persua-sive. But much of the language that he uses in the chapter conclusions and in the final chapter unnecessarily obfuscates. The political realities of this African state as seen from the hinterland of the Equateur Region are sufficiently complex without the intrusion of arcane language from the social sciences.

GARY L. FOWLER

University of Illinois
Chicago

WELFIELD, JOHN. *An Empire in Eclipse: Japan in the Postwar American Alliance System: A Study in the Interaction of Domestic Politics and Foreign Policy.* Pp. xiii, 513. Atlantic Highlands, NJ: Athlone Press, 1988. No price.

Given a more simple title such as *Japan since 1945* or *The New Postwar Japan,* this book might well be used as a second-semester college textbook for a course on the history of modern Japan. The lengthy and complicated title, together with Welfield's remarks in the preface and conclusion, however, suggest that writing a textbook was not his original inten-tion. Rather, he seems to have had in mind a sophisticated study of Japanese-U.S. relations as a scheme of analysis for international rela-tions in general. He does not succeed in this, coming up mainly with the not-so-original idea that "nations have neither permanent friends nor permanent enemies" and that "international soci-ety has always been complex, fluid and unstable."

But this failure of grand design does not diminish the book's value as a solid and wide-ranging presentation of both historical facts and insightful analysis of the history of postwar Japan, together with, in chapter 1, a well-done introduction to Japanese traditions. Utilizing a multitude of Japanese sources, including the major newspapers, and living in Japan, Welfield produces what may be described as an inside-Japan portrayal of the politics, economics, and foreign relations of the progress of Japan's recovery from the disasters of World War II. There are 14 chapters, each divided into 7 to 12 subdivisions. For example, chapter 2, entitled "The Postwar International Order and the Origins of the San Francisco System, 1945-1952," contains 11 quite detailed subheadings covering various phases of the Occupation period, including "Japan's Planning for Defeat," "Yoshida Shigeru's Vision," "Ashida Hitoshi and Katayama Tetsu," and "The 1951 Dulles-Yoshida Negotiations and Japan's Refusal to Rearm," among others. Chapter 3, entitled "Japanese Rearmament, 1945-1955," contains such subsections as "The Government Section of SCAP and Ashida Hitoshi Modify General MacArthur's Pacifist Constitution," "Yoshida Shigeru's Tentative Preparation for Rearmament," "The Police Reserve Force and the Expanded Maritime Safety Force," and "The Establishment of the Defense Agency and the Self-Defense Forces, March 1954."

Skipping ahead, chapter 6, "The 1960 Security Treaty Crisis," has such subsections as "The Crisis," "The Treaty," "The Impact of Conservative Party Factional Policy Conflicts," and so on. Chapter 9 is "Domestic Politics, Foreign Policy and the Reversion of Okinawa, 1960-1972."

As can be seen from this listing, the chapter titles and subsection headings are both lengthy and, it could be said, somewhat strange. Perhaps the book would be better off without them? But the content, in terms of both presentation of historical facts and explanations thereof, is not only solid but presents a great deal of information about Japanese politics and decision making not easily available. Because of the anomalies of organization, the book is not the sort of standard-style text that teachers of Japanese history and foreign relations might like it

to be, but in the relative absence of such on the period after the Pacific War, it is both welcome and useful, to be recommended especially for fairly sophisticated students, who would not be bothered by the anomalies.

HILARY CONROY

University of Pennsylvania
Philadelphia

EUROPE

BEISSINGER, MARK R. *Scientific Management, Socialist Discipline, and Soviet Power.* Pp. viii, 363. Cambridge, MA: Harvard University Press, 1988. $30.00.

SCOTT, HARRIET FAST and WILLIAM L. SCOTT. *Soviet Military Doctrines: Continuity, Formulation, and Dissemination.* Pp. xii, 325. Boulder, CO: Westview Press, 1988. $45.00.

The two works reviewed here are particularly timely in an era when traditional assumptions are being challenged by a Gorbachev regime that is beset by severe economic difficulties and a sullen, cynical, apathetic population. Such an unfavorable environment raises anew questions of discipline, performance, and the need for greater individual productivity when the old nostrums of central control, coercion, and terror are no longer fully appropriate or acceptable. The Soviet armed forces — the source of national pride, regime legitimation, and coercive diplomatic leverage — are increasingly parasitical under such conditions.

Beissinger's study, based on extensive documentation and archival research and interviews with Soviet managers undergoing a three-month training period in the USSR, is a tightly argued, well-written survey of the course of Soviet managerial history. Beissinger asks how successive Soviet regimes have ensured central control over an unlimited bureaucratic apparatus that habitually stagnates and ossifies. How can bureaucratic structures be adapted to changing economic conditions that demand more efficient use of resources and a more participatory, enthusiastic work force? How can one shift from the Stalinist model of campaigning, storming, coercion, and terror to new methods that guarantee responsive structures and quantitative and qualitative economic transformations? Early in the 1920s how could Western models of efficiency like Taylorism or scientific management be technocratically applied without sacrificing central control and ushering in Western free-market concepts?

The Party was periodically ensnared in a dilemma; how could it act like a manager — for efficiency — and enforce bureaucratic discipline and mobilize society simultaneously? This role conflict eventually helped lead to Khrushchev's demise and undermined Kosygin's reform. Currently Gorbachev and others call for discipline and reform, centralized planning and market mechanisms. The dilemma — or cycle, as Beissinger depicts it — repeats itself. Can Red and expert both function within the same person or organization? Beissinger doubts it, as do I.

Beissinger's work will take its place alongside those of Fainsod, Azrael, Parrott, and other major writers on Soviet ideology and organizational behavior. Its combination of general observations on Soviet organizational and bureaucratic behavior and detailed, descriptive case studies is very effective, and the reader, even the nonspecialist, will find great value in it.

The Scotts' volume is a major, almost encyclopedic study of the doctrine, tactics, and organization of the Soviet armed forces. They argue that Soviet military doctrine, like the passion for total control that Beissinger observes, "impacts all aspects of Soviet life, whether it be the military-political education of Soviet youth, the location of new industries, or scientific exchange with the noncommunist world." It prepares the country for the possibility of future war, conventional or nuclear, and the preemption of surprise attacks. Doctrine often precedes the weapons needed to operationalize it, but the expectation is that it is only a matter of time before plans become reality.

The Scotts may identify declared intentions with capability, which does not automatically follow. How much is the doctrine meant to

provide an operational guide to future force structures, weapons, and tactics and how much of it is mere morale raising? The Scotts concede this in part by saying that stripped of its Marxist-Leninist trappings, Soviet doctrine differs from what is taught in American military academies by stressing defeat of the enemy in depth, which is congenial to a continental mass power; the creation and prompt replacement of reserves, increasingly important in U.S. planning for budgetary reasons and due to a smaller regular force structure; and defeat of the enemy, violated by the United States in Korea and Vietnam. Soviet performance in Afghanistan raises doubts on this latter point.

The Scotts believe that Gorbachev needs a breathing space to gain time to improve the performance of the civilian economy in order to provide the increasingly technologically sophisticated weapons needed in the future. We should not, accordingly, substitute wishful thinking about Gorbachev's words and intentions for the realities of brute Soviet military power. But the Soviet economic crisis, as Moscow itself increasingly admits, may be worse than many of us thought. Gorbachev may be pressured into making major defense cuts as well as providing more consumer goods for an impatient, disbelieving population than was originally planned.

The two studies raise the question of how much Gorbachev thinks he can break with or wants to break with the past with respect to the fine line between continuity and reform. They provide a rich context for providing tentative answers.

ROGER HAMBURG

Indiana University
South Bend

MEARSHEIMER, JOHN J. *Liddell Hart and the Weight of History.* Pp. xi, 234. Ithaca, NY: Cornell University Press, 1988. $24.95.

B. H. Liddell Hart's stream of books, articles, and columns for the London *Daily Tele-*

graph and *Times* made him the most widely read military theorist in the Western world between the two world wars. His high visibility gained him influence as a military adviser to the highest levels of the British government and propelled him into a prominent place in post-World War II military thought. History has largely passed Liddell Hart down to posterity as a clairvoyant who consistently drew the correct lessons from World War I, predicted the course of World War II, and influenced those who fought it correctly. Mearsheimer has raised an undercurrent of skepticism about this record to the surface of military history.

This book is a meticulously documented and argued case for the prosecution. Mearsheimer finds Liddell Hart guilty of inconsistent thinking, of reading the lessons of World War I incorrectly in the final analysis, of failing to predict the course of World War II in the final analysis, of rewriting his personal intellectual history in the post-World War II period to launder the record, and of using the World War II German generals responsible for the blitzkrieg to help him with the laundry. It is a powerful case. Major figures in military historiography have helped build the case for the prevailing view, and their dialogue with Mearsheimer should further open up the story of Liddell Hart and the important events surrounding him. The reader who wishes to join the discussion at its point of departure is well advised to read Mearsheimer's analysis in conjunction with the only other full-length study of Liddell Hart, Brian Bond's *Liddell Hart.*

EDWARD HAGERMAN

York University
Toronto
Ontario
Canada

SHORROCK, WILLIAM I. *From Ally to Enemy: The Enigma of Fascist Italy in French Di-* *plomacy, 1920-1940.* Pp. xii, 355. Kent, OH: Kent State University Press, 1988. $35.00

Although this book does a competent and at times interesting job when it discusses French diplomacy, it irritates the reader for a number of reasons.

First and foremost is the almost complete failure to take Italian sources into account. While Shorrock has delved into French, English, and even German documentary collections of various types, he did not do the same for Italy — a curious failure given the availability of Italian documents, the book's focus on fascist Italy, and the pleasant working conditions at Rome's Archivio centrale dello stato. Thus, while on a given matter Shorrock refers to primary documents when analyzing French policy, the corresponding reference to France's fascist interlocutor is almost always a secondary source. Indeed, just as serious, Italian and English secondary literature is scarcely represented, especially the former. For example, ignorance of Richard Webster's study of Italian industrial imperialism before World War I leaves one ill equipped to discuss fascist Italy's ambitions in Eastern Europe. Furthermore, on those rare occasions when Shorrock refers to Italian primary documents, he prefers the English translation; the Ciano diaries are a case in point.

Given this fundamental failing, Shorrock cannot really shed new light on the diplomatic incidents with which he is concerned, even conceding his exhaustive research in French archives.

The book also demonstrates failures of interpretation. For example, Shorrock discusses Pierre Laval's controversial negotiations with Mussolini and the disputed contention by which the French statesman allegedly granted the Duce a free hand in Ethiopia. Instead of concentrating on the major issue, Shorrock is primarily concerned with saving Laval's reputation, arguing that this incident did not prove that Laval admired fascism. Fair enough. But Shorrock also defends Laval on the ground that while it appears probable that Laval did indeed grant the free hand, Mussolini did not understand that Laval "conceded" it on condition that the Italian dictator not use it. Frankly, no one else would have understood either.

Shorrock's general thesis is that French policy aimed from the very beginning to mollify Mussolini in order to achieve greater security against Germany. I have no argument with this position. But while this policy was understandable in the 1920s even though the "strident" Italian antifascists consistently warned French statesmen — by the way, what indeed was the antifascist role? — by the 1930s it became less comprehensible. Perhaps Shorrock could have gone out on a limb and considered the cynicism of French diplomacy between the wars, instead of continually defending it.

SPENCER M. DI SCALA

University of Massachusetts
Boston

SIMKINS, PETER. *Kitchener's Army: The Raising of the New Armies, 1914-16.* Pp. xvi, 359. New York: St. Martin's Press, 1988. $67.50.

General Henry Wilson denounced Lord Kitchener's "ridiculous and preposterous army" as the "laughing stock of every soldier in Europe." Historians by and large have decried Kitchener's constitutional inability to delegate authority, his hostility to extradepartmental interference, his failure to give a clear lead on conscription, his autocratic bearing, and his extended absences from Britain before 1914. Simkins, a historian at the Imperial War Museum, joins recent American and Canadian scholars such as G. H. Cassar, P. Fraser, and K. Neilson to revise this negative image. Simkins depicts Kitchener as the talisman of victory and the symbol of unity, and he credits him with raising thirty divisions of the New Armies by June 1916, "a national achievement of colossal proportions."

The first half of the book describes how the New Armies actually were raised. Fully one-half of the 5.7 million soldiers that Britain put in the field were volunteers. In creating Britain's first-ever mass citizen army, Kitchener relied heavily upon civilians at the local level. The fact that 38 percent of the armies were raised other than through the War Office is a reflection of Edwardian civic pride, a last manifestation of Edwardian liberalism. Instead of being rent asunder by the triple threat of Ireland, labor, and suffragettes, Simkins argues, "Liberal England" was held together by strong bands of local loyalties.

The second half of the book traces the experiences and impressions of officers, noncommissioned officers, and men who made up the New Armies. The majority volunteered out of a sense of duty and obligation. Others rallied to the colors out of economic necessity, a sense of patriotism, peer pressure, or simply to escape depressing jobs; some even went in the belief that they were off to fight the French! The highest percentage of volunteers came from the professions and the entertainment industry. Twenty million recruiting leaflets and 2 million posters directed an unrelenting propaganda barrage at Britain's able-bodied males and largely drowned out the antiwar protests of the Union of Democratic Control, the Independent Labour Party, and the No Conscription Fellowship. In short, the war pulled the diverse strata of society together and welded them into a coherent whole. To be sure, there were severe overcrowding, shortages of materials, lack of equipment as well as uniforms, and an abysmal shortage of the weapons of trench warfare such as howitzers, mortars, grenades, and machine guns. There also remained a yawning gap between the tactical doctrine of the troops at the front in France and those training at home; the post of inspector general of training was not established until June 1918. Yet this air of unreality and amateurishness was overcome by the glue of social cohesion provided by a powerful sense of local rather than purely national identity.

Simkins documents his story meticulously from numerous unpublished official and private papers, diaries, letters, and memoirs as well as with printed materials. He has provided the first comprehensive description of Kitchener's New Armies, a most welcome addition to the growing literature on Britain in World War I.

HOLGER H. HERWIG

Vanderbilt University
Nashville
Tennessee

SUNY, RONALD GRIGOR. *The Making of the Georgian Nation.* Pp. xviii, 395. Bloomington: Indiana University Press, in association with Hoover Institution Press, Stanford, CA, 1988. $45.00. Paperbound, $17.50.

McNEAL, ROBERT H. *Stalin: Man and Ruler.* Pp. xvi, 389. New York: New York University Press, 1988. $34.95.

Here are two very different books, both concerned in some measure with Soviet policy, and both produced by excellent scholars in the field.

Suny begins his volume with an extensive, erudite, and encyclopedically dense description of Georgia from ancient times to the Russian conquest. In this complex and agonizing history of a people located at the crossroads of the world and set upon over centuries by neighbors and conquering nations — Iranian, Byzantine, Arab, Turk, Mongol — we are faced with names of literally hundreds of princes, dozens of tribes, tens of geographic areas, often with alternative spellings appended. Readers must in any case persevere, for although Suny's tour-de-force research on ancient and medieval times is of greatest interest to historians, his material on Georgia after the Russian conquest makes fascinating reading for anyone.

To me, the most interesting segment of the book is that dealing with Georgia before the Bolshevik conquest. Here Suny analyzes Georgian response to Russian czarist rule, which he describes as a "mixture of benefits and burdens"; the problems and effects of peasant emancipation and imperial reform; and particularly the rise of social democracy in its specific

cast of Menshevism, adopted, Suny feels, because of a strongly elective party tradition and the Georgian radicals' natural concern with the demands of nationality. Indeed, Suny's description of the "extraordinary achievement" of the Mensheviks before the Russian invasion of 1921 is sympathetic and striking. Subsequent material deals with Georgian reaction to various policies originated in Moscow, none of which was especially adapted to this unique environment, and includes interesting material on Beria plus a thoughtful analysis of contemporary trends.

Suny urges us to abandon the inadequate "totalitarian model" in Soviet studies and to consider the complex personality of Stalin as a key factor in Russia's modern history. This is what McNeal so successfully does in his extraordinary new biography of Stalin. Stalin has surely become for us a mythic figure, whose contribution to Russian development is dominated by legends we have molded on the basis of particular dramatic reports — which may or may not be accurate since they derive, for the most part, from his enemies. In this fine study, McNeal insists that we reexamine the real Stalin. Without rejecting out of hand the evidence with which we are familiar, he insists that we review the old myths on the basis of new scholarship: new materials that have emerged since Stalin's death and many historic documents, of which McNeal has superior knowledge.

Here, then, is Stalin from the vantage point of 1988. He is, for example, extremely close to Lenin in the years from 1919 to 1922, much more so than Trotsky biographers would have us believe. As an administrator, he is excellent because he is positive and efficient and gets things done. He is "in his way" a "deeply committed Marxist, Leninist, and a champion of class struggle," although we too often think of him as caring only about himself. In the 1920s, he is the image of the man of the people. He plays a smaller day-to-day role in collectivization and industrialization than we have presumed and displays a far more angry — and often unwise — unwillingness to accept even temporary defeat. His fanaticism in the terror, McNeal believes, reflected elements in Soviet society, and some scholars may take exception to McNeal's analysis of the Kirov murder and subsequent events. In McNeal's description, Stalin becomes less remote and more human: he dislikes his wife but cares for his small daughter; he has a considerable sense of humor but is given to fits of anger; he drinks too much. McNeal's Stalin may upset some American scholars, but it upsets myths, too, and demands that we do some rethinking.

Both of these volumes represent excellent contributions. They belong on the bookshelf of any individual with an interest in the Soviet past.

DEBORAH HARDY

University of Wyoming
Laramie

VIOLA, LYNNE. *The Best Sons of the Fatherland: Workers in the Vanguard of Soviet Collectivization.* Pp. x, 285. New York: Oxford University Press, 1987. $29.95.

THORNILEY, DANIEL. *The Rise and Fall of the Soviet Rural Communist Party, 1927-1939.* Pp. xiii, 246. New York: St. Martin's Press, 1988. $42.50.

For more than a decade the dullness and grayness of Soviet politics in the final years of Brezhnev and his successors were matched by a blandness and vacuity in the study of Soviet politics in the West. The official revival of the deservedly defunct totalitarian model; the continuing emphasis on Kremlinology; and high politics, terror, and coercion highlighted the isolation of the Soviet field from other social sciences. Soviet politics enjoyed the dubious distinction of being the only field in area studies in which the majority of the practitioners loathed and despised their subject.

In the last four years, Gorbachev's rise to power and his attempts to reinvigorate the Soviet polity and economy have greatly altered the atmosphere in Moscow. So, too, have they seemingly aided in the rejuvenation of the Western study of the Soviet Union. These two studies

by Lynne Viola and Daniel Thorniley, then, in some sense, are the Western fruits of *glasnost* and *novaya myshlenie.*

They have much in common in their approach to Soviet history. First, their shared topic, collectivization and the rural party organization, is in itself daring since this area has traditionally been reserved as the domain for an alleged totalitarian regime ruthlessly using force to crush a hapless peasantry. Instead, these books show the complexity of the movement, and the Viola work in particular emphasizes the genuine revolutionary enthusiasm for collectivization in a segment of the population. Second, while the field traditionally has emphasized the Stalinist perspective from above, these works look at the social base for Stalinism and revolution. Third, similarly, traditional works have focused on Moscow and its desires while these works look at the localities and the center-locality interaction. Finally, they both, although more so the Viola work, seek to correct a traditionally very negative view of Stalinism.

Viola's work is indisputably the better of the two books. Her volume is a superb, remarkably mature first effort by a young American specialist. Her focus on the 25,000 workers sent to aid the collectivization effort late in 1929 provides many fresh insights into this vital campaign. Using hitherto unavailable archival sources, she develops a fascinating, complex, and variegated picture of collectivization. Individuals of the 25,000 come to life, the revolutionary aspects and social base of Stalinism are strongly delineated, and the intricate center-peripheral relationships are richly drawn. The usual monochromatic gray view of the Soviet Union in the 1930s — with notable exceptions such as Getty and Davies — now gives way to a kaleidoscopic view of Soviet realities. Truly this volume represents a bravura performance in Viola's first time out.

While less exciting and rewarding, the Thorniley volume is still a solid, skillful effort. It fills in the organizational details of the rural party organization from 1927 to 1939. Especial attention is paid to revising the traditional views of rural purges and center-local relations. The mystery of the sharp decline of the rural party organization in the middle 1930s is strongly emphasized. One comes away from this volume with a better grounding in an important but often neglected subject.

One can quibble with both volumes. They both could use more editing. Viola should realize that a 36 percent drop-out rate over a short period of time is significant, while Thorniley should question more why the center could tolerate the demise of the rural party organization in the middle 1930s. Overall, though, they are a strong contribution to the literature.

JONATHAN R. ADELMAN

University of Denver
Colorado

WOOLF, STUART. *The Poor of Western Europe in the Eighteenth and Nineteenth Centuries.* Pp. ix, 240. New York: Methuen, 1986. $57.50.

Poor families in need of assistance are well advised to apply for a bed rather than money. Such was the kind of advice that needy residents of early nineteenth-century Florence took seriously when they sought help from the Congregation of San Giovanni Battista, the city's main institution for home relief. The Congregation's directors believed that providing a bed was preferable to granting a cash subsidy because a bed would meet not only material need but also a moral purpose by preventing the sexual promiscuity that could readily arise if a pubescent daughter or niece continued to sleep in the bed of her parents or aunt and uncle. Poor parents were undoubtedly aware of the directors' moral concerns, and they were thus quick to cite similar concerns in their written requests for beds. Some recipients sold the beds they were given and thereby got the money they no doubt wanted in the first place. So it was that the rules of charity, made and used as they were to enforce the mores of donors, could also be manipulated by the resourceful poor.

This example of charity at work illustrates one of the main themes in Stuart Woolf's collection of eight essays. All but one have previously been published, but five appear here for the first time in English. The first essay, written specially for the book, is the only one that justifies the book's rather broad title. It surveys issues and developments principally in England, France, and Italy. Here Woolf argues persuasively that poverty and the poor should be studied in connection with both the economy and the life cycle of the family. Although that approach correctly calls attention to the vulnerability of families to fragmentation and descent into indigence, he should point out that Europeans who lacked the protecting shield of family – widows, youthful migrants, the aged – made up the poorest of the poor. Where others would emphasize differences between Protestant and Catholic responses to poverty, Woolf stresses a common pattern of institutional response via the establishment of hospitals and foundling homes for the deserving poor and penal workhouses for detestable beggars and vagrants. He also suggests that poverty ought to be studied not merely as an economic condition but as a social construct that enabled elites to enforce the acceptance of the existing social order through the manipulation of aid.

The other essays take up specific problems related to Italy. One explores the relationship between the laboring poor, proto-industrialization, and the formation of the working class, while the remaining six examine aspects of poverty and assistance in Tuscany and Florence during the Napoleonic regime (1808-14). The centralization of decision making under that regime and the French concern to see a good portion of Italian wealth tapped not for the poor but for the imperial treasury had a debilitating effect on the existing poor-relief system. The *monti di pietà* ("pawn shops"), for example had previously been an effective part of that system but were nearly ruined by siphoning off their revenues to pay state debts.

The last three essays explore a remarkable collection of evidence: some 5000 surviving applications for aid to the Congregation of San Giovanni Battista during the years 1810-12. Here we learn how nuclear families variously contracted or expanded into more complex units to deal with adversity and that the handling of requests for assistance was hardly a pro forma or impersonal matter. In selecting deserving families, deputies of the Congregation visited applicants in their homes and studied character references from parish priests. The Congregation favored widows and large families in temporary difficulties over young families with two adult wage earners. The quid pro quo for all assistance was to conduct oneself in keeping with the Congregation's social and moral expectations. Applicants suspected of selling previously donated beds were therefore duly noted and dropped from the list of worthy poor.

This book allows us to follow Woolf's research over some 15 years. The earliest essay, on the administration of poor relief under the Napoleonic regime (1971-72), and two recent ones on charity and the poor in Florence (1984 and 1985) are all based on archival research and make solid contributions. Others are more successful in posing interesting questions than in providing full answers. Woolf's decision to reprint articles without changes is fair enough but results in a good deal of repetition. Nevertheless, this book is a useful addition to the sparse literature in English on the problem of poverty in eighteenth- and nineteenth-century Italy. Besides being informative, it contains suggestive ideas, and one hopes that Woolf, or others, will pursue them further.

ROBERT M. SCHWARTZ

Mount Holyoke College
South Hadley
Massachusetts

UNITED STATES

AMAKER, NORMAN C. *Civil Rights and the Reagan Administration.* Pp. xxvii, 224. Washington, DC: Urban Institute Press, 1988. $29.95. Paperbound, $17.95.

With the possible exception of the massive increase in the federal deficit, perhaps no other single aspect of the Reagan so-called revolution has been the subject of more intense debate and controversy than has the Reagan record on civil rights. Amaker's book is above all else a lucid,

detailed, lawyerly written narrative of the Reagan administration's actions — and inaction — as regards civil rights issues. For the eight years he was in office, Amaker argues, President Reagan and the administration he led were essentially committed to turning back most, if not all, of the legislatively and judicially obtained civil rights gains of the 1950s and 1960s. He contends that all of the immediately preceding administrations, from Presidents Eisenhower to Carter, had taken measures to implement various court-ordered and legislatively mandated civil rights directives. The Reagan administration, on the other hand, came to power rejecting the very fundamentals of civil rights. As put by D. Lee Bawden in the foreword to Amaker's book, "At the core of the Reagan effort was rejection of the concepts of affirmative action, redress of discriminatory practices unless intent could be proved, and compensation for the effects of discrimination unless victims could be identified."

The agency most responsible for the Reagan drubbing of civil rights was, according to Amaker, the United States Justice Department, specifically its Civil Rights Division, which for most of the Reagan years was headed by Assistant Attorney General William Bradford Reynolds. But this was a situation filled with paradox. The function of the Justice Department, as constitutionally determined and commonly understood, is to enforce laws that are either passed by Congress or decreed by the courts. Up until the Reagan administration, Amaker argues, the U.S. Justice Department was indeed in the forefront in enforcing federal laws that forbade segregation and racial discrimination. Under Eisenhower and Kennedy, federal troops were used, albeit sometimes reluctantly, to enforce the landmark *Brown* vs. *Board of Education* decision. Under Jimmy Carter there was a "sweeping reorganization of the equal employment opportunity effort in his Reorganization Plan No. 1 of 1978." The plan, according to Amaker, "represented a clear presidential direction that the civil rights laws were to be vigorously enforced." Thus, under Carter, the Justice Department became known as "one that took its law enforcement responsibilities seriously."

But even more important has been the Justice Department's corollary responsibility to bring suits against individuals, agencies, or organizations suspected of violating federal laws, including laws protecting the rights of racially defined minorities and women. If suits were not actually initiated by the Justice Department, the department was nonetheless typically on the side of private plaintiffs in discrimination cases. For example, before Reagan, both the National Association for the Advancement of Colored People and the Justice Department were on the same side in practically all school-desegregation cases before the courts. But beginning with Nixon and reinforced under Reagan, a pattern emerged in which lawyers for private plaintiffs repeatedly found themselves on the opposite side of U.S. attorneys in school-desegregation cases.

As articulated by Amaker, the Reagan record on civil rights is essentially one of "foot dragging," nonenforcement, urging the courts not to decide on certain civil rights cases, and, most distressing, resisting all notions of group discrimination. In order to illustrate his basic point of a Reagan retreat from civil rights, Amaker walks us through a detailed, if at times laborious, lawyerlike discourse on the specific juridical actions taken by the administration relative to the five areas that have been most prominently associated with civil rights: education, federally assisted programs, housing, employment, and voting. Amaker contends that attempts to curtail judicially mandated minority protections and guarantees in all five areas indicate an overall tendency within the administration to view discrimination with blinders on. Only in cases where there were identifiable victims could one speak of discrimination. The government, furthermore, "has no affirmative responsibility to deal with the systemic and institutional causes that in the past, and currently, account for the wide divergence in both achievement and opportunity between blacks and women and white men."

While it might be simplistic, and even imprudent, to refer to the Reagan administration as racist, what is abundantly clear is that, in the Reagan era, race assumed preeminence on two fronts. First, it had become an important linchpin in a larger attempt to restructure and redefine the world ideologically; and, second, racial meanings and interpretations were projected as subject matters for political or ideological debates. The Reagan worldview held that human beings were at their productive best when they were free of the state and all its encumbering rules and regulations. Affirmative action laws, decrees, and ultimatums, along with cumbersome trade restrictions, were seen as additional instances of government intrusion on the free spirit. They should be actively resisted. But more important, the whole issue of race was a burden the American society was trying to rid itself of. The administration presented itself as doing more than its fair share in the struggle against all forms of racism, including the racism of affirmative action. It is in this light that the statement of U.S. Civil Rights Commission Chair Clarence Pendleton, Jr., that we are "working on a color-blind society that has opportunities for all and guarantees for none" must be read. Pendleton was one of President Reagan's few black appointees.

BERNARD D. HEADLEY

Northeastern Illinois University
Chicago

COOPER, PHILLIP J. *Hard Judicial Choices: Federal District Court Judges and State and Local Officials.* Pp. 374. New York: Oxford University Press, 1988. $34.00. Paperbound, $15.95.

BARROW, DEBORAH J. and THOMAS G. WALKER. *A Court Divided: The Fifth Circuit Court of Appeals and the Politics of Judicial Reform.* Pp. xiv, 274. New Haven, CT: Yale University Press, 1988. $29.95.

If you like books that tell a good story and make you think, you will enjoy *Hard Judicial Choices* and *A Court Divided.* They are lively accounts of some uncommon — and uncommonly controversial — activities of federal judges, clearly written, with ample background and technical assistance for the nonspecialist, broadly grounded in documents and interviews, and guaranteed to raise questions about the outer limits of the judicial role.

Hard Judicial Choices is a collection of five case studies, to be read separately or together, of federal district judges who felt they had no choice but to ride herd on state and local governments, forcing compliance with the Constitution by means of complex remedial decrees. The cases concern open housing in Parma, Ohio; school desegregation in Detroit; the right to treatment in mental hospitals in Alabama; the rights of prisoners in overcrowded antiquated prisons in Ohio; and police misconduct in Philadelphia.

In Parma, to take one case, the National Association for the Advancement of Colored People and the American Civil Liberties Union charged that local decisions on low-income housing were aggravating rather than easing racial segregation in metropolitan Cleveland. Parma, a nearly all-white suburb, opposed open housing for fear of attracting blacks and argued that it had no obligation to relieve housing problems in the inner city. The upshot was a court decree aimed not simply at creating open housing in a reluctant community but also at overcoming the reluctance itself by mandating, among other things, educational and public-information programs for officials, residents of Parma, and prospective residents of the new housing.

In a more ordinary federal case, a single order to behave might suffice. In a case such as Parma, however, where unconstitutional practices are pervasive and court orders are resisted by the community and their elected officials, the trial judge must be jurist, politician, and administrator in one and fashion broad, effective remedies. He or she must be in close touch with local officials as long as it takes to see the work through. Court-ordered school desegregation, as in the Detroit case, is the most widely known — but as *Hard Judicial Choices* demonstrates, not the only — example of this drawn-out process.

At times the judges in these cases seemed to many to have exceeded their authority. Certainly, they all drew criticism, even abuse. In Cooper's view, however, they did what they had to do to secure compliance, and no more. They were not free-lance social engineers.

A Court Divided describes the 18-year struggle over whether to enlarge or divide the overburdened federal Court of Appeals for the Fifth Circuit, which covers Texas, Louisiana, Mississippi, Alabama, Georgia, and Florida. Some feared that enlarging the court beyond the traditional nine members per circuit would make it unwieldy and less collegial, but others contended that dividing it would also divide and weaken a hardy bloc of moderates willing to enforce civil rights in the face of strong public opposition. Arch-conservative James O. Eastland of Mississippi, chairman of the Senate Judiciary Committee, favored division, specifically at the Mississippi River to isolate the two moderates he least liked in a new Texas-Louisiana circuit, where they would no longer trouble Mississippi. When the judiciary, regionally and nationally, began to lean toward the plan favored by Senator Eastland, moderate judges Richard Rives and John Minor Wisdom launched a discreet but effective campaign to let influential people in and out of government know that civil rights in the South were at stake.

Under pressure, then, the Judicial Conference of the United States, chaired by the chief justice, with representatives from each of the circuits, tabled the division of the Fifth Circuit and recommended its enlargement from 9 to 13 members, a plan approved by Congress in 1966. In the years following, the work load of the court continued to grow, and calls for a new circuit resumed. By 1980, however, President Carter had appointed two women, a black, and a Hispanic to the court, and incentives to maintain the old Fifth were largely gone. Congress put Texas, Louisiana, and Mississippi in a new Fifth Circuit and made Alabama, Georgia, and Florida the Eleventh. The division was inevitable, but the moderates had conducted an important holding operation during trying times.

Each of these fine books tells the story of judges who assumed nontraditional roles to protect what they believed was the integrity of the judicial process.

ROBERT J. SICKELS

University of New Mexico
Albuquerque

CRESPI, IRVING. *Pre-Election Polling: Sources of Accuracy and Error.* Pp. x, 205. New York: Russell Sage Foundation, 1988. $17.50.

During the 1988 elections, the United States was blanketed by preelection polls on almost every level of politics. On the presidential level, we were told by some pollsters that Dukakis led by 18 points in July and that Bush led by 13 points in October. We now know that Bush won by 8 points in November.

In the face of the proliferation and omnipresence of poll results, Irving Crespi has written a timely but disturbing book. It presents the results of his exhaustive analysis of a large number of polls in a large number of different types of elections. The work of thirty pollsters, including those associated with national, state, academic, and private polling organizations, is surveyed in terms of methodology used and degree of accuracy achieved.

Crespi defines accuracy as the size of percentage difference between a poll's measurement of the successful candidate's share of voter preference, with undecideds excluded, and that candidate's actual victory margin on election day. Using this definition, Crespi finds that the mean margin of error for the 430 post-1979 polls reviewed was 5.7 points, a figure that is "roughly three to four times as large as what would be expected through chance alone." This is a troubling conclusion, given the pervasiveness of preelection polls and their potential impact on so many aspects of the electoral process.

Some 98 percent of preelection polls are now conducted by telephone. This presents immediate problems since telephone samples tend to underrepresent minorities and since high refusal rates in telephone surveys are reported by many pollsters. Crespi writes that "special measures apparently need to be taken to insure proper minority representation in telephone polls" and that "conducting repeated call backs to achieve a high completion rate within a narrow time frame will contribute to poll accuracy."

Several additional characteristics of accurate polling are particularly worthy of note. Polls taken in high-turnout — 56 percent or better — elections tend to be more accurate than polls taken in low-turnout — below 33 percent — elections. Polls that report a large number of undecideds — 18 percent or more — tend to be more error prone than polls that report a small number — 9 percent or less — of undecideds. Also, the timing of preelection polls is vital to their accuracy. Crespi tells us that "only if interviewing is conducted within days of the election is there a strong likelihood that a poll will provide an accurate measure of voting behavior."

Since preelection polling has become so important in American politics and since a significant body of methodological literature on such polling is lacking, Crespi has produced an important and valuable book. It should be required reading for all those who conduct polling and for those who rely on the results of polling. While the scientific and specialized nature of the book will make it of unlikely interest to a general readership, this should not detract in any way from the book's contributions.

ROBERT E. GILBERT

Northeastern University
Boston
Massachusetts

HARGROVE, ERWIN C. *Jimmy Carter as President: Leadership and the Politics of the Public Good.* Pp. xxv, 211. Baton Rouge: Louisiana State University Press, 1988. $24.95

SPENCER, DONALD S. *The Carter Implosion: Jimmy Carter and the Amateur Style of Diplomacy.* Pp. ix, 162. New York: Praeger, 1988. $38.95.

The assessments of the presidency of Jimmy Carter have been appearing with some regularity since he left the White House in January 1981. These two books are a part of the growing body of evaluations.

The volume by Erwin C. Hargrove is from the Miller Center Series on the American Presidency. The series of monographs in which participating scholars report the insights they have gained from oral-history interviews constitutes a useful series of retrospectives on the Carter presidency.

Jimmy Carter entered the presidency with a demanding policy agenda. He wanted comprehensive solutions to problems faced by the nation, and he believed in a process of decision making through "centralized collegiality." Part of Carter's problems reflected the fact that his policies fell between liberal and conservative poles: too cautious for the first and too radical for the second.

Many of President Carter's difficulties stemmed from his reluctance to deal forthrightly with the politics of getting his program implemented. Hargrove says, "Carter focused on substantive issues when he should have been giving much of his attention to the politics of the situation." It was often extremely hard for Carter to make compromises. Yet he did so out of necessity. Political concerns became more important in the Carter calculus as time moved nearer to the fight for reelection to a second term.

The growing gulf between Carter and Senator Edward Kennedy was a breach that deeply affected the second half of Carter's term. One of the central dilemmas was how to revive the economy without inflation. But by February 1980 the inflation rate had hit 18 percent, an overriding factor in Carter's defeat for a second term.

In the area of foreign policy making, much attention is given to the sharp difference between the views and methods of Carter's two principal advisers, Secretary of State Cyrus Vance and National Security Adviser Zbigniew Brzezinski. These conflicts permeated the foreign policy field. Nevertheless, there were some significant attainments: the Panama Canal Treaty, the Egypt-Israel Mediation and the Camp David Accords, normalization of relations with China. But Hargrove says flatly that the policymaking process employed during the Iranian revolution

was chaotic, and the Soviet invasion of Afghanistan "had a more profound effect on Carter than any other unanticipated event in his administration." The Afghanistan invasion decisively tipped the scales in favor of Brzezinski over Vance. As the 1980 election approached, the beleaguered administration of Jimmy Carter appeared to have been overtaken by events.

The Carter Implosion: Jimmy Carter and the Amateur Style of Diplomacy is an almost unrelieved negative critique of Carter's handling of foreign affairs. Spencer says, "In the 1976 campaign Carter rhetoric implied that amateurism somehow constituted an essential qualification for high office in that year." The book is a series of essays about a "self-consciously amateur style of diplomacy."

In the aftermath of Vietnam and Watergate, Jimmy Carter's promise never to lie to the American people had a strong moral appeal to the electorate. Carter's tremendous emphasis on human rights as a central focus of foreign policy reflected this moral premise.

Carter's rhetorical attacks against Soviet tyranny undoubtedly had an adverse impact on U.S.-Soviet relations. The Spencer book focuses particular attention on the invasion of Afghanistan, the debacle in Iran, the growing difficulties in Nicaragua, and the "Malthusian nightmare" in Africa. The failures of the Carter presidency in the conduct of foreign policy are heavily attributed to moral posturing and an amateur style of diplomacy. This mode of diplomacy, Spencer writes, exhibited "an unfortunate proclivity for ignoring as if with distaste the historic realities of power."

Both of these books will arouse controversy in the ranks of presidential scholars, but they help put the troubled presidency of Jimmy Carter in perspective.

RAYMOND H. GUSTESON

Ohio University
Athens

KOLKO, GABRIEL. *Confronting the Third World: United States Foreign Policy 1945-*

80. Pp. xiii, 332. New York: Pantheon Books, 1988. $24.95. Paperbound, $15.95.

This substantial volume by Gabriel Kolko is an illuminating study on the involvement of the United States with the Third World since the inception of the postwar era. Kolko unravels, systematically and methodically, the complicated web of relationships between the United States and the Third World from the early declaration of policy positions by the leaders in Washington to actual intervention by America in the developing countries. As a comprehensive treatise on the subject, this work is primarily descriptive, though it is secondarily analytical where policy implications of the American behavior are discussed and options suggested. In the core of the study Kolko dissects three decades of the American role in the developing countries, when fundamental social changes were sweeping the world and European colonialism was gradually being replaced by an American globalist activism.

The book, however, is not merely a chronicle of events that took place in modern times but focuses on analysis of actions and responses as the United States and the developing countries interacted in their search for outcomes that were at cross-purposes. As a revisionist historian of considerable prominence, Gabriel Kolko provides a novel perspective to the analysis of a subject matter that has received a one-sided treatment in both the popular media and the world of scholarship.

The book is divided into four parts according to historical periods since World War II; each period is linked with others by a thread of mutually interwoven issues. In a case-study fashion, Kolko focuses on several Third World countries and finds a common pattern in American actions toward them, based on common assumptions, motives, and objectives that characterized the American involvement. Kolko provides effective documentation that the American intrusion into the Third World, while neither wanted nor welcomed, was primarily for the purpose of creating opportunities for American business to operate freely and profitably. The overall strategy of the policymakers in Washington was to advance the economic interest of the United States through gaining either access to or control of the markets and natural resources of the developing countries. American security needs were equated with ensuring a preponderant role of the United States in an integrated world economic order, unchallenged and unsurpassed by any other power. The rhetoric of the Communist threat and Soviet expansionism was conveniently used to emplace compliant leaders as heads of Third World regimes who willingly served as instruments of American policy. Kolko asserts that the welfare of the Third World countries, either in terms of economic development or in terms of building democratic institutions, was rarely an American concern. The U.S. decision makers really did not much care whether there was repression or violation of human rights as long as political stability was maintained within various countries and at the regional levels.

Given the cynicism upon which the American policy was based, argues Kolko, its failure was inevitable. The Third World countries should have been left alone to their own fates, Kolko suggests, and that would have spared the United States frustration, agony, and domestic divisiveness, to say nothing of the animosity of the peoples in developing countries.

This richly textured work is highly readable and intellectually challenging, especially for those who would go out of their way to seek the views of others with whom they disagree. The book enhances our understanding of a crucial subject and is likely to make a significant contribution to scholarly debate on U.S. foreign policy toward the Third World.

GHULAM M. HANIFF

St. Cloud State University
Minnesota

LANOUE, DAVID J. *From Camelot to the Teflon President: Economics and Presidential Popularity since 1960.* Pp. xiii, 125. Westport, CT: Greenwood Press, 1988. $33.95.

This work is a detailed description of the use of Box Jenkins time-series analysis techniques — including autoregressive-integrated-moving-average (ARIMA) modeling — to test two hypotheses relating economic conditions to presidential popularity.

The "asymmetry hypothesis" borrows heavily from psychology and argues that people are more aware of and concerned about negative information than positive information. As a result, bad economic conditions — measured in terms of rising inflation rates and declining real disposable income — should generate disapproval of the administration in power. Good economic conditions — low inflation, increasing real personal income — should have little, if any, impact on public attitudes.

The "partisan differences" hypothesis states that voters think differently about the ability of the two political parties to handle the economy. Republican presidents are evaluated in relation to recession and Democratic presidents in relation to inflation levels.

The hypotheses are tested using quarterly data covering the period 1961-85. Several noneconomic variables are used as control variables. They include inaugural, or the start of a new administration; rally, or short-lived dramatic events; Watergate; and the Vietnam war.

One chapter is devoted to a discussion of the existing literature on economics and politics. It not only presents the areas of disagreement within this literature but deals with the various methodological differences as well. Another chapter is devoted to the basic research design and the operationalizing of the variables. Lanoue carefully and clearly outlines the time-series techniques used. The model and the various ways it was tested are then presented. Throughout the discussion, Lanoue specifies the limitations of his data and the analysis techniques.

Lanoue's model shows the two hypotheses to be interrelated. Rising inflation rates have a negative effect on presidential popularity; falling inflation rates have no impact. These negative impacts are present only for Democratic administrations. Recession — as measured by declining real disposable income — leads to a decline in presidential popularity. Recovery from recession leads to a return in popularity.

The separate effect of party could not be sorted out due to the fact that in the period examined, the major recessions all occurred during Republican administrations.

Despite the clarity of the writing and the separation of the methodological details from most of the substantive discussion, this work is most appropriate for advanced undergraduate, graduate, and research collections.

ANNE PERMALOFF

Auburn University
Montgomery
Alabama

MUTCH, ROBERT E. *Campaigns, Congress, and Courts: The Making of Federal Campaign Finance Law.* Pp. xx, 217. New York: Praeger, 1988. $42.95.

This is a detailed history of philosophical, legislative, and judicial aspects of election campaign funding regulation in the United States.

At the philosophical level, Robert Mutch focuses on the ancient conflict between rich and poor, and he contrasts two perspectives. First, there is the egalitarian idea that the wealthy should be hindered from using all their financial power in campaigns because it gives them an unfair advantage. Against this is the notion that the wealthy should be permitted to contribute to election campaigns without limit because such contributions are protected as free speech by the Constitution, together with the Burkean argument that the wealthy, as valued and useful members of society, should be allowed the means of defending themselves. Mutch argues that, unlike most areas of American politics, where basic philosophical divisions are obscured and often ignored, these bedrock schisms figure prominently in election campaign funding conflicts.

Federal campaign limitation initiatives have been started primarily by scandals, beginning with the discovery that Theodore Roosevelt's 1904 presidential campaign was partly funded by corporations. Since then, Teapot Dome and Watergate have fueled further reform efforts.

Scandals allow middle-class good-government groups to use the opinion of the temporarily attentive public to pressure Congress to enact changes. Mutch maintains that the campaign funding regulation process will never end. Since limits on contributions are invariably circumvented, and money quickly finds its way back into the hands of campaigners, new abuses will appear.

This study is devoid of partisan or ideological bias and is exceedingly well researched. It provides an excellent bibliography of books, articles, congressional sources, and court cases.

Despite these strengths, the book could have been improved with only small increases in its length. Explanations of statutes and court cases could have been made more useful with the addition of summaries. Although Mutch's explanations of legislative and judicial developments are easily understood, a reader wishing to use this work for reference purposes will be obliged to follow long histories before a particular point becomes clear.

Throughout this work the classic images are presented of Democrats as being the ones most hurt by large contributions and therefore the chief advocates of reform and Republicans as the major beneficiaries of contributions and the major opponents of reform. But in the last few years moneys of political action committees have tended to gravitate toward incumbents of either party and therefore primarily toward Democrats. At present, Republicans speak most fervently in favor of change. The battle is no longer a simple one between rich and poor.

CARL GRAFTON

Auburn University
Montgomery
Alabama

SOCIOLOGY

BOGDAN, ROBERT. *Freak Show: Presenting Human Oddities for Amusement and Profit.* Pp. xiii, 322. Chicago: University of Chicago Press, 1988. $29.95.

In this richly textured social and cultural history, Robert Bogdan illuminates a disappearing part of American life: the freak show, the world of "Otis, the Frog Man"; the "Hovarth Midgets"; Eli Bowen, "The Legless Wonder"; "The Korean Siamese Twins"; "Pasqual Piñon, the Two-Headed Mexican"; "The Wild Men of Borneo"; "Tom Thumb"; "The Bearded Lady"; and the traveling circus. This work started as a study of the cultural practice of exhibiting human beings with physical, mental, and behavioral anomalies. It was organized by two key notions, later discarded, that disability is associated with evil and that disabled persons are often mistreated. True, Bogdan found degradation of the disabled, but he also discovered that such persons often achieved fame, fortune, and enhanced social status. He was led to examine the social worlds of the freak shows, including exhibitors, promoters, and those persons who feigned physical and mental abnormalities or who were presented as novelty acts, including non-Western exhibits, such as "Figi Cannibals," "Ancient Aztecs," and "Zula Giants." He confined his historical investigation to the period of the sideshow's greatest popularity, 1840-1940.

A single thesis structures this text. Freakishness is not a quality of a person; it is something that is created out of a set of social practices. His work, organized in 10 chapters, unravels these practices. It leaves the reader with the sense that modern-day advocates of the civil liberties of the disabled lack a ready audience. Those disabled who have found a place in the freak show appear to be quite proud of their accomplishments and regard these advocates as persons who would put them out of work.

Bogdan finds, then, that the freak existed only in the spaces and the practices that the popular culture created. These spaces were ambiguous and fraught with an ideological struggle that turned in several directions at the same time. The popular culture needed freaks as a way of containing and defining the disabled person; the freaks' presence defined what was normal. The production of social texts that depicted freaks, in billboards, photographs, posters, and films, served to keep in front of the public recurring images of deformed persons as entertaining cultural oddities. This was a money-making business. These texts produced freaks. These meanings — odd versus normal; entertainment and making money; degradation versus self-enhancement — collided once the world of the freak was actually entered. Robert Bogdan is to be thanked for entering this world and exposing its limits and its possibilities. In so doing, he shows all of us another side of ourselves that we otherwise prefer to keep hidden.

NORMAN K. DENZIN

University of Illinois
Urbana-Champaign

HAYES-BAUTISTA, DAVID E., WERNER O. SCHINK, and JORGE CHAPA. *The Burden of Support: Young Latinos in an Aging Society.* Pp. xvi, 196. Stanford, CA: Stanford University Press, 1988. $32.50.

Using the literary device of a worst-case scenario for the state of California to introduce their topic, Hayes-Bautista, Werner, and Chapa propose a conceptual model of a future age-ethnic stratification of that state. Based upon demographic trends and projections, the model predicts a future in which a predominantly Anglo — that is, European American — elderly population will depend on a heavily Latino — that is, Hispanic working-age population. Given current patterns of educational and income inequity, the authors ask if these future young Latinos will be both able and willing to provide such support.

Extensive demographic data from California and Mexico are presented in support of the argument that by the year 2030 age and ethnicity will be correlated in California; those aged 65 and older will be overwhelmingly Anglo while the majority of the working-age population will consist of minority-group members, primarily Latinos. While the baseline predictions presented are grounded in moderate assumptions, alternatives using assumptions of no new immigration and a sudden immigration influx with a return to moderate levels are also discussed, so that the reader is given a range of possibilities. Demographic concepts such as the age pyramid

and dependency ratio are clearly explained, making the text quite accessible to those with little or no training in that field.

Using current data on educational and income attainment of Californian Latinos, as compared to Anglos, the implications of the predicted age-ethnic stratification for our ability to provide adequate income and health care to future cohorts of elders and younger people alike are explored. The picture of the year 2030 painted in this book is not bright. In addition to the difficulties presented by demographics alone, this picture is colored by the injustice — and shortsightedness — of the expectation of today's baby-boomers that their old age will be funded by those children who are currently underserved by the educational and health-care delivery systems.

While the focus of this analysis is on Latinos and Anglos in California, other major ethnic groups are also taken into account. Although this state is examined in isolation from the rest of the nation, the potential for the occurrence of similar phenomena in other states with large Latino populations is discussed.

Certainly the issues raised in this book are important. The authors' contention that today's policy decisions will determine our future in unanticipated ways is valid. Policy suggestions to deal with many of the issues raised in the book are presented. Unfortunately, the choices are presented as being between young Latinos and elderly Anglos, rather than between human services and other types of federal budget items, such as the military. This is particularly troubling because it assumes — indeed, promotes — future age and ethnic conflict rather than a reordering of national priorities.

LINDA LISKA BELGRAVE

Case Western Reserve University
Cleveland
Ohio

IZOD, JOHN. *Hollywood and the Box Office, 1895-1986.* Pp. xii, 240. New York: Columbia University Press, 1988. $30.00. Paperbound, $15.00.

The adage that "art anticipates reality" is both inspiring and frightening. John Izod's compelling narrative of the motion picture dependency on market forces, the costs of production, and rivalries over distribution excludes any privileged position for art in the history of filmmaking as a business. It is an actual history that both Adam Smith and Karl Marx would find confirming of their separate representations of capitalism.

Izod's book does not at all have any intention of sustaining or rejecting the theories of Smith or Marx. What he does accomplish, with great skill, is to establish cogently and concretely the essential determinative role of capital formation, innovations and technical inventions, and cycles of economic growth and recession in the development of the movie industry. Perceptive attention is paid to the decisive function of investors, bankers, creditors, vertical control structures, oligopoly, cartels, trusts, and the internecine competition of the great studios Paramount, Metro-Goldwyn-Mayer, and Warner Brothers. With a masterful command of the published literature on the business of filmmaking, Izod divides his history into 15 distinct periods from 1895 until 1986. He tells a story that begins with the invention of cameras and projectors, the role of the nickelodeons in showing the first films and in identifying the popular audiences that would determine the future of the motion picture industry.

Izod ends his history with a description of the multiplex chambers that in today's shopping centers are the heirs of the dream palaces of the 1920s and 1930s. He does not permit himself any aesthetic judgments on this unromantic conclusion to his history. He does, in his role of historian and accountant, underline the critical contribution of hot buttered popcorn to the bottom line of profit and loss of the contemporary motion picture industry. The rules of the game in the world of finance capitalism have ordained and continue to assure our cinematic oneiric pleasures.

EDWARD T. GARGAN

University of Wisconsin
Madison

LAUREN, PAUL GORDON. *Power and Prejudice: The Politics and Diplomacy of Racial Discrimination.* Pp. xv, 388. Boulder, CO: Westview Press, 1988. $34.95. Paperbound, $19.95.

To one unlearned in the scope and magnitude of racial discrimination in recent times, *Power and Prejudice* is shocking. To one enlightened by Western philosophy and science, *Power and Prejudice* is a jolt to the conscience.

Paul Gordon Lauren has prepared an exhaustive historical record of racial prejudice as public policy from the time of Aristotle to Ronald Reagan, in international as well as domestic political affairs, with an emphasis upon racism in twentieth-century diplomacy. The record culminates in the United Nations' Decade for Action to Combat Racism and Racial Discrimination (1973-83), in which South Africa's policy of apartheid was the major focus of attention. History does not easily distinguish between apartheid, slavery, and genocide, however. Each of these policies has been more or less grotesque, but the declared rationale has been the same in each: inferior nonwhite races are naturally subject to the will of the superior white race, and public policy toward nonwhites must be such as to preserve the integrity and well-being of whites lest the former contaminate the latter.

History does not reveal by what accident of culture white came to be considered superior and colored inferior, since there is mounting evidence that civilization under white leadership is bent on self-destruction. On the other hand, Lauren makes it clear that white and colored are relative terms and that any racial element finding itself in a position of dominance over another will soon develop racial prejudice, perhaps more out of fear of the tables being turned than any innate sense of righteousness. One is left with the conclusion that racial discrimination is inherent in human nature, that any kind of difference between peoples is a potential source of misunderstanding, fear, and prejudice. It is ironic that one of the great scientific breakthroughs of modern times, Darwin's theory of evolution, gave rise to unscientific social

Darwinism, which has become a convenient excuse for racial discrimination in the twentieth century.

If there is a shortcoming in the work, it is in what other reviewers might describe as its greatest virtue, the narrow scope of the study. *Power and Prejudice* is a history of racial prejudice, but racial prejudice is inextricably intertwined with religious prejudice and both may be dependent upon economic advantage as the causal variable. Lauren raises both religious dogma and economic status as related to racism in this easy-reading and carefully documented monograph. I regret that he did not explore the possibility of a causal relationship.

HOWARD D. NEIGHBOR

University of Texas
El Paso

OVED, YAACOV. *Two Hundred Years of American Communes*. Pp. xvi, 500. New Brunswick, NJ: Transaction Books, 1988. $39.95.

A dedicated member of a kibbutz since boyhood, Yaacov Oved makes it plain that his book was "conceived, written and published in a communitarian spirit." Such ardor suggests special pleading, but, in reality, Oved's long experience with communal living has served to release him from the problems of bias far more than it has embroiled him. He writes serenely as neither the cynic scorning those who would be perfect nor a visionary dreamer of utopia. He proves to be a trustworthy guide who can deliver bad news without flinching, yet also convey the very special optimistic emotion of commune participants that detached observers are not in a good position to understand.

To strike the important balance between advocacy and objectivity, Oved has divided his study in two. In the first section he follows a brief chapter, "Communes in the History of the United States," which stresses the counterpoint between frontier and immigrant idealism that has given America a uniquely instructive communal history, with the lengthiest section of his book, 16 chapters describing seventy of the most representative communes from the mid-1730s to the mid-1930s. Oved's references show a wide grasp of the published literature, along with some use of the journals and records of the communes themselves and visits to key sites. The cascade of eccentric characters and picaresque adventures that tumbles out of the record leaves one impressed with the force of wishful thinking and the disappointment repeatedly wreaked in the name of morality, property, and normality.

The second half of the book draws general themes out of the melee. After analyzing the ideological principles of the communes and their effects on management, family, and cultural expression, Oved acknowledges that they mostly add up to "a collection of pathetic and sad case histories." Yet the few exceptions, especially the stable and persistent Hutterite and Bruderhof communes, reassure Oved that "a preordained sentence of the fateful inevitability of breakup is not at all inherent in the history of communes." The prime ingredients for sustained success, Oved concludes, with systematic attention to detail, are a slow rate of change, "controlled seclusion," family solidarity, emotional attachment to fixed values, and effective transformation of charismatic personal leadership into respected institutions.

In his epilogue, bringing the story briefly up to date, Oved lets his partisanship carry him too far. Without substantiation he makes a dubious distinction between the transient communalism of the late 1960s, which ended a thirty-year period of remission, and the allegedly more sensible and lasting communes of the 1970s. Against the conventional wisdom that the Reagan era has exalted self-regard over community, Oved proclaims the 1980s to be a period of worldwide communal revival, with America once more playing the leading role. Surely, Oved exaggerates when he tries to support that hopefulness by describing Hutterite and Bruderhof activity as two "large movements" on the current scene. Yet one might argue at least the possibility for renewed efforts at creating communities in a world where the cold war seems to be diminishing and the needs of suffering people are escalating. Those who would reflect on such potentiality, as well as those who wish simply to know more about the fascinating and important history of communalism in America, will benefit from Oved's thorough and carefully integrated study.

ALAN LAWSON

Boston College
Chestnut Hill
Massachusetts

VIGIL, JAMES DIEGO. *Barrio Gangs: Street Life and Identity in Southern California.* Pp. xv, 202. Austin: University of Texas Press, 1988. $22.50. Paperbound, $8.95.

The nation's current and growing concern with the sale and use of illegal drugs, the underclass, and the wanton violence of drive-by shootings has caused a renewed focus on youth gangs. Gangs have been an urban problem as long as there have been large numbers of immigrants in American cities. Gangs of Chicano youths are found in Mexican American communities, or *barrios.* James Diego Vigil's *Barrio Gangs* presents an analysis of these gangs in southern California using two complementary methodological approaches: the life histories of individual gang members and the structural history of the circumstances that create gangs.

Vigil explains the existence of Chicano gangs with the concept of multiple marginality. His examination of the life histories of the regular gang members, those with the deepest gang involvement, revealed that they were commonly marginalized in many aspects of American life. In addition to its greater inherent plausibility, this multicausal explanation has a further advantage over prior monocausal theories of gang membership; it can explain why different youths have different degrees of gang involvement. Vigil shows us that in addition to the regular member with a deep, long-term commitment to the gang, there are many Chicanos who are peripheral, temporary, or situational

members. Each type of less committed gang member is marginalized on fewer dimensions than the regular member.

Regular gang members are marginalized on many different dimensions. Their parents typically are in economically marginal situations. If employed, they have low-paying, unsteady jobs. The families of gang members are unstable and under stress. Fathers are often absent due to death, incarceration, or separation. Future gang members have serious problems with school as soon as they start. Unable to find support or guidance from either family or school, the *barrio* streets become the major locus of socialization for these children as early as age seven. On the streets they form close friendships with the peers who will later be their fellow gang members. Also on the street they learn the *cholo* culture, the Chicano gang norms for dressing, speaking, partying, walking, and living. The gang becomes an important element in members' psychological development and the defining aspect of their identity. They will be involved with the gang and gang activities well into their adult years. Committed gang membership is thus the cumulative result of economic, familial, educational, and residential marginality.

Vigil's other methodology, structural historical analysis, reveals the very important finding that *barrio* gangs are not a transitory phenomenon. Unlike the gangs of European immigrants, some *barrio* gangs have been in continuous existence long enough for as many as 12 or 14 successive age cohorts of members to pass through their ranks. The persistence of *barrio* gangs is due to continuous immigration from Mexico and the persistence of economic marginality even among third-generation Mexican Americans.

Vigil quotes the response of a youth program director to a question about the causes of gang formation: "We don't want to understand the problem, we just want to stop it." *Barrio Gangs* is a major contribution to our understanding of the problem of Chicano gangs, and it indicates the types of large-scale change needed to stop it. It presents a framework that can inform future research on gangs of any racial or ethnic group. This book should be read by all who are interested in either understanding or solving one of the most serious problems of our times.

JORGE CHAPA

University of Texas
Austin

VINOKUR, MARTIN B. *More Than a Game: Sports and Politics*. Pp. xiv, 155. Westport, CT: Greenwood Press, 1988. $37.95.

More Than a Game: Sport and Politics is another in a relatively long line of treatises that assert that it is naive and unrealistic to view sport as separate and above social, economic, and, more specifically, political activity. According to Vinokur, economists and sociologists have done a reasonably good job making a case for the seriousness of sport to society, but political scientists have totally neglected sport as it is linked to political socialization, formation of political culture, and development of national identity. *More Than a Game* is the outcome of the melding of Vinokur's academic background with his personal enthusiasm for sport and his direct experience with international sport as a tour director for goodwill tennis competition in Europe.

Even though the title of this text suggests a broad view of the relation of sport to politics, the focus is on international sport, with a concentration on the sport programs of Eastern Europe, namely, Romania and East Germany. The latter are utilized as case studies in Vinokur's investigation of several hypotheses about the relationship of sport and political activity. These propositions generally proclaim that the more serious sport is to citizens, the more likely a government will use sport as a vehicle of policy and control; that sport is replacing other cultural activities as a basis for international exchange; that sport organizations are tools of the government in the political socialization of a country's youth; and that "sport is an essential instrument serving the national and political integration of a country."

In all cases, government activity is the independent variable and sport is the dependent variable.

Vinokur's analysis is guided by a structural-functional orientation that evaluates the role of sport at each of three levels: physical education in school, mass leisure and recreation, and elite international competition. The functional paradigm is adequately applied at a societal level but does neglect the potential dysfunctions of sport. In addition, the functions of sport for community and individuals are not reviewed. Vinokur describes various research techniques, such as content analysis and time-diary review, as being the basis upon which his conclusions are drawn. Except for a few personal interviews, however, it is obvious that Vinokur did not implement these techniques; he depended upon the work of others. Thus little original research is reported in this study. The case studies include succinct descriptions of Romanian and East German sport and educational systems, but they are superficial in analysis and understanding: four unstructured interviews and personal experience do not make an adequate data base. The analysis contained in *More Than a Game* ultimately depends upon a research base that Vinokur declared, in the first pages of the text, to be inadequate and incomplete.

The premise of *More Than a Game* is good: expose the myth that sport and politics do not mix. But the analysis is superficial at best, and generalization is limited because the coverage is restricted to only a few national experiences with sport and politics. The discussion does not include detailed analyses of such dramatic examples of how sport and politics mix as the case of South Africa, the African Olympic boycotts, the use of sport by the Cuban government, and the United States' strategic use of Ping-Pong diplomacy. Seminal volumes on sport and politics by Lever, Hoberman, Kanin, Allison, Espy, and Gruneau are not included or reviewed. In addition, the lack of a thorough review of the Marxist, neo-Marxist, and critical thinking on the role of sport is a major oversight. Some of the descriptive material, such as that on the Olympic boycotts and their aftermath, is very good; most, however, is readily available from other sources and thus is not original or enlightening. Finally, too many scholars have felt that personal experience and intense interest are sufficient bases for the analysis of the role of sport in society. They are not. Sport studies requires the intense theoretical and methodological attention that any scholarly subfield deserves. It must move from an interest that is secondary, casual, and fun to one that is primary, consuming, and serious. *More Than a Game* does not reflect the latter.

JAMES H. FREY

University of Nevada
Las Vegas

ECONOMICS

BAIROCH, PAUL. *Cities and Economic Development: From the Dawn of History to the Present.* Translated by Christopher Braider. Pp. xxii, 574. Chicago: University of Chicago Press, 1988. $49.95.

Paul Bairoch, professor of economic history at the University of Geneva, has written a comprehensive, comprehensible, and competent overview of urbanization. In scope, it is a work recalling Mumford's *City in History*. Bairoch is heavily influenced by the French Annales School. He works with sources from a wide range of disciplines.

The ambitious theme is the set of relations between urbanization and economic development, with recorded history as the time span and the whole world as stage. Cities, Bairoch shows, appear early in human prehistory, relatively simultaneously, and in many places. He argues that adapting agriculture and adapting to agriculture, humanity adapted the city as well. Ever since, there have been reciprocal relations between the city and economic development.

Following this introductory statement, Bairoch works out this theme in three settings: traditional Western society, the modern world following on the industrial revolution, and the Third World, linked more recently to developed regions by colonial ties.

The first millennia saw some rather precipitous shifts in the urban population, though cities survived. Bairoch's analysis shows that the early world was more highly urbanized than most scholars would allow. Given that agricultural surplus was small but population growth higher in rural areas than in cities, which needed immigration to survive, we see the sources of the continuing link between the two domains.

In traditional Western societies, 15 to 20 percent of the population lived in cities. This level remained stable from the classical era to the beginning of the industrial revolution. Bairoch characterizes the city in this period, as well as later, as the arena for change, for technological innovation. With the upheavals brought on by the industrial revolution, new cities and a new urbanization arose. Mobility was facilitated, new markets arose, and greater agricultural productivity came about, in good measure brought on by the growth of cities. But it was only quite recently that urban populations have been able to replenish themselves: cities in the nineteenth century and earlier were basically unhealthy and relied on immigration from rural areas.

The colonial domain had been urbanized prior to contact with Europe. Modern colonization de-urbanized the prior cities and lightly urbanized many of the conquered areas. A different urbanization arose, and, significantly, it was one that was not based on industry. The link, however, did add to the urbanization of Europe. In recent years, we have witnessed an urban explosion in the Third World — a consequence of rural population surplus occasioned by the demographic transition — yet this has not been associated with higher agricultural production. It leads to a series of urban and rural problems. Bairoch, sadly, concludes that this is the one instance where urbanization has impeded development and encouraged a concomitant rise in welfare.

Looking to the future, Bairoch anticipates for the rapidly urbanizing Third World a deepening in the misery quotient. Giant cities of the next generation — such as Mexico City, with a population in the 20-30 million range — will have enormous problems, with no solutions in sight. This is a grim ending for a story that otherwise evokes the city-based sources of enrichment and civilization.

As an economic historian, Bairoch casts his net wide: literature from these fields but also writings from geography, anthropology, demography, and other disciplines. The impressive bibliography, comprising well over 500 items, shows familiarity with the classics but also offers the scholar specialized monographs and technical publications, mainly in English and in French. An all too brief technical appendix outlines his own efforts to adjust and improve on extant population and urbanization estimates — drawn from a wide range of sources — which are the framework on which his arguments rest.

A synthetic work of such grand scope will, of course, lend itself to criticism that certain subjects, such as the governance of cities, are insufficiently covered, that one or another epoch or region — for example, Eastern Europe — is given short shrift, that the work of one or another predecessor with similar ambitions — for example, Erwin Gutkind — is apparently overlooked. Yet one leaves this volume with the feeling of positions intelligently argued and related to the existing state of theory and knowledge. One also has the pleasure of reading a book unusually well written. It will long both be a standard and stimulate new thought on the central issues of urban and economic growth.

THOMAS A. REINER

University of Pennsylvania
Philadelphia

DAVIDSON, GREG and PAUL DAVIDSON. *Economics for a Civilized Economy.* Pp. x, 213. New York: Norton, 1988. $22.95.

While this small volume pays much attention to the economic policies adopted by the Reagan administration, it is more generally an indictment of the conservative economic view that seems to have gripped the nation — and the world — in the 1980s. It argues for the tempering influence of civilized ideals on conservative

economic logic. Otherwise, there is danger that, at least in economic matters, the world will sink into barbarism. Already, the economic policies of, say, Ronald Reagan or Margaret Thatcher are widely viewed as barbaric.

One of the great paradoxes of the twentieth century is that Reagan campaigned for office on issues related to civic values — for example, the importance of family, community, and religion — while his administration followed policies based only on self-interest and, therefore, on fear. Perhaps that is why he is an extremely popular human being but not an extremely popular president.

There are two basic tenets of conservative economics: first, that individuals are governed solely by self-interest and, second, that the standard conservative economic analysis is value free. Together, these two tenets lead to the view that economic outcomes are inevitable. It then becomes easy, if uncivilized, to blame the victim and, therefore, to follow policies that hurt precisely those persons whom, presumably, one wishes to help. Moreover, the cure for any problem now involves simply providing the right monetary incentives. For example, according to conservatives, a tax cut would provide incentives to business and labor and, thereby, release the entrepreneurial spirit needed to pull the economy out of the doldrums. But, while it reduced everyone's taxes, Reagan's tax cut in the early 1980s was a give-away to the rich. Ironically, all the effects, good and bad, of the tax cut were predictable from Keynesian — that is, old-fashioned liberal — economics.

These two tenets seem also to have polluted liberal economic analysis recently. Liberals still believe in a civilized income distribution and full employment. But now they are between a rock and a hard place; their economic skills will not serve their ideals. It is a myth, created by economists of all stripes, that economics is a hard — not a social — science.

Civilized government will require a marriage between the self-interest aspects of conservative doctrine and liberal civic values. As it stands, conservative economics suggests motivating individuals through fear and/or appetite while liberal economics would motivate people only by altruism or a sense of community ideals. Somehow, a happy medium between these two views must be found.

The first few chapters of this book tell us what is wrong with economists. This is a non-technical and quite readable treatment of economic theory. In most respects, these views are untainted by philosophy and are held by conservatives and — former? — liberals alike. Nevertheless, being untempered by altruism or civic values, they suggest to the conservative that the main macroeconomic problem is inflation, which can — should? — be beaten with a barbaric recessionary policy. Several chapters then argue that, in fact, the main economic problem in an entrepreneurial economy is not inflation but unemployment, that is, recession. From this viewpoint, it is not the least helpful that conservatives refer to the "natural rate of unemployment." With the problem of unemployment in mind, a chapter is devoted to civilized policies for controlling inflation. Clearly, the volume is most concerned with macroeconomic questions.

Throughout, the policy failures of untempered conservative doctrine are demonstrated by the experience of the Reagan years, although, sometimes, the book goes as far back as Carter, Ford, or Nixon. Of course, such conservative dogma is not limited to the United States or Reagan; it also informs the policies of Margaret Thatcher's Britain and, importantly, of the International Monetary Fund. For this reason, this volume also discusses recent international questions, such as the debt crisis. It calls for and discusses a civilized global economy.

While this book's concern is with economics, it is highly readable by a general audience. I heartily recommend it to everyone. It might better inform the views of the civilized. Nevertheless, it should be required reading for those wedded to conservative doctrine.

JON HARKNESS

Queen's University
Kingston
Ontario
Canada

DAWISHA, KAREN. *Eastern Europe, Gorbachev and Reform: The Great Challenge.* Pp. xiii, 268. New York: Cambridge University Press, 1988. $12.95.

During the Gorbachev ascendancy, the Soviet Union was in economic, political, and moral decline domestically. Expenditures on the Soviet arms buildup had long exceeded the country's capability to pay for them and also maintain the population's standard of living. Gorbachev came to power obviously believing that socialism, being a dynamic and transitional system, was capable of reforming itself not only in the USSR but also in Eastern European countries.

Economic reforms in the past fifty years have become integral parts of the process of improving the sluggish performance of Soviet socialist systems. In the pantheon of reforms, Gorbachev's is probably a hallmark. For all practical purposes, these reforms, both in style and content, represent modest changes in the system, though the authorities vociferously refute that the proposals represent aberrations from the basic Marxist-Leninist covenants. Placing the reforms in historical perspective, these reforms could be considered the Enlightenment stage of Soviet socialism. The Western Enlightenment originated and spread atomistically, while in the Soviet systems enlightenment had to be imposed from the top, which created its own new set of problems.

Neither policymakers nor students of international affairs can afford to underestimate the potential for change that has been unleashed. Gorbachev's reform campaign in Eastern Europe moved beyond the canons of conventional wisdom.

Karen Dawisha presents a lucid, well-structured picture of the causes leading to the reforms and of the difficulties encountered by the policymakers in making them operational.

Projections of the long-run potential, whether and to what degree these reforms will succeed, fall outside the scope of this treatise. Many of the Eastern European leaders, who were installed and protected by Soviet power, may feel threatened and vulnerable as a result of the "new openness" being proclaimed by Moscow. Meantime, the perception continues to grow that the cold war is grinding to an end.

With this, a crucial and substantive question is raised by Dawisha: in promoting the notion that the reform in the Soviet Union could beneficially spill over and stimulate similar processes in Eastern Europe, does Gorbachev not fear a repetition of previous upheavals, when the results in Eastern Europe resulted not in the perfection of socialism but in its near collapse? The greatest challenge to Gorbachev, therefore, will not be in promoting change but in preventing the bursting of pent-up desires for change among the Eastern European population from engulfing his own program and aspirations.

The first part of the book focuses on the nature of the challenge presented by Eastern European aspiration for the reform. It details the basic Soviet conception of the region and briefs us on some factional views that claim that the Soviet Union's enormous geopolitical stake in the region overrides the risk in promoting reforms in the Eastern Bloc.

Part 2 addresses the way the new challenges will be met. By switching policy and moving beyond the use of force and threat, there will be a new relationship with the West, and the impact of that relationship is discussed. Dawisha sees light emerging at the end of the tunnel and believes that the new policies will fuel, perhaps unwittingly, the popular yearning in Eastern Europe for the end of the East-West division.

PETER S. ELEK

Villanova University
Pennsylvania

HOUNSHELL, DAVID A. and JOHN KENLY SMITH, Jr. *Science and Corporate Strategy: Du Pont R&D, 1902-1980.* Pp. xx, 756. New York: Cambridge University Press, 1988. $34.50.

A new kind of industry burgeoned during the late nineteenth century. Electrical, chemical, photographic, and telecommunications companies — companies, in other words, that relied on recent scientific discovery for the technologies they exploited — had achieved great size and command of vast resources by the turn of the century. Recognizing their dependence on science, they sought ways to institutionalize and systematize the search for improved products and processes — ways, in brief, to harness science to corporate ends. Historians and social scientists had not missed this phenomenon, but two books published in 1977 reminded us of its peculiar importance: David F. Noble's *America by Design: Science, Technology, and the Rise of Corporate Capitalism* (Knopf) and *The Visible Hand: The Managerial Revolution in American Business,* by Alfred D. Chandler, Jr. (Harvard University Press).

A key link in the new relations between business and science took the form of the industrial research laboratory. Again, scholars have long noted its significance, but several recent studies have suggested new answers to how it happened and why it mattered: Reese V. Jenkins's *Image and Enterprise: Technology and the American Photographic Industry* (Johns Hopkins University Press, 1975), George Wise's *Willis R. Whitney, General Electric, and the Origins of U.S. Industrial Research* (Columbia University Press, 1985), and Leonard S. Reich's *Making of American Industrial Research: Science and Business at GE and Bell* (Cambridge University Press, 1986). *Science and Corporate Strategy* now joins this select group.

Hounshell and Smith are both academic historians. Subsidized by Du Pont but guaranteed full access to company records and complete freedom to draw their own conclusions, they enjoyed an unusual opportunity, of which they have taken full advantage. We now have an extremely detailed, fully documented, clearly written, and enormously informative narrative history of one of the pioneer industrial research and development laboratories, with sophisticated analyses of the role of research and development in a particular though changing corporate setting over most of a century, the problems of decision making with respect to research management and organization, and the careers — whether successful or not — of every significant Du Pont research project. Hounshell and Smith offer, in fact, almost an embarrassment of riches. Fortunately, they also provide help. Their introductions to the book as a whole and to each of its five parts, plus their conclusion, effectively guide the reader through their analysis, while the individual chapters furnish the evidence in fascinating detail. Scholars in business and economic history and the history of science and technology will deem the book indispensable. Others may find it makes for splendid browsing, to say nothing of reference.

BARTON C. HACKER

Oregon State University
Corvallis

SIGLER, JAY A. and JOSEPH E. MURPHY. *Interactive Corporate Compliance: An Alternative to Regulatory Compulsion.* Pp. xii, 211. Westport, CT: Greenwood Press, Quorum Books, 1988. $39.95.

In this book, Jay Sigler and Joseph Murphy present a program for redefining government and industry relationships in a manner that would ensure that currently mandated social policies would be effective in practice. Beginning with an insightful analysis of the development of the government's adversarial role vis-à-vis business from one of sponsor and protector in the early days of the Republic, they note that confrontational relationships serve the interests of neither business nor society. To maintain cost competitiveness, business needs to guard against litigation and is reluctant to create compliance programs independently for fear that the data generated may be used against it in court. But business leaders are amenable to realistic cost-effective regulation. Government regulators, on the other hand, either create paper-and-pencil measures of compliance with little social benefit or create complex and expensive models beyond the ability of either industry or society to support.

Administrative regulation is only one form of social control. Criminal law techniques are appropriate when the objective of social policy is deterrence but ineffective when the goal is compliance. Fines primarily penalize stockholders.

The system of interactive compliance proposed is one that recognizes forms of social control other than legal sanctions and the extent of interdependence between government and industry. Relying on the knowledge developed by social scientists in behavioral modification, Sigler and Murphy propose a system in which business would be rewarded financially for taking leadership roles in developing model programs to be used by others in the industry and for the costs of compliance. If the notion of management by exception is employed, only miscreant noncompliers would be punished. This notion recognizes that effective behavioral change needs to be learned and that those that carry on these activities within the firm are in fact surrogate government representatives whom society should be willing to compensate for the costs of program design and compliance.

Implementation of this plan requires major changes in legislation and in activities of regulatory agents to create a relationship of trust between business and government. First, business needs to be assured of consistent legislative protection from litigation as a result of compliance activities. Second, the government needs to undertake the responsibility of making laws understandable and known to citizens. Finally, regulatory agents need to be held accountable for their advice. The result would be more comprehensive and workable legislation and more effective implementation. In conclusion, Sigler and Murphy describe a model of the operation of interactive compliance between the Federal Trade Commission and a hypothetical firm in regard to antitrust legislation.

This volume is a welcome addition to a literature that tends toward normative models with little attention to the needs of implementation or the role of applied social science in policy formulation.

CAROLYN R. DEXTER

Pennsylvania State University
Harrisburg

SMITH, MICHAEL PETER. *City, State, and Market: The Political Economy of Urban Society.* Pp. x, 252. New York: Basil Blackwell, 1988. $34.95.

Since the publication of his path-breaking 1979 book, *The City and Social Theory,* Michael Peter Smith has become one of this country's leading urban social theorists. In *City, State, and Market,* Smith continues to evidence that he is one of the most important of the political scientists working on urban politics. This insightful book is organized around stimulating critiques of three major theoretical approaches often offered to explain oscillating urban development in the United States: the market-capitalist perspective, the welfare-liberal perspective, and the structural-Marxist perspective.

After a brief introductory chapter summarizing his key themes and underscoring his point that "politics matters," Smith discusses in chapters 2-4 the character and development of the U.S. welfare state in comparison with the welfare states in other capitalist societies. He shows how the U.S. welfare state, rooted in New Deal and Great Society programs, has been legitimated by a pervasive ideology asserting that unbridled market-centered economic growth automatically reduces inequality and social divisions and generates sufficient tax revenues to pay for a variety of social programs. Yet this widely believed assertion has not been borne out in reality, and in chapter 2 Smith shows that the actual effect of these state policies has been the creation of new social divisions in U.S. society, including social and spatial inequalities that have contributed to the emergence of right-wing politics aimed at sharply reducing the welfare state.

In chapter 3, Smith turns to the structural Marxist — for example, "capital logic" — explanations of the crisis of contemporary welfare-state capitalism. Faulting advocates of this perspective for accenting economic explanations and for failing to factor in adequately the historically specific political — and cultural — structures of the United States, Smith argues that structuralist explanations have not provided

an understanding of the rise and fall of urban political movements. He also develops an important argument about the "fiscal welfare state," his phrase for state aid to capitalists in such forms as tax expenditures. In discussing governmental action, both the structuralist Marxists and the market capitalists focus on direct governmental expenditures, not the vast array of indirect subsidies provided to business through the tax system.

Perhaps because the market-capitalist perspective has been the dominant perspective during the 1980s, Smith devotes considerable attention in chapter 5 to leading theorist Milton Friedman. There Smith lays out the basic assumptions of the market-capitalist theory and demonstrates with devastating and scalpel-like precision that the scholarly visions of a depoliticized "free and natural market" are decidedly fictional. The market is fundamentally political. In chapter 6 Smith examines the implications of this free-market perspective for urban political policy, and in chapter 7 he moves from theory to the implemented urban policy of the Reagan administration. He shows in detail the differences between the illusions of the free-market ideology and the realities of the active and far-reaching use of the state by so-called conservatives to carry out the Reagan administration's Sunbelt-oriented policies of military spending and economic growth.

In the last section of the book, Smith examines the close relationship between the changing character of the global political economy and the changing character of urban politics in the United States. Capitalist competition has led not only to capital flight to low-wage countries but also to the creation of Third-World-type urban enterprise zones within the United States, areas with many tax and labor concessions to corporate investors. The establishment of enterprise zones has involved close working relationships between presumably conservative capitalists and politicians.

Smith's analysis is a frontal challenge to the reigning capitalist market viewpoint in the various urban social sciences, including sociology, economics, and political science. His analysis provides a deep critique of such books as Brian

J.L. Berry and John Kasarda's *Contemporary Urban Ecology* (New York: Macmillan, 1977), which has been influential in establishing a capitalist market perspective in urban ecology and sociology. Such social scientists have for the most part accepted uncritically the workings of the dominant market and the processes of capital accumulation. Similarly, economists Katharine Bradbury, Anthony Downs, and Kenneth Small, in their book *Urban Decline and the Future of American Cities* (Washington, DC: Brookings Institution, 1982), argue that market forces are so powerful and constructive that it is "folly" to try governmental policies that ignore the capitalist market in guiding economic change. And political scientist Paul E. Peterson, in his book *City Limits* (Chicago: University of Chicago Press, 1981), has argued that local government officials seek to enhance the general welfare of their particular cities and thus pursue economic growth, in partnership with market — business — interests, a growth that Peterson views as benefiting all urban residents. In Peterson's perspective, "the interests of cities" are roughly identical with those of local industrialists and investors. Smith's analysis demonstrates rather convincingly that these sociologists, economists, and political scientists do not provide a sufficient or critical analysis of either the U.S. state or U.S. capitalism.

In contrast to this market-knows-best perspective, Smith provides overwhelming evidence that certain groups in U.S. politics, including urban politics, have far more power than others to shape political decisions and institutions. Just as markets favor powerful capitalist investors over ordinary consumers, the political process favors powerful business and other groups over ordinary voters. Moreover, in spite of their free-market ideology, conservative business leaders make great use of the state to further their own interests. This has led to urban policies in which there are clear winners and losers. U.S. society is in reality skewed toward the few and the powerful, yet legitimated ideologically as favoring the common welfare. Neither U.S. markets nor U.S. political arrangements are neutral or hermetically separated. One of Smith's major contributions is to demonstrate

that the U.S. economy and U.S. politics are not separate "containers" but rather are part of an integrated political-economic whole. From his perspective there is no economics without politics — and no politics, especially in a capitalist society, without economics.

JOE R. FEAGIN

University of Texas
Austin

WEAVER, R. KENT. *Automatic Government: The Politics of Indexation.* Pp. xii, 276. Washington, DC: Brookings Institution, 1988. $31.95. Paperbound, $11.95.

This book is an effort to understand what R. Kent Weaver views as a puzzle in contemporary U.S. public policy: why policymakers have been increasingly willing to adopt indexation as a central component of programs and thus surrender considerable control over them.

Indexation involves the establishment of a base figure for an element of the program; the creation of an index to measure change, usually in wages or prices or both; and finally the adjustment of the base to reflect changes in the value of the index. The last twenty years have seen a steep increase in the number of indexed programs. Approximately 30 percent of the federal budget is directly tied to the consumer price index, and another 20 percent is indirectly linked to it.

Weaver's first three chapters treat two main topics: an analysis of the goals of policymakers, cast in terms of rational-choice theories; and an overview of indexation in terms of the scope and timing of indexed programs and the fiscal circumstances present when they were created.

With respect to politicians' goals, Weaver analyzes the payoffs to policymakers in terms of claiming credit, avoiding blame, and making good policy. He concludes that an a priori treatment of these ends is inconclusive. This leads to a historical treatment, qualitative and quantitative, of indexed programs. Weaver concludes that indexation is most likely to be used in benefit programs, has occurred historically in three periods, and has involved primarily commodity price supports, federal retirement, means-tested benefit programs, and social insurance. The most recent surge in indexed programs ended in the 1970s.

To explain these patterns is more difficult, and Weaver is able only to suggest that both credit claiming and blame avoidance were probably important in legislators' decision rules. More important, Weaver argues, were the inflation of the 1970s and the concern over the budget deficit of the 1980s. While both help account for the overall attractiveness of indexation, neither helps in explaining why some program types were much more likely to be indexed than others.

In further pursuit of the solution to the indexation puzzle, Weaver presents six chapter-length case studies on social security, food stamps, congressional pay, dairy price supports, minimum-wage policy, and federal income taxes. These studies, brief but very solid, lead to the book's final section.

Weaver's final conceptualization of indexation choices rejects both rational-choice and policy-overload explanations. Informed by the case studies, he concludes that indexing-related policies must surmount four "hurdles": establishing support, establishing the plausibility of indexing, tailoring indexation proposals to meet the objections of clients, and, finally, tailoring indexing proposals to meet the objections of policymakers. None of these would be inapplicable to any policy arena or program provision.

If any portion of the final part of the book speaks to the unique aspects of indexation, it is probably that which discusses the intersection of the inflation of the 1970s and the demands for benefits from large numbers of beneficiaries. Legislators, faced with these pressures, adopted what was essentially a mini-max strategy designed to avoid blame. In Weaver's words, "The cases also suggest that blame-oriented objectives and strategies — when the political environment gives rise to them — are an especially powerful influence on policy-makers' behavior."

The book, which begins with a puzzle, does not ultimately solve it in a direct, parsimonious way. What Weaver has accomplished, however, is a work that carefully utilizes several theoretical approaches and several types of data. All these are handled surely, and Weaver is especially skillful at not letting a particular theoretical approach outpace his data. The case studies, especially, present enough variety in circumstances to assure this.

This is a skillful piece of work that applies a number of tools of contemporary social science, in terms of both types of data and theoretical approaches, to a puzzle that yields only partially to them.

PHILLIP L. GIANOS

California State University
Fullerton

WEISBROD, BURTON A. *The Nonprofit Economy.* Pp. ix, 251. Cambridge, MA: Harvard University Press, 1988. $22.95.

In 1983, the last year for which comprehensive data are available, there were almost 3 million for-profit corporations in the United States and almost 900,000 nonprofit organizations. In spite of its relative size and rapid growth, the nonprofit sector has thus far drawn relatively little attention from economists. Weisbrod argues that this sector plays a significant role in the economy and merits detailed analysis.

Weisbrod provides a valuable tourist guide to the nonprofit sector. The essence of the nonprofit association is that no one connected with the organization may legally receive any profits. Further, to receive tax benefits, the organization must be so designated by the Internal Revenue Service. Among the almost 900,000 nonprofits in 1985, contributions to over 360,000 were tax deductible on the donor's tax return.

Not only does Weisbrod provide a statistical sketch of the sector; he also attempts to develop a theoretical rationale for its existence. When information about a good or service is costly to acquire, sellers may often be rewarded by misleading consumers. In this situation, Weisbrod argues, nonprofits are often viewed as more trustworthy. This, he suggests, explains the multitude of nonprofit firms in the health and education sectors. The theoretical framework, which draws from both the public-choice literature and some of the work on asymmetric information, is quite general and raises a great many interesting questions about the design of institutions in society. Much remains to be done.

In addition to the conceptual issues, Weisbrod explores a variety of other questions concerning nonprofits. Are there economies of scale? Apparently there are, to a limited degree. How important are donations relative to sales of goods or services as sources of revenue? Around 20 percent receive more than 90 percent of their money from donations. What are the implications of sales by nonprofits for private market suppliers? He analyzes the tremendous importance of voluntary labor to the sector and discusses the relationship between the supply of labor and the tax system. Finally, he asks whether nonprofits are really different. He examines industries in which proprietary and nonprofit firms coexist, the medical-care sector, and concludes that there are differences, with nonprofits appearing to provide consumers with more information.

The Nonprofit Economy is an interesting monograph, more for the questions it raises than for the answers it provides. Weisbrod has made the case for the importance of studying the nonprofit sector and, more specifically, for gathering the detailed data needed for a comprehensive examination of this sector.

G. S. GOLDSTEIN

Library of Parliament
Ottawa
Ontario
Canada

OTHER BOOKS

ADAMS, RICHARD NEWBOLD. *The Eighth Day: Social Evolution as the Self-Organization of Energy.* Pp. xvii, 292. Austin: University of Texas Press, 1988. $35.00.

BORDO, MICHAEL D. and LARS JONUNG. *The Long-Run Behavior of the Velocity of Circulation: The International Evidence.* Pp. xiv, 181. New York: Cambridge University Press, 1987. No price.

BOURDIEU, PIERRE. *Homo Academicus.* Pp. xxvi, 344. Stanford, CA: Stanford University Press, 1988. $29.50.

BOWMAN, JAMES S. and FREDERICK A. ELLISTON, eds. *Ethics, Government, and Public Policy: A Reference Guide.* Pp. 341. Westport, CT: Greenwood Press, 1988. No price.

BROWN, JEROLD E. and PATRICK D. REAGAN, eds. *Voluntarism, Planning, and the State: The American Planning Experience, 1914-1946.* Pp. xix, 168. Westport, CT: Greenwood Press, 1988. No price.

BURNETT, SCOTT S., ed. *Korean-American Relations: Documents Pertaining to the Far Eastern Diplomacy of the United States.* Vol. 3, *The Period of Diminishing Influence, 1896-1905.* Pp. xiii, 304. Honolulu: University of Hawaii Press, 1989. No price.

BURROW, J. W. *Whigs and Liberals: Continuity and Change in English Political Thought.* Pp. xi, 159. New York: Oxford University Press, 1988. $39.95.

CANAK, WILLIAM L., ed. *Lost Promises: Debt, Austerity, and Development in Latin America.* Pp. xii, 244. Boulder, CO: Westview Press, 1989. $37.00.

CARNOVALE, MARCO and WILLIAM C. POTTER, eds. *Continuity and Change in Soviet-East European Relations: Implications for the West.* Pp. viii, 238. Boulder, CO: Westview Press, 1989. Paperbound, $24.50.

CEADEL, MARTIN. *Thinking about Peace and War.* Pp. 222. New York: Oxford University Press, 1987. $29.95.

CHILD, JACK. *Antarctica and South American Geopolitics: Frozen Lebensraum.* Pp. 248. New York: Praeger, 1988. $39.95.

CHISHOLM, DONALD. *Coordination without Hierarchy: Informal Structures in Multiorganizational Systems.* Pp. xiv, 273. Berkeley: University of California Press, 1989. $30.00.

COLE, LEONARD A. *Clouds of Secrecy: The Army's Germ Warfare Tests over Populated Areas.* Pp. xi, 188. Totowa, NJ: Rowman & Littlefield, 1988. No price.

COLLENDER, STANLEY E. *The Guide to the Federal Budget: Fiscal 1990.* Pp. xvi, 179. Washington, DC: Urban Institute Press, 1989. $28.50.

DALTON, RUSSELL J. *Politics in West Germany.* Pp. xx, 376. Glenview, IL: Scott, Foresman/Little, Brown, 1989. Paperbound, $12.76.

DE SILVA, K. M. et al., eds. *Ethnic Conflict in Buddhist Societies: Sri Lanka, Thailand, Burma.* Pp. 220. Boulder, CO: Westview Press, 1988. $38.50.

DE VRIES, MARGARET GARRITSEN. *Balance of Payments Adjustment, 1945 to 1986: The IMF Experience.* Pp. xi, 336. Washington, DC: International Monetary Fund, 1987. Paperbound, $14.50.

DEERING, CHRISTOPHER J. *Congressional Politics.* Pp. 352. Chicago: Dorsey Press, 1989. Paperbound, $19.75.

DMITRIEV, BORIS. *A Policy Keeping the World on Edge.* Translated by Dmitry Belyavsky. Pp. 280. Moscow: Progress, 1987. Paperbound, $3.95.

FELDER, ELLENE A. and ANDREW HURRELL. *The U.S.-Brazilian Informatics Dispute.* Pp. xv, 59. Washington, DC: Johns Hopkins University Foreign Policy Institute, 1988. Paperbound, $7.00.

FELTON, JOHN RICHARD and DALE G. ANDERSON. *Regulation and Deregulation of the Motor Carrier Industry.* Pp. x, 210. Ames: Iowa State University Press, 1989. $24.95.

FERLING, JOHN, ed. *The World Turned Upside Down: The American Victory in the War of Independence.* Pp. x, 250. Westport, CT: Greenwood Press, 1988. No price.

FREEMAN, RICHARD B. and CASEY ICHNIOWSKI, eds. *When Public Sector Workers Unionize.* Pp. 428. Chicago: University of Chicago Press, 1988. $49.00.

FREMON, DAVID K. *Chicago Politics Ward by Ward.* Pp. xii, 372. Bloomington: Indiana University Press, 1988. Paperbound, $14.95.

FURTWANGLER, ALBERT. *American Silhouettes: Rhetorical Identities of the Founders.* Pp. viii, 168. New Haven, CT: Yale University Press, 1987. Paperbound, $10.95.

GALIULLIN, RUSTAM. *The CIA in Asia: Covert Operations against India and Afghanistan.* Pp. 144. Moscow: Progress, 1988. Paperbound, $4.95.

GAVLIN, M. and L. KAZAKOVA. *Elitist Revolution or Revolution of the Masses?* Pp. 205. Moscow: Progress, 1988. Paperbound, $4.95.

GIBNEY, MARK, ed. *Open Borders? Closed Societies? The Ethical and Political Issues.* Pp. xvi, 199. Westport, CT: Greenwood Press, 1988. No price.

GREBENNIKOV, V. V., ed. *Rights of Soviet Citizens: Collected Normative Acts.* Pp. 374. Moscow: Progress, 1987. $11.95.

GROVES, ROBERT M. et al., eds. *Telephone Survey Methodology.* Pp. xx, 581. New York: John Wiley, 1988. No price.

GUIDIERI, REMO, FRANCESCO PELLIZI, and STANLEY J. TAMBIAH, eds. *Ethnicities and Nations: Processes of Interethnic Relations in Latin America, Southeast Asia, and the Pacific.* Pp. 407. Houston, TX: Rothko Chapel, 1988. $22.50.

HALLORAN, RICHARD. *Serving America: Prospects for the Volunteer Force.* Pp. x, 71. New York: Priority Press, 1988. Paperbound, $8.95.

HANCOCK, M. DONALD. *West Germany: The Politics of Democratic Corporatism.* Pp. 192. Chatham, NJ: Chatham House, 1989. Paperbound, $12.95.

HARDY, DEBORAH. *Land and Freedom: The Origins of Russian Terrorism, 1876-1879.* Pp. xiii, 212. Westport, CT: Greenwood Press, 1987. $37.50.

HARRIS, RICHARD A. and SIDNEY M. MILKIS, eds. *Remaking American Politics.* Pp. x, 334. Boulder, CO: Westview Press, 1989. $33.00.

HARTFORD, KATHLEEN and STEVEN M. GOLDSTEIN, eds. *Single Sparks: China's Rural Revolutions.* Pp. xi, 216. Armonk, NY: M. E. Sharpe, 1989. $35.00.

HAUNER, MILAN and ROBERT L. CANFIELD, eds. *Afghanistan and the Soviet Union: Collision and Transformation.* Pp. xi, 219. Boulder, CO: Westview Press, 1989. $38.50.

HESS, EARL. *Liberty, Virtue, and Progress: Northerners and Their War for the Union.* Pp. viii, 154. New York: New York University Press, 1988. $35.00.

HODGES, TONY and MALYN NEWITT. *São Tomé and Príncipe: From Plantation Colony to Microstate.* Pp. xviii, 173. Boulder, CO: Westview Press, 1988. $34.95.

HOGWOOD, BRIAN. *From Crisis to Complacency? Shaping Public Policy in Britain.* Pp. 264. New York: Oxford University Press, 1987. $45.00.

ISARD, WALTER. *Arms Races, Arms Control, and Conflict Analysis: Contributions from Peace Science and Peace Economics.* Pp. xxv, 529. New York: Cambridge University Press, 1988. Paperbound, $9.95.

JACOBS, MARILYN S. *American Psychology in the Quest for Nuclear Peace.* Pp. 208. New York: Praeger, 1989. $39.95.

JANNUZI, F. TOMASSON. *India in Transition: Issues of Political Economy in a Plural Society.* Pp. xiii, 164. Boulder, CO: Westview Press, 1989. Paperbound, $21.50.

JENSON, JANE, ELISABETH HAGEN, and CEALLAIGH REDDY, eds. *Feminization of the Labor Force: Paradoxes and Promises.* Pp. xii, 295. New York: Oxford University Press, 1988. $39.95.

JOHN, BETTY, ed. *Libby: The Alaskan Diaries and Letters of Libby Beaman, 1879-1880.* Pp. x, 236. Boston: Houghton Mifflin, 1989. Paperbound, $8.95.

JOHNSON, KERMIT D. *Realism and Hope in a Nuclear Age.* Pp. vi, 133. Atlanta, GA: John Knox Press, 1988. Paperbound, no price.

KROMER, ROBERT. *New Weapons and NATO: Solutions or Irritants?* Pp. ix, 185. Westport, CT: Greenwood Press, 1987. $35.95.

LaRUE, L. H. *Political Discourse: A Case Study of the Watergate Affair.* Pp. xi, 172. Athens: University of Georgia Press, 1988. Paperbound, $10.00.

LEAGUE OF WOMEN VOTERS OF PENNSYLVANIA. *Key to the Keystone State.* 4th ed. Pp. xvi, 238. University Park: Pennsylvania State University Press, 1989. Paperbound, $12.95.

LEE, MANWOO, RONALD D. McLAURIN, and CHUNG-IN MOON. *Alliance under Tension: The Evolution of South Korean-U.S. Relations.* Pp. viii, 229. Boulder, CO: Westview Press, 1988. $35.00.

LeMAY, MICHAEL C., ed. *The Gatekeepers: Comparative Immigration Policy.* Pp. 232. New York: Praeger, 1989. $39.95.

LERNER, LAWRENCE W. and DONALD W. TREADGOLD, eds. *Gorbachev and the Soviet Future.* Pp. vii, 284. Boulder, CO: Westview Press, 1988. $43.50.

LINCOVE, DAVID A. and GARY R. TREADWAY, comps. and annotators. *The Anglo-American Relationship: An Annotated Bibliography of Scholarship.* Pp. 432. Westport, CT: Greenwood Press, 1988. $49.95.

LONG, SAMUEL, ed. *Political Behavior Annual.* Vol. 2. Pp. x, 184. Boulder, CO: Westview Press, 1989. Paperbound, $40.00.

LOUSCHER, DAVID J. and MICHAEL D. SALAMONE. *Technology Transfer and U.S. Security Assistance: The Impact of Licensed Production.* Pp. xvi, 201. Boulder, CO: Westview Press, 1987. Paperbound, $23.50.

McCRACKEN, GRANT. *The Long Interview.* Pp. 87. Newbury Park, CA: Sage, 1988. Paperbound, $6.00.

McKEE, DAVID L. *Growth, Development, and the Service Economy in the Third World.* Pp. 146. New York: Praeger, 1988. No price.

MEDLAND, WILLIAM J. *The Cuban Missile Crisis of 1962: Needless or Necessary.* Pp. viii, 167. New York: Praeger, 1988. $35.95.

MILLER, MARTIN A. *The Russian Revolutionary Emigres, 1825-1870.* Pp. xii, 292. Baltimore: Johns Hopkins University Press, 1986. $32.50.

MITCHELL, C. R. and K. WEBB, eds. *New Approaches to International Mediation.* Pp. 268. Westport, CT: Greenwood Press, 1988. $45.00.

MONKKONEN, ERIC. *America Becomes Urban: The Development of U.S. Cities & Towns, 1780-1980.* Pp. xvi, 332. Berkeley: University of California Press, 1988. $25.00.

MONTGOMERY, JOHN D. *Bureaucrats and People: Grassroots Participation in Third World Development.* Pp. xviii, 140. Baltimore: Johns Hopkins University Press, 1988. $22.50.

MORGAN, DAVID R. *Managing Urban America.* 3d ed. Pp. xiii, 351. Pacific Grove, CA: Brooks/Cole, 1989. $25.00.

MORGAN, KEVIN and ANDREW SAYER. *Microcircuits of Capital: Sunrise Industry and Uneven Development.* Pp. 321. Boulder, CO: Westview Press, 1988. $45.00.

NOYELLE, THIERRY, ed. *New York's Financial Markets: The Challenges of Globalization.* Pp. ix, 126. Boulder, CO: Westview Press, 1989. $32.50.

NYE, JOSEPH S., Jr. and JAMES A. SCHEAR, eds. *On the Defensive? The Future of SDI.* Pp. xv, 206. Lanham, MD: University Press of America, Aspen Institute for Humanistic Studies, 1988. Paperbound, $12.75.

PALMER, JOHN L., TIMOTHY SMEEDING, and BARBARA BOYLE TORREY, eds. *The Vulnerable.* Pp. xxiii, 458. Washington, DC: Urban Institute Press, 1988. $36.50.

PETERSON, M. J. *Managing the Frozen South: The Creation and Evolution of the Antarctic Treaty System.* Pp. xi, 283. Berkeley: University of California Press, 1988. $35.00.

PLAS, JEANNE M. and KATHLEEN V. HOOVER-DEMPSEY. *Working up a Storm: Anger, Anxiety, Joy, and Tears on the Job—and How to Handle Them.* Pp. 299. New York: Norton, 1988. $19.95.

POWELL, WALTER W., ed. *The Nonprofit Sector: A Research Handbook.* Pp. xiii, 464.

New Haven, CT: Yale University Press, 1987. Paperbound, $21.95.

PUSHKAREV, SERGEI, VLADIMIR RUSAK, and GLEB YAKUNIN. *Christianity and Government in Russia and the Soviet Union: Reflections on the Millennium.* Pp. xii, 166. Boulder, CO: Westview Press, 1989. Paperbound, $21.95.

QUANDT, RICHARD E. and HARVEY S. ROSEN. *The Conflict between Equilibrium and Disequilibrium Theories: The Case of the U.S. Labor Market.* Pp. viii, 102. Kalamazoo, MI: W. E. Upjohn Institute for Employment Research, 1988. No price.

REGENS, JAMES L. and ROBERT W. RYCROFT. *The Acid Rain Controversy.* Pp. xviii, 228. Pittsburgh, PA: University of Pittsburgh Press, 1988. Paperbound, $12.95.

ROHR, JOHN A. *Ethics for Bureaucrats: An Essay on Law and Values.* 2d ed. Pp. 352. New York: Marcel Dekker, 1989. $45.00.

RUESCHEMEYER, MARILYN and CHRISTIANE LEMKE, eds. *Quality of Life in the German Democratic Republic: Changes and Developments in a State Socialist Society.* Pp. xiii, 242. Armonk, NY: M. E. Sharpe, 1989. $40.00.

RUNYAN, WILLIAM McKINLEY, ed. *Psychology and Historical Interpretation.* Pp. xiii, 306. New York: Oxford University Press, 1988. Paperbound, $13.95.

RUSSETT, BRUCE M. and HARVEY STARR. *World Politics: The Menu for Choice.* 3d ed. Pp. xiv, 619. New York: W. H. Freeman, 1989. $24.95.

RUSSIN, SUZANNE STURMTHAL, ed. *Democracy under Fire: Memoirs of a European Socialist, Adolf Sturmthal.* Pp. xvi, 207. Durham, NC: Duke University Press, 1989. $29.95.

RYAN, MIKE H., CARL L. SWANSON, and ROGENE A. BUCHHOLZ. *Corporate Strategy, Public Policy and the Fortune 500: How America's Major Corporations Influence Government.* Pp. vi, 249. New York: Basil Blackwell, 1987. $34.95.

SCHEMAN, L. RONALD. *The Alliance for Progress: A Retrospective.* Pp. xxv, 272. New York: Praeger, 1988. $42.95.

SCHROEDER, W. WIDICK and FRANKLIN I. GAMWELL, eds. *Economic Life: Process Interpretations and Critical Responses.* Pp. ix, 269. Chicago: Center for the Scientific Study of Religion, 1988. $26.95.

SELIGMAN, LESTER G. and GARY R. COVINGTON. *The Coalitional Presidency.* Pp. 176. Pacific Grove, CA: Brooks/Cole, 1989. Paperbound, $17.75.

SHARMA, URSULA. *Women's Work, Class, and the Urban Household: A Study of Shimla, North India.* Pp. 213. New York: Tavistock, 1987. Paperbound, $15.95.

SOŁTAN, KAROL EDWARD. *The Causal Theory of Justice.* Pp. xii, 265. Berkeley: University of California Press, 1987. $30.00.

SOUTH, NIGEL. *Policing for Profit: The Private Security Sector.* Pp. xi, 180. Newbury Park, CA: Sage, 1988. Paperbound, $16.95.

STALLINGS, BARBARA and ROBERT KAUFMAN, eds. *Debt and Democracy in Latin America.* Pp. vii, 232. Boulder, CO: Westview Press, 1989. $29.00.

STEINBRUNER, JOHN D., ed. *Restructuring American Foreign Policy.* Pp. xii, 260. Washington, DC: Brookings Books, 1989. $29.95.

STRAUSS, LEO. *Liberalism Ancient and Modern.* Pp. 276. Ithaca, NY: Cornell University Press, 1989. Paperbound, $8.95.

SUMM, G. HARVEY and TOM KELLY, eds. *The Good Neighbors: America, Panama, and the 1977 Canal Treaties.* Pp. xiii, 160. Athens: Ohio University/Swallow Press, 1988. Paperbound, $11.00.

SVIREZHEV, YURI M. et al. *Ecological and Demographic Consequences of a Nuclear War.* Translated by L. Goering. Pp. 112. Berlin, German Democratic Republic: Akademie-Verlag, 1987. $15.95.

UTLEY, ROBERT L., Jr., ed. *Principles of the Constitutional Order: The Ratification Debates.* Pp. ix, 187. Lanham, MD: University Press of America, Tocqueville Forum, 1989. Paperbound, $12.50.

UYS, PIETER-DIRK, comp. *P. W. Botha in His Own Words.* Pp. 176. New York: Penguin Books, 1987. Paperbound, $4.95.

VANO, GERARD S. *Canada: The Strategic and Military Pawn.* Pp. 163. New York: Praeger, 1988. $35.95.

VOYDANOFF, PATRICIA and LINDA C. MAJKA, eds. *Families and Economic Distress: Coping Strategies and Social Policy.* Pp. 306. Newbury Park, CA: Sage, 1988. Paperbound, no price.

WARNER, EDWARD L., III and DAVID OCHMANEK. *Next Moves: An Arms Control Agenda for the 1990s.* Pp. xi, 163. New York: Council on Foreign Relations, 1989. Paperbound, $10.95.

WARREN, ELIZABETH. *The Legacy of Judicial Policy-Making: Gautreaux v. Chicago Housing Authority, the Decision and Its Im-*

pacts. Pp. xii, 97. Lanham, MD: University Press of America, 1988. $14.75.

WEISS, FRANK D. et al. *Trade Policy in West Germany.* Pp. xii, 167. Tubingen: Mohr, 1988. Paperbound, $42.50.

WILLIAMS, BRETT. *Upscaling Downtown: Stalled Gentrification in Washington, D.C.* Pp. xi, 157. Ithaca, NY: Cornell University Press, 1988. Paperbound, $8.95.

WILLIS, DAVID P., ed. *Health Policies and Black Americans.* Pp. 531. New Brunswick, NJ: Transaction Books, 1989. Paperbound, $19.95.

ZASLAVSKAIA, TAT'IANA I. *A Voice of Reform.* Pp. xix, 191. Armonk, NY: M. E. Sharpe, 1989. No price.

INDEX

Argentina
  disappearances in, 136-37
  and human rights, 52, 135
  see also Buenos Aires
Ashkenazi Jews in Israel, 127
ASSESSING ISRAEL'S RECORD ON HUMAN
  RIGHTS, Rita J. Simon, 115-28
Autopsy, to document arbitrary killing, 137

Basic Principles on the Independence of the Judi-
  ciary, 79
Brazil, and human rights, 52-53, 135
British Raj, 126-27
Buenos Aires, penal-system deaths in, 61-63
Bush administration, and human rights, 27, 38, 39-40

Capital punishment, 75, 82-83
Caracas Declaration, 74-75
Carter administration, and human rights, 22-23
CHALIDZE, VALERY, *Perestroika*, Socialism, and
  the Constitution, 98-108
Chernobyl, nuclear-plant explosion at, 97
Chile
  and human rights, 132
  and U.S. foreign policy, 32-34
China, and human rights, 133
Civil liberties, 7-8, 115-28
Civil rights, 7-8, 11, 109-14
CIVIL RIGHTS IN THE SOVIET UNION, Arkady
  I. Vaxberg, 109-14
CLARK, ROGER S., Human Rights and the U.N.
  Committee on Crime Prevention and Control,
  68-84
Code of Conduct for Law Enforcement Officials and
  the Principles of Medical Ethics, 73-74
Committee on Crime Prevention and Control, 68-84
CORILLON, CAROL, The Role of Science and Sci-
  entists in Human Rights, 129-40

Declaration of Basic Principles of Justice for Victims
  of Crime and Abuse of Power, 76, 77
Declaration on the Protection of All Persons from
  Being Subjected to Torture and Other Cruel,
  Inhuman or Degrading Treatment or Punish-
  ment, 72-73
Democratic countries, and human rights abuses, 36,
  37, 38-39

Distributive justice, 27, 29
Domestic Violence Resolution, 76, 77-78
Drug abuse, 149

Economic rights, 11, 27, 29, 103, 106, 107
Einstein, Albert, 130
Enlightenment, 48-49, 55
Environmentalism, and human rights, 138-39

Fang Lizhi, 133
Forensic anthropology, 136
Forensic pathology, 137
FOX, ELAINE R. and LISA ROTH, Homeless Chil-
  dren: Philadelphia as a Case Study, 141-51

Glasnost, 91-93
GLASNOST—THE DAWN OF FREEDOM? Rich-
  ard Schifter, 85-97
Gorbachev, Mikhail, reforms of, 85-97, 99
Guatemala, and U.S. human rights policy, 37

Health professionals, role in torture, 134-35
Helsinki Final Act, 88
HENKIN, LOUIS, The Universality of the Concept
  of Human Rights, 10-16
HOMELESS CHILDREN: PHILADELPHIA AS A
  CASE STUDY, Elaine R. Fox and Lisa Roth,
  141-51
Homeless population
  characteristics of, 142-43
  children in, 147-50
  in Philadelphia, 141-51
Housing, affordable, availability of, 145, 149
Human rights
  definition of, 8, 11
  universality of, 11-15, 47-48
  as a Western idea, 12, 14, 16, 48, 55
HUMAN RIGHTS AND THE U.N. COMMITTEE
  ON CRIME PREVENTION AND CONTROL,
  Roger S. Clark, 68-84
HUMAN RIGHTS AS AN INTERNATIONAL
  ISSUE, Louise I. Shelley, 42-56
Human Rights Committee, 113
HUMAN RIGHTS IN THE REAGAN ERA: ACCEP-
  TANCE IN PRINCIPLE, Aryeh Neier, 30-41
HUMAN RIGHTS, THE NATIONAL INTEREST,
  AND U.S. FOREIGN POLICY, Jerome J.
  Shestack, 17-29

191

International Court of Justice, 112
International Covenant on Civil and Political Rights, 113
Intifada, 116-17
Iran
  and human rights, 134, 136
  and U.S. foreign policy, 40-41
Israel, and human rights, 56, 115-28, 134

Juvenile justice, 76-77, 82-83

King, Mary-Claire, 136-37
Kirkpatrick, Jean, 24-25, 31, 34
Kissinger, Henry, 21-22
Koryagin, Anatoly, 132

Latin America
  and human rights, 47, 48-50, 52-53, 132
  penal-system deaths in, 57-67
  see also names of countries
Lefever, Ernest, 31-32
Legal aid, 84
Locke, John, 12

Malaysia, and human rights, 133
Mexico City, penal-system deaths in, 64
Milan Plan of Action, 76, 78
Minnesota Lawyers International Human Rights Committee, 137
Minnesota Protocol, 137
Model Agreement on the Transfer of Foreign Prisoners, 78-79
Mohamed, Ismail, 133-34
Moscow Tribune, 112

National Academy of Sciences, 133, 138
National interest, 19-21
National security, 24-26, 31
National security doctrine, 47, 49-50
NEIER, ARYEH, Human Rights in the Reagan Era: Acceptance in Principle, 30-41
News coverage
  of the *intifada*, 117, 126
  of penal-system deaths in Latin America, 57-67
Nicaragua, and human rights, 132-33

Olivares, Ramiro, 132

Pakistan, and human rights, 135
Perestroika, 91, 102, 113
PERESTROIKA, SOCIALISM, AND THE CONSTITUTION, Valery Chalidze, 98-108

Peru, penal-system deaths in, 63-64
Philadelphia, homeless families in, 141-51
Philippines, and U.S. human rights policy, 35-36
Poland, and human rights, 134
Police intervention in citizens' activities, 121-22
Political rights, 11
Poverty, 144-45
Psychiatry, and human rights abuses, 132, 134
Public housing, 145

Reagan administration, and human rights, 23, 26, 30-41
Reagan, Ronald, assessment of the USSR by, 87-88
Recommendations on the Treatment of Foreign Prisoners, 78-79
RIGHT TO LIFE AND LATIN AMERICAN PENAL SYSTEMS, THE, Eugenio Raúl Zaffaroni, 57-67
ROLE OF SCIENCE AND SCIENTISTS IN HUMAN RIGHTS, THE, Carol Corillon, 129-40
ROTH, LISA, *see* FOX, ELAINE R., coauthor
Rushdie, Salman, 41

Sakharov, Andrei, 133
SCHIFTER, RICHARD, *Glasnost* — The Dawn of Freedom? 85-97
Science and scientists, and human rights, 129-40
Sephardic Jews in Israel, 127
Sexism, 150
SHELLEY, LOUISE I., Human Rights as an International Issue, 42-56
SHESTACK, JEROME J., Human Rights, the National Interest, and U.S. Foreign Policy, 17-29
Shultz, George, 36
SIMON, RITA J., Assessing Israel's Record on Human Rights, 115-28
Snow, Clyde, 136
Social rights, 11, 27, 29, 103, 106, 107
Socialism, 103-8
Somalia
  and human rights, 134, 139
  and U.S. human rights policy, 34-35
Soros Foundation, 112-13
South Africa, and human rights, 133-34
Stalinism, 100, 101
Standard Minimum Rules for the Treatment of Prisoners, 71-72
Standards Guaranteeing Protection of the Rights of Those Facing the Death Penalty, 75
State security and secrecy, 139-40

Torture, 72-73, 134-35

Turkey, and U.S. foreign policy, 39-40

U.N. Charter, 13

United Nations Standard Minimum Rules for the
    Administration of Juvenile Justice (Beijing
    Rules), 76-77
Universal Declaration of Human Rights, 11, 13
UNIVERSALITY OF THE CONCEPT OF HUMAN
    RIGHTS, THE, Louis Henkin, 10-16
Uruguay, and human rights, 52
U.S. foreign policy, and human rights, 17-29, 30-41, 46
USSR
    civil rights in, 109-14
    Constitution of, 101-3, 106-8, 111
    dictatorship in, 86, 91, 104
    emigration from, 89, 90, 92, 111, 114, 139-40

and human rights, 46, 48-49, 51-52, 85-97, 103, 132,
    134
    secession from, 108

VAXBERG, ARKADY I., Civil Rights in the Soviet
    Union, 109-14
Vienna Concluding Document, 111-12

WOLFGANG, MARVIN E., President's Welcome at
    the Ninety-First Annual Meeting, 7-9
World War II, 43-44

Yugoslavia, and U.S. human rights policy, 36-37

ZAFFARONI, EUGENIO RAÚL, The Right to Life
    and Latin American Penal Systems, 57-67

Forthcoming!

INTERNATIONAL HUMAN RIGHTS
Universalism versus Relativism

by ALISON DUNDES RENTELN,
University of Southern California

Are human rights universal? Universalists and cultural relativists have been debating this question for a long time. Cultural relativists have been criticized for claiming that human rights are a Western construct and that some cultures have no such concept. Renteln disagrees with this idea, claiming that it is possible to create structural equivalents to rights in all cultures. She argues that cross-cultural empirical research can provide universal human rights standards. This is demonstrated through the existence of one such universal right—measured retribution.

International Human Rights is an important book that provides a fresh and unusual combination of abstract theory and empirical evidence. It will interest scholars and students in political science, anthropology, sociology, and philosophy.

Frontiers of Anthropology, Volume 6
1990 (Winter) / 240 pages (tent.) / $35.00 (c) / $16.95 (p)

SAGE PUBLICATIONS, INC.
2111 W. Hillcrest Dr.
Newbury Park, CA 91320

SAGE PUBLICATIONS LTD
28 Banner Street
London EC1Y 8QE, England

SAGE PUBLICATIONS INDIA PVT LTD
M-32 Market, Greater Kailash I
New Delhi 110 048 India

Here's one reason why you need more life insurance... and three reasons why it should be our group insurance.

Family responsibilities increase and change—a new baby, a job change, a new home. Your family could have a lot to lose *unless* your insurance keeps pace with these changes.

Now, here's why you need *our* group term life insurance.

First, it's low-cost. Unlike everything else, life rates have *gone down* over the past 20 years. And, because of our buying power, our group rates are low.

Second, you will continue to receive this protection even if you change jobs, as long as you remain a member and pay the premiums when due.

Third, our wide range of coverage allows you to choose the insurance that's right for you. And you can protect yourself and your entire family.

It's insurance as you need it. So check your current insurance portfolio. Then call or write the Administrator for the extra protection you need.

UP TO $240,000 IN TERM LIFE INSURANCE PROTECTION IS AVAILABLE TO AAPSS MEMBERS.

Plus these other group insurance plans:
Major Medical Expense Insurance
Excess Major Medical
In-Hospital Insurance
High Limit Accident Insurance
Medicare Supplement

The AAPSS Life Plan is underwritten by New York Life Insurance Company, New York, New York 10010 on form number GMR.

**Contact Administrator,
AAPSS Group Insurance Program**
Smith-Sternau Organization, Inc.
1255 23rd Street, N.W.
Washington, D.C. 20037
800 424-9883 Toll Free
in Washington, D.C. area, 202 296-8030